A COSMOPOLITAN JOURNEY?

For Dad

A Cosmopolitan Journey?

Difference, Distinction and Identity Work in Gap Year Travel

HELENE SNEE
University of Manchester, UK

Routledge
Taylor & Francis Group

LONDON AND NEW YORK

First published 2014 by Ashgate Publishing

2 Park Square, Milton Park, Abingdon, Oxfordshire OX14 4RN
711 Third Avenue, New York, NY 10017

Routledge is an imprint of the Taylor & Francis Group, an informa business

First issued in paperback 2018

British Library Cataloguing in Publication Data
A catalogue record for this book is available from the British Library.

The Library of Congress has cataloged the printed edition as follows:
Snee, Helene.
    A cosmopolitan journey? : difference, distinction and identity work in gap year travel / by Helene Snee.
        pages cm
    Includes bibliographical references and index.
    ISBN 978-1-4094-5303-1 (hardback)
    1. Educational leave. 2. Leave of absence. 3. Travel. 4. Youth.
5. Cosmopolitanism. I. Title.
    HD5257.S64 2014
    331.25'763--dc23
                                                                    2013044003

ISBN 978-1-4094-5303-1 (hbk)
ISBN 978-1-138-37986-2 (pbk)

Contents

Acknowledgements

I would like to thank the many people who contributed to this book in one way or another, including the staff and students (past and present) in Sociology at the University of Manchester. In particular, I am grateful to Alan Warde for his guidance over the years. Special thanks (and citations!) to Wendy Bottero for all her help above and beyond the call of duty. I would also like to thank Fiona Devine for being so supportive during the writing of this book, and Nick Crossley, Sue Heath and Mike Savage for their invaluable insights along the way.

I would also like to thank the young people whose gap year stories were the foundation of this study and who kept me entertained (and occasionally envious) with their 'tales from the road'. Special thanks to the participants who took the time to talk to me about their travels.

I am very grateful to my family and friends, especially my mum Jean and my sister Elizabeth for their love and encouragement, and for the moral support I've received at various stages from: Jo Mylan; Helen Norman; Desmeana Johnson; Andrew Jackson; Katherine Davies; and Lucy Simmers. Last, but certainly not least, thank you to Steven Cook, for everything (you are my favourite).

List of Abbreviations

AoIR	Association of Internet Researchers
CV	Curriculum Vitae
ICS	International Citizen Service
LSYPE	Longitudinal Study of Young People in England
UCAS	Universities and Colleges Admissions Service
VSO	Voluntary Service Overseas

Chapter 1
Introduction

Does travel broaden the mind and help you to 'find yourself'? This book explores whether 'gap year' travel is a way for a young person to become 'cosmopolitan': a global citizen who is open to cultural difference. Alternatively, are gap year experiences a way for privileged youth to claim they are doing something 'worthwhile' without really learning anything about their place in the world? In this book, I suggest gap years can reproduce standard ways of thinking about difference, and are shaped by historical legacies and dominant ideas about value and worth.

Gap year travel is encouraged by the education sector, government bodies and career guidance literature. When A Level results are released, national newspapers run special features offering suggestions for gap year activities and projects. These articles urge young people to use their time out wisely:

> 'A gap year is still one of the most worthwhile experiences you can have', says Marcus Sherifi, travel editor at Gapyear.com. 'You learn about yourself, gain independence, learn about other cultures and societies … it really makes you a more rounded person'. (Thorne 2013: n.p.)

Such benefits are inherently tied to the idea of being cosmopolitan: mobile, engaged with the world, and eager for new experiences.

In this book, I explore the stories of 'gappers'[1] and how their narratives offer insight into cosmopolitanism as a social and cultural practice. I consider how young people engage with difference, and how they understand this; how cosmopolitanism is tied up with ideas about good taste (and cultural distinctions) in travel; and how cosmopolitan gap year experiences are a resource for identity work. Running throughout the book is a theoretical concern with understanding self-development, and whether the legacies of social class and global inequalities guide young people's gap years along standard scripts.

This chapter introduces gap years in popular culture and academic research. It notes that gap years are a popular activity, but one that is taken by individuals who are relatively privileged. I explore the public debate over what sort of gap year is beneficial for young people and the places they visit, and the emphasis that is placed on doing something worthwhile. The chapter then outlines the

---

1 I use the term 'gapper' to refer to young people on gap years.

history, growth and popularity of youth travel, from the Grand Tours of the seventeenth and eighteenth centuries, through the Hippy Trail of the 1960s, to the British Princes William and Harry volunteering overseas. These 'alternative' experiences have influenced wider tastes in travel, driven by the rise of the new middle classes who are keen to demonstrate they are 'not tourists'. I then summarise the 'problems' of alternative tourism that are relevant to gap year travel: concerns over who benefits from volunteer tourism; independent travel as a means of accumulating valuable cultural resources; and the role of travel in narrating self-identity.

Introducing the Gapper

To begin, we need to define gap year travel and introduce the gapper, who is a recognisable figure in UK popular culture. In 2000, the profile of gap years was raised when the heir to the British throne Prince William undertook a volunteering placement in Chile (Simpson 2005a: 9). A British television advertisement for coffee features an incompetent but well-meaning gap year student working on a coffee plantation in Kenya (Kenco 2006), while William Sutcliffe's novel *Are You Experienced?* (1997) provides a satirical account of the backpacker trail in India, in which the central character is a 19 year-old British gapper. The stereotypical gapper is a potentially rich source of comedy, such as Orlando, the 'Gap Yah' student created by a young comic who was a viral video success in 2010. Orlando 'thinks nothing of getting Mummy and Daddy to pay for him to travel the world, doing a bit of charity work here and cocaine smuggling there, on his gap year between Harrow and St Andrews University' (Law 2011: n.p.). There are also similar types of youth travel in other national contexts, like the 'big OE' (overseas experience) in Australia and New Zealand (Inkson and Myers 2003).

An oft-cited definition of gap years is 'any period of time between 3 and 24 months which an individual "takes out" of formal education, training or the workplace, and where the time out sits in the context of a longer career trajectory' (Jones 2004: 8). This is a broad definition, which recognises that gap years do not necessarily involve overseas travel, and may be taken at various stages in life. For example, gap years might be spent in the UK; 'adult' or 'career break' gap years are for older people who take shorter periods of time out; and 'silver gappers' are retired people who use their exit from the workplace as an opportunity to travel. In this book I focus on a particular type of gapper, as the stories explored are written by young people who have finished their A Levels and are progressing on to university.

Already we can see that these people are fairly privileged: they live in a developed country, are able to attend tertiary education,[2] and are in a position to take a year off to travel overseas. The consequences of focusing on this group are discussed in Chapter 4, although it is worth noting here that the wide range of alternative gap year stories that would fit within Jones's definition are not captured in this sample. The reasoning behind such a decision was to narrow down the analysis to a critical examination of the figure of the gap year student that is enshrined in popular culture, and how the discourses that surround gap years may or may not come to bear on how young people actually represent their experiences. These young people describe both 'structured' and 'unstructured' gap year activities. Structured placements refer to: 'the involvement of [a] providing organisation in setting up, managing and facilitating the activities' (Jones 2004: 30). Unstructured activities are independently organised and typically involve backpacking. Both types of overseas experiences are represented in this book.

To gather gap year narratives, this study employed qualitative 'blog' analysis. Weblogs, or blogs, are web documents of dated entries or 'posts', often (but not always) similar to a journal. According to Wakeford and Cohen, contemporary blogging conventions include:

> regular and frequent updating, whether writing, photos or other content; the expectation of linking to other bloggers and online sources; a month-by-month archive; the capacity of feedback through comments to the blog; a particular style of writing which is often characterised as spontaneous and revelatory. (Wakeford and Cohen 2008: 308)

The features of blogs, and the methodological and ethical issues associated with using these sources in social research, will be explored in more detail in Chapter 4, in which I consider how gap year blogs provide access to gap year stories. One such story, hosted on a UK national newspaper's website, briefly became famous in 2008. This single blog post, and the public reaction to it, introduces the key debates that surround the seemingly innocuous practice of young people broadening their horizons and becoming more knowledgeable about the world.

---

2 Despite the expansion of higher education in the UK, it is important to remember that less than half of young people will study at university. The Higher Education Initial Participation Rate (the probability that a 17-year-old will participate in higher education by age 30) was 49 per cent in 2011/12 (Department for Business Innovation and Skills 2013). It is still not the path of the majority of young people. Moreover, as will be explored below, the act of taking a gap year can be seen as an effort to stand out in the context of credential inflation.

'Meet Max Gogarty'

> Meet Max Gogarty – 19, from north London, spends his money on food, booze and skinny jeans, writes for *Skins*[3] in his spare time. He's off to India and Thailand to have a good time, and you can join him in his weekly blog. (*The Guardian* 2008: n.p.)

On 14 February 2008, *The Guardian's* 'Travel' section published the first post of a gap year traveller, Max Gogarty, as part of a planned series. Max is positioned as a young man with typical interests but some cool credentials. It is also clear that he is fairly affluent and middle-class. Taking a gap year is common among his peers as he states that 'all my friends are going'. As many backpackers before him, Max values the freedom of independent travel: 'I'm free to roam. That's the beauty of doing it by myself'. He highlights the cosmopolitanism of gap year travel by claiming the places he will visit are a 'world away' from home. Travelling to India and Thailand is scary, but also a way of finding 'culture and enlightenment'. Max also makes a tongue-in-cheek reference that this is an excuse to have a good time – youthful hedonism disguised as self-development. 'I'll do my best to tell of the debauched beach parties, the dodgy days with "washing machine" tummy, the messy late-night stumblings into bars and, of course, all that bullshit about finding myself' (*The Guardian* 2008 n.p.).

On the surface, this seems like a harmless enough enterprise, but the negative public response to Max's post is fascinating. By the morning of the following day it received around 500 comments, many of which were edited or deleted by *The Guardian* moderators due to vitriolic personal abuse. A great deal of the outrage seems to have been because Max's father is a freelance journalist who writes for the same paper. Links to the blog appeared on internet forums and other blogs, Max's family expressed their shock at how the incident spiralled,[4] and comments were closed on following day.

The comments include:

> posh 19 year old goes to Thailand to find himself amongst all the other 'gappers', and we can follow his every move? wow ...

> Moneyed youngster goes travelling to the usual places to get drunk and meet girls? ... a stroke of genius ...

---

3 A popular and controversial UK television teenage drama series.

4 An amusing aside to this story is that the Wikipedia page on 'Nepotism' was edited so that Max's name appears 'alongside Kim Jong-il of North Korea and George W Bush' (Davies 2008: n.p.). It is hard not to feel sorry for Max being placed in such company.

Don't forget, poverty is sad, but kinda authentic and like ennobling, mmmhmmm. Why does nobody go looking for themselves in Belarus? … (*The Guardian* 2008 n.p.)

The people commenting on Max's post are *angry* about his privilege, suggesting that the people who go on gap years are 'posh' and 'middle-class', travelling 'for life experience on daddy's money'. They also criticise gappers looking for authenticity and exoticness in the global South. As we will see, the comments are similar to academic criticisms of cosmopolitan consumption. But is there a contradiction at work here? Max is derided because he has been given opportunities that other people do not have access to: he is *able* to take a gap year (and then, of course, write about this for a national newspaper). It is unfair that not everyone can get this life experience. Yet the comments also suggest that it is meaningless, boring, a cliché for moneyed youth. Behind the official accounts of the gap year as something open to all for self-development, we can observe symbolic struggles over meaning and worth, and indications of inequalities on a national and global scale.

Max's story provides clues to some critical issues in gap year travel:

- Why might we criticise the relationship between gappers and the people and places they visit? For example, why does Max highlight the 'difference' of such places?
- What do young people get out of gap year travel, and does it reproduce class privilege? Is Max displaying middle-class taste and gaining valuable cultural resources?
- Are gap years really about self-development? Or, to paraphrase Max, is this business about 'finding yourself' a load of nonsense?

These concerns – of difference, distinction and identity work – are explored in this book through the narratives of gap year travellers who, like Max, write blogs about their gap years. In doing so, it critically reflects on the idea of these travels as 'cosmopolitan journeys'. The following section sets the scene and discusses how many young people take gap years, who takes them, and why.

Mapping Out the Gap Year

Rates of Participation

A report by the marketing organisation Mintel (2005) estimates that some 50,000 young people take a gap year between school and university or further education. However, as noted by Jones (2004), it is difficult to quantify participation in gap years, as there is no comprehensive source of data that would capture this information.[5] There are three main difficulties in trying to establish the number of young people who take gap years overseas between school and university: distinguishing gap years spent overseas from time out spent in the UK; distinguishing young people on pre-university gap years from other age groups; and the variety of activities in which young people can engage (work, volunteering, leisure travel, and so on). A potential source of data would be figures on UCAS deferred places, which is 'the number of applicants who apply to defer their entry to higher education to the following year' (UCAS 2013: n.p.). This does not reflect those who defer their place but spend this time in the UK, nor does it capture those who apply to university during their year out.

An analysis of data from the Longitudinal Study of Young People in England (LSYPE) (Crawford and Cribb 2012) finds that 12.5 per cent of young people intended to take a gap year before university at age 18 when surveyed in 2008, although only 6.6 per cent had done so when they were resurveyed the following summer.[6] If we take the population of young people in England aged 18 in the university intake year 2008/9, which was 683,900 (Department for Business Innovation and Skills 2011), we can arrive at a rough estimate of 45,000 young people on self-defined gap years during this period.[7] How many of these gap years involve time spent overseas? According to the LSYPE data, the most popular activity is work in Britain, and over 80 per cent of young people on gap years spend at least some time earning money at home. Some young people combine this with periods of travel as well. Crawford and Cribb identify two types of gappers: young people who intend to take a gap year, and those who do not. Travelling, working abroad and volunteering abroad is more common among the first group, with more than half spending some time on travel, whereas those who do not plan a gap year are more likely to use their year out to retake exams (Crawford and Cribb 2012: 28). It is clear, then,

---

5 Jones (2004) suggests a 'sensible estimate' of 250,000–350,000 young people per year, which incorporates young people aged between 16 and 25 and involved in a wide range of activities (including time spent in the UK). The figure is drawn from both quantitative data (via the Universities and Colleges Admissions Service (UCAS) and the Office of National Statistics' Labour Force Survey) and qualitative data (from university admissions advisers and gap year providers).

6 However, a further 6.2 per cent had accepted a place at university and would be attending the following year, suggesting they were involved in activities that they did not categorise as a 'gap year', e.g. in full-time education (Crawford and Cribb 2012: 23).

7 Of course, this figure should be treated with caution, not least because the higher education participation rate is higher for the LSYPE cohort than the wider population. Moreover, this estimate excludes young people from Wales, Scotland and Northern Ireland.

that overseas gap years before university are a popular activity, in that tens of thousands of young people are involved. However, there is also evidence that these sorts of gap years are more likely to be taken by relatively privileged individuals.

Who are the Gappers?

In a review of gap year provision, Jones (2004) notes some common gapper characteristics: White; women outnumbering men; relatively affluent; an over-representation of grammar school and private school backgrounds; and an under-representation of people with disabilities. We can see parallels between the gapper population and inequalities in higher education (Jones 2004: 52). This profile is repeated in the analysis of the LSYPE cohort of those more likely to take a gap year: White; from higher socio-economic backgrounds; and from independent schools. Gappers are also more likely to attend high-status universities (Crawford and Cribb 2012: 29–30). Again, there are differences between young people who plan to take gap years and those whose year out is unintended:

> there are at least two distinct groups of gap year takers: one plans to take a gap year, applies to and accepts a place at university before they leave school, is more likely to go travelling, has higher ability and comes from a more affluent socio-economic background, and is much more likely to take up their place at university on their return; the other is less likely to have planned to take a gap year, typically hasn't applied for and accepted a place before they leave school, is more likely to have worked and/or continued in full-time education during their 'gap year' and tends to come from a lower socio-economic background (although still significantly higher than the average socio-economic background of non-students). These individuals are far less likely to go on to university at the end of their 'gap year'. (Crawford and Cribb 2012: 6)

So, while the term gap year may be used to describe a range of activities, the type of gap years explored in this book are those associated with the activities of young people who are in a position of relative privilege compared to their peers. It is important to remember that context will affect rates of participation. The gap year narratives in this book were written in 2006–2007, which was a different, pre-recession landscape, and we might expect financial pressures to have had some impact. Participation in pre-university gap years has also been affected by changes in education policy, including the recent rise in tuition fees in the UK. There was a marked decrease in deferred places among 18 year olds in 2011/12, which was the academic year before the new fees of up to £9000 were introduced (Department for Business Innovation and Skills 2013).

Young people went to straight to university after school to avoid these fees. In 2011/12, 2.7 per cent of accepted applicants deferred their place, compared to 6 per cent the previous year (UCAS 2013: n.p.). Rising university costs may put pressure on future uptake, although one gap year organisation suggests a year out is 'breathing space' to ensure that young people choose the 'right path': 'With university fees ever increasing, a gap year can be a perfect option for anyone not totally sure of their life path to find out what they really want from life and rev up the energy to go for it' (Philpott 2013: n.p.). While the future of overseas gap years is uncertain, they remain surrounded by discourses that they may still be beneficial for young people if conducted *in the right way*.

The Benefits of Gap Year Travel

Young people are encouraged to take gap years between school and university by careers advice websites, press articles and, unsurprisingly, gap year providers. Gap year travel is framed as something different to trips that are solely concerned with leisure. In these public discourses, gap years offer young people an opportunity to see the world, and are viewed as potentially educational, helping them to develop desirable skills. There is some disagreement over what is worthwhile, however. The issue of what counts as a valuable gap year experience is important, as 'a university degree is not enough to make one employable as credentials do no more than permit entry into the competition for tough-entry jobs rather than entry into the winner's enclosure' (Brown and Hesketh 2004: 2).

For the most part, the image of gap years is that they are beneficial. Although there are a variety of activities that young people engage in during their time out, one newspaper article suggests that:

> at its core, the concept of a gap year is reassuringly stable – as are the potential benefits of taking one. There's the lure of the open road for those inclined to travel; the chance to challenge yourself; plus it's an opportunity to learn new skills and have life-altering experiences along the way. (Thorne 2013: n.p.)

Advice on the UK Government's website stresses that gap years are a form of learning that 'can do wonders for your skills, confidence and CV [Curriculum Vitae]' (Directgov 2012: n.p.). Such advice usually suggests that this should be instrumental and strategic, and orientated towards benefits for university and subsequently a graduate career. Consequently, gap years are viewed as something that can be used in university and job applications. According to another newspaper article, a year out 'will give you something impressive to add to your CV. Employers and university admissions officers love gap year students and the skills they acquire' (Ford 2005: n.p.). The message that there will be a future 'pay-off' to taking a gap year is reinforced by gap year providers: 'Employers and university staff increasingly attach importance to evidence of enterprise, maturity and sustained commitment both within and outside formal education' (Year Out Group 2013).

These discourses suggest that gap years give young people a competitive edge in the context of credential inflation (Heath 2007) and the economic downturn: 'Today's tough job market means gappers must ensure a year out will leave behind a sprinkling of CV fairy dust' (Tobin 2009: n.p.). There is a perception that a well-planned gap year will 'trump a generic degree every time' (Griffiths 2009: n.p.). Indeed, gap years receive official support, with successive UK governments funding overseas volunteering programmes. In 2009, the Labour Government collaborated with the charitable organisation Raleigh International to subsidise gap year placements in response to the 'shrinking' graduate job market (Sugden 2009: n.p.). Although this scheme was for university graduates (rather than pre-university gappers), it indicates the legitimisation and institutionalisation of gap years as a means of self-development. Entitled the 'Graduate Bursary Award' programme, it provided graduates with subsidised placements on 10-week Raleigh expeditions to Borneo, Costa Rica and Nicaragua, or India. The subsequent Coalition Government has established the International Citizen Service (ICS), funded by the Department for International Development. ICS works with volunteering and development organisations to provide 10 to 12 week placements for 18 to 25 year olds, meeting all direct costs but asking young people to generate at least £800 through fundraising (ICS 2013: n.p.). Announcing ICS, the Prime Minister David Cameron stated the scheme is a way to 'give thousands of our young people, those who couldn't otherwise afford it, the chance to see the world and serve others' (Birdwell 2011: 9).

One point of contention in these public debates is the relative benefits of independent travel versus volunteering. Volunteering has the moral advantage of altruism, meaning that gappers can 'make a difference' rather than engage in 'the selfish, carefree connotations of backpacking' (Shepherd 2008: n.p.). Moreover, volunteering is seen to provide the added cosmopolitan benefit of a more authentic engagement with difference (Lyons et al. 2012). According to one article, 'Travelling is all very well, but to get a real slice of life in a foreign country, you need to walk in the shoes of the locals' (Ford 2005: n.p.). Alternatively, independent travel carries with it the connotations of adventure and social status. The director of the travel company Lonely Planet argues in favour of backpacking during a pre-university gap year: 'I think you can tell the difference between someone who has seen the world, travelled and challenged themselves, and someone who hasn't' (Thorne 2013: n.p.).

Another point of public debate concerns the benefits of gap year volunteering for the host communities. One online commentator asks: 'Is gap year volunteering a bad thing?':

> We're teaching our next generation of leaders that development work is easy, and that their skills are so valuable to the people abroad that it is worth donating money to send them to help. And we're teaching them that, just because they come from the UK or the US, they are in a position of superiority over the people they are going to 'serve'. (Papi 2013: n.p.)

A Demos report on ICS suggests young people do gain something from volunteering, but notes many have doubts about the community benefits (Birdwell 2011). This was widely reported in the press, who picked up on the idea of gap years as 'colonialism'. Subsequently, the 2013 London Library Student Prize[8] asked students to submit essays on the theme: 'Gap Years: A New Form of Colonialism?' The winning article, however, defends gap years, suggesting that they engender global citizenship and awareness of international inequalities (Nave 2013). The commercialisation of gap year placements has also led to the rise of 'chads', or charity adventurers. These young people still want to do something useful but also remain independent, and consequently organise their own expedition to raise money for charity. According to the founder of gapyear.com, Tom Griffiths, this is 'the last bastion of raw travel adventure' (Shepherd 2008: n.p.). Even simply taking a (short) break can be framed as beneficial if it is justified by providing the young person with some respite before knuckling down to serious study at university.

There are some clear symbolic struggles over what kinds of gap year are most beneficial, and the public debates foreshadow those in gap year research. Running throughout all of the discourses, however, is an emphasis on making gap years strategic and worthwhile. The head of UCAS, Mary Curnock Cook, even declared the 'death of the gap year' in 2010, suggesting that the environment was so competitive that they should be re-framed as 'bridging years'. Curnock Cook argues that young people should not be concerned with leisure activities during any periods of time out:

> Conceptually a gap year has been when young people take a nice break and go out and see the world … By calling it a bridging year instead, you stress that it should be used in a focused way to support an application to the course or university you are targeting. (Barrett 2010: n.p.)

Other commentators also question the use of the term gap year, placing the responsibility on young people to make these strategic decisions in order to gain a competitive advantage:

---

8 This is a competition for final year undergraduates run by the London Library in collaboration with *The Times* newspaper and the graduate recruitment website *Milkround*. The winning article is published in *The Times*.

The very term gap year is a misnomer; it implies a space to be filled, something passively waiting rather than a period when a young adult will be actively constructing an identity and taking responsibility for their own lives in a way unlikely to be matched by friends going straight to university or college. (Price 2008: n.p.)

As gap years are only temporary, and the graduate job market is difficult, time is viewed as a precious commodity. Consequently, young people are urged to 'use the time wisely' (Ford 2005) and to 'make productive use of your time out' (Reed 2012). Even just travelling can be beneficial if understood in this way, as long as 'personal goals and objectives' are emphasised to potential employers so that this is 'time well spent' (Tobin 2009: n.p.). Tom Griffiths from gapyear. com goes as far as stating that overseas gap years are 'not about travel and volunteering' but are concerned with a 'constructive use of time' for young people to shape their path through life (Griffiths 2009: n.p.).

Cosmopolitanism and Gap Year Travel

Griffiths's comments are rather disingenuous, given that taking an overseas gap year, as opposed to one at home, provides particular kinds of benefits. Lyons et al. suggest that gap years are promoted as a 'de facto form of civics education that promulgates an acceptance and tolerance of cultural diversity and engenders the development of global citizenship' (Lyons et al. 2012: 365). Exposure to difference, and having knowledge of the world, is increasingly beneficial. According to Johan, taking gap years overseas mean that young people learn to deal with different cultural contexts, which is an important resource in the context of globalisation: 'adaptation to different national cultures and tolerance of diversity are regarded as both valuable ... and bring benefits contributing to success in education and employment' (Johan 2009: 142). There are parallels with young people embarking on international education. In their work on student mobilities, Brooks and Waters note that young people studying overseas are seen to gain a cosmopolitan sensibility, providing 'inter-cultural learning, [a] global outlook and understanding of "difference"' (Brooks and Waters 2011: 15). They point to Mitchell's concept of the 'strategic cosmopolitan', who is 'motivated ... by understandings of global competitiveness, and the necessity to strategically adapt as an individual to rapidly shifting personal and national contexts' (Mitchell 2003: 388). Yet this focus on future benefits has implications for the status of gap years as cosmopolitan journeys. Cosmopolitanism has political and moral dimensions of global citizenship, tolerance and universalism. Rizvi (2009) argues that such concerns are not the primary focus of international students. Instead, studying overseas is a way to gain positional advantage, given that the global economy 'increasingly prizes the skills of intercultural experiences and a cosmopolitan outlook' (Rizvi 2009: 260). There are comparable concerns with gap year cosmopolitanism, given the emphasis that is placed on making this time out worthwhile for the young people involved.

Youth Travel and Alternative Tourism

The Tourist and the Traveller

The desirability of gap years as a way for young people to demonstrate their cosmopolitanism can be placed in the wider context of 'good taste' in travel, and the development of independent youth travel as a sign of status. Seeing travel as an educational experience that provides young people with important cultural knowledge harks back to the era of the Grand Tour in the seventeenth and eighteenth centuries, when the young elite of Europe would tour the sites of high culture (Craik 1997). One of the most common axes of distinction in contemporary leisure travel is the tourist versus the traveller (Wang 2000). Indeed, many of the young people's gap year narratives explored in this book stress the difference between their activities and those of tourists. Youthful, independent travel is part of a historical trend in which 'proper travel' is positioned in opposition to mass tourism. MacCannell argues that this intellectualised discourse is nostalgia for clear-cut distinctions between the classes (MacCannell 1999: 107). For MacCannell, tourism emerged as a search for authenticity in modern complex societies. He draws on Goffman's (1959) distinction between the 'front' and the 'back', and suggests that what tourists hope to see on their travels is the intimate and real in the authentic 'back stage' space. However, MacCannell argues tourists actually experience something in-between, a 'staged authenticity' (MacCannell 1999: 92–98). According to MacCannell, the perceived authenticity of an experience gives travel its value. These desires share some clear parallels with cosmopolitanism as an orientation to engage with difference on a real, rather than superficial level. As will be discussed, however, the idea that some cultures may be able to provide authenticity leads to problematic framings that can commodify difference and position 'the Other' as 'less developed' and hence more 'real'.

Despite the influence of MacCannell's arguments in the study of tourism, Urry (2002) suggests that tourism is not always a search for authenticity. Instead, Urry argues tourists are looking for escape from their everyday lives, although authenticity may determine what is extraordinary (Urry 2002: 12). Gap years may offer such a (temporary) escape. In addition, the concept of 'post-tourists' developed by Feifer (1985) suggests some individuals know that tourism is not authentic, and are ironic and playful in enjoying different types of settings, always aware of their outsider status (cited in Urry 2002: 91). In contrast to this ironic playfulness, gap years are shaped by trends that place proper travel in opposition to mass tourism. One influence on the development of gap years is 'backpacking', or independent travel.

Backpacking as an Alternative

Backpacking is often positioned as a youthful antidote to the consumerist pleasures of mass tourism. It emerged as an alternative activity in the second half of the twentieth century in the context of other countercultural youth movements. Cohen locates backpacking in 'the social and political upheavals of the 1960s: the student revolution and the Vietnam War' (Cohen 2004: 55). Backpacking began to emerge in academic and popular literature in the 1990s, although earlier studies of independent travel include Cohen's (1973) study of 'drifters' (O'Reilly 2006: 1000). This typology of youth travellers notes the 'drifter' as the ideal, travelling without itinerary, destination or even purpose (Cohen 1973; 2004). The value here is in authentic, non-institutionalised experiences. Increasingly, however, independent travel relies on institutional structures such as youth travel operators, which Cohen sees as a gap between ideology and practice, analogous to MacCannell's concept of staged authenticity (Cohen 2004: 49). Although backpacking practices may be institutionalised, empirical studies note the continuing resonance of this discourse of alternative travel. Backpackers still construct symbolic communities that are positioned in opposition to tourism. For example, Loker-Murphy and Pearce find that backpackers 'want to … participate in a wide range of activities, many of which help them to understand and experience the "real"' (Loker-Murphy and Pearce 1995: 840–841). These concerns have remained fairly constant since backpacking's countercultural beginnings, according to Welk (2004).

The kudos and 'coolness' of this history is not lost on the gap year industry. The gap year provider organisation gapyear.com makes a specific link between the history of alternative travel and the organised volunteering and structured placements offered by their companies. After considering the 'history of the gap year', which touches on the Hippy Trail to India in the 1960s, the Magic Bus trips of the 1970s,[9] the development of the independent travel company Lonely Planet, and pioneering volunteering organisations like Project Trust and Raleigh International, the article suggests there are some common themes:

> We may smile now when we think of those bearded guys and beaded girls catching the bus to India, but they wanted a genuine experience. They wanted to grow as a group and as individuals. People will always want to test and challenge themselves, to gain new experiences, and that's exactly what gap years are all about. (Sherifi 2013: n.p.)

---

9 An overland bus trip from London to Kathmandu run by a young Australian.

What started out as a countercultural movement now has considerable influence on more 'mainstream' practices.

The figure of the backpacker is seen by Richards and Wilson as the model for contemporary tourists (Richards and Wilson 2004: 253). As argued by Urry (2002), forms of tourism need to be considered in relation to wider economic, social and cultural processes. The move to post-Fordist consumption, for example, has resulted in a growth in 'flexible' travel rather than package holidays (Urry 2002: 14). Moreover, structural changes have meant an increase in the service class, and in particular the 'new petit bourgeoisie' who are 'stronger on cultural rather than on economic capital' (Urry 2002: 80). Cultural capital is knowledge, objects and experiences with legitimate cultural value that can be exchanged for future benefits (Bourdieu 1984; 1997[1986]). As will be explored in Chapter 3, cultural capital is a scarce resource and is not equally distributed. The new middle classes may not be able to afford 5-star holidays but they can draw on their cultural knowledge in order to have experiences with an alternative form of status – much like gappers. These shifts in consumption practices can be summed up by the idea of 'real' holidays that place an emphasis:

> on travel rather than tourism, on individual choice, on avoiding the package holiday-maker, on the need to be an educated traveller, and on a global operation that permits individual care and attention. (Urry 2002: 96)

Structural changes and the rise of the new middle classes have driven the growth of independent travel to a wider audience, drawing on the history of backpacking as an activity with non-mainstream status. Munt suggests:

> the new petit bourgeoisie are best conceived as ego-tourists, who search for a style of travel which is both reflective of an 'alternative' lifestyle and which is capable of maintaining and enhancing their cultural capital. (Munt 1994: 108)

This can also be seen in relation to wider concerns like environmentalism, driving an interest in 'eco-tourism' and 'responsible travel' as good taste among certain sectors of the middle classes. Mowforth and Munt summarise these trends as 'sea, sun, sand and sex' being replaced with 'travelling, trekking and trucking' (Mowforth and Munt 1998: 53).

Volunteer Tourism

One sector that has grown as part of this alternative tourism field is volunteer tourism. These tourists 'volunteer in an organized way to undertake holidays that might involve aiding or alleviating the material poverty of some groups in society, the restoration of certain environments or research into aspects of society or environment' (Wearing 2001: 1). The growth of volunteer tourism has been driven by the growth of gap year companies, often offering placements in the global South (Butcher and Smith 2010; Lyons et al. 2012). Wearing (2001) argues that volunteer tourism is progressive, and concerned with offering a genuine alternative to the exploitation of communities by the mass tourism industry. For Lyons et al. (2012), these practices are *potentially* cosmopolitan, given their associated concern with global citizenship. Moreover, the cross-cultural interactions that occur through volunteering are often viewed as facilitating the understanding of different cultures and the issues facing communities (Raymond and Hall 2008: 531). An alternative take on altruistic motivations for 'making a difference' is that this is a sign of the individual morality of contemporary 'life politics' (Butcher and Smith 2010). As will be seen, however, some researchers are highly critical of volunteer tourism, which is one of the 'problems' of alternative travel.

The 'Problems' of Alternative Tourism and Gap year Travel

The history of youth travel illustrates three key themes which will be developed throughout this book. Firstly, some research into the growing gap year industry questions the model of development offered in volunteer tourism placements and their potential for encouraging cross-cultural understanding. Secondly, the benefits of gap year travel are promoted as a means of gaining status and advantageous skills, but there are concerns over its role in perpetuating inequalities. Finally, gap years are considered as a way for young people to undertake identity work at transitional moments.

Historical Legacies in Volunteer Tourism

The traveller's desire to gain access to authentic difference certainly has relevance for thinking about cosmopolitanism, but also comes with a problematic legacy. The growth of leisure travel, initially by the elite, missionaries and explorers, is bound up with modernity and colonial expansion, leading Simpson to conclude that tourism 'grew out of both the social and physical conditions of colonialism, and consequently adopted many of the same values' (Simpson 2005a: 45). For Simpson, this results in gap years being more concerned with the exotic than exploring the political and structural context of difference. The focus of Simpson's critique is volunteer tourism in the 'Third World', despite its claim to offer an ethical alternative to mainstream tourism. Indeed, there is a growing body of literature that questions the benefits of volunteer tourism, especially as the sector becomes increasingly commercialised (Lyons et al. 2012). The idea that volunteering in any context is automatically a 'good thing' is a normative assumption. Critical reflection on the benefits for both volunteers and the communities they engage with is crucial (Holdsworth and Quinn 2012).[10]

Research into the gap year phenomenon has tended to focus on structured placements, especially volunteering, in the global South. This work, and that of Simpson (2004; 2005a; 2005b) in particular, has been hugely important in providing a critique of the growing and increasingly commercialised gap year industry. In this study, however, I explore a wider range of activities that are defined by the young people who undertake them as gap years. This includes times spent in 'developed' countries and gap years that involve backpacking.

Class and Good Taste in Independent Travel

According to Munt (1994), independent travel is a way of accumulating cultural capital: knowledge, objects and experiences that are deemed to have legitimate cultural value and that are associated with higher social status and class inequalities (Bourdieu 1984; 1997[1986]). So, does gap year travel help young people to develop good taste? This depends on how we classify 'legitimate culture'. Craik (1997) considers how tourist activities are seen as rewarding and enriching experiences, and evaluates the idea of contemporary cultural tourism in the model of the Grand Tour. For Craik the 'truly self-improving tourist' is in the minority and limited to the privileged social classes – just like the young elite from the seventeenth and eighteenth centuries (Craik 1997: 120). However, what is the contemporary relevance of Craik's definition of 'highbrow' culture: opera, museums, art galleries, etc.? While these may remain classed activities, alternative forms of cultural knowledge are also valuable. The 'cultural omnivore thesis' (Peterson 1992; Peterson and Simkus 1992; Peterson and Kern 1996) suggests that being able to appreciate a range of cultural activities is now considered to be good taste. According to Peterson, people of high status have a 'taste for everything': 'status is gained by knowing about, and participating in (that is to say, by consuming) many if not all forms [of cultural activities]' (Peterson 1992: 252).

Backpacking and other modes of independent travel are often framed as an alternative to mass tourism, offering more authentic experiences, and gap years can draw on the status associated with these travel practices. We can see parallels between a desire to engage with the real life of the Other when travelling and a cosmopolitan openness to difference. Alternative travel is also particularly popular among certain sections of the middle classes with high cultural capital. In the next chapter, I expand on the idea of cultural cosmopolitanism as good taste that is associated with privileged groups. As this chapter has shown, it is

---

10 The authors make this point with reference to UK-based volunteering but note the parallels with criticisms of overseas gap years.

young people in a position of relative advantage who are more likely to take overseas gap years between school and university. Moreover, gap years are also promoted as a way for young people to make themselves more employable, so that they provide individuals who are already privileged to gain future benefits. This book consequently considers the role of gap years in the reproduction of advantage.

Travelling to 'Find Yourself'

Finally, 'identity work' is a concept that runs through much of the literature on travel. As Richards and Wilson (2004) note, the idea that there is a 'true self' that can be uncovered through travel is well-established: 'one of the classic notions about backpacking is that people travel to find themselves' (Richards and Wilson 2004: 262). Empirical studies of backpackers and independent travellers support this idea. For example, Desforges (2000) argues that travel provides backpackers with new experiences that can be mobilised for identity narratives. These ideas are also used in work on gap years. Gap years take place at transitional points in young people's lives, which leads Johan to suggest that overseas travel allows young people to use the difference between 'home' and 'away' to narrate their self-identity (Johan 2009: 142). This work can be continued after they return home according to King (2011), who finds that undergraduates draw on their gap years to define their emerging identities. However, we might consider to what extent our 'identity' is a matter of individual narration, and think about who is in a position to be able to tell stories about their cosmopolitan self.

Gap years are an example of how practices that purport to be cosmopolitan operate within particular social and cultural contexts. These are shaped by historical legacies and shared ideas about value and worth. In this book, I use Bourdieu's concept of habitus, a 'system of durable, transposable dispositions' (Bourdieu 1990: 52), in order to explore these ideas. The dispositions of the habitus, which guide our action, are a result of being embedded in a particular social context. Individuals are pre-adapted to appropriate ways of acting through the internalisation of their social circumstances (Bourdieu 1990: 560). Alternative perspectives, discussed here as theories of 'reflexive modernisation', suggest that traditional social structures (such as class divisions) have less influence over our lives, and see our experience of the world as individualised (Beck 1992; Giddens 1991). Consequently, another concept that is referred to throughout this book is 'reflexivity', the 'ability [of people] to reflect on the social conditions of their existence' (Beck 1994: 174). In other words, people have to think and deliberate, rather than take their place in the world for granted. Reflexivity is also used with reference to cosmopolitanism to describe critical and active engagements with difference (Kendall, Woodward and Skrbis 2009).

Theories of identity that argue our notions of self are increasingly individualised neglect the continuing relevance of collective understandings – 'us and them' – in order to tell particular stories. Identity is not just objective (determined by social structures) or subjective (a question of individual experience) but also emerges in an *intersubjective context*. Intersubjectivity is the relations between people, the 'mutual influence and accountability' that also shapes social action (Bottero 2010: 20). In the concluding chapter to this book, I argue for an alternative perspective that builds on Bourdieu's theory of practice to offer a new take on self-development through gap year travel. By doing so, we can engage with wider sociological debates surrounding cosmopolitanism, cultural taste and identity work.

Structure of the Book: A Gap Year Itinerary

Chapter 2 starts with a definition of the multi-dimensional concept of cosmopolitanism, with a focus on considering gap years in relation to their cultural elements. As gap years are increasingly commercialised and driven by market demands, the chapter asks if there are conflicts between cultural cosmopolitanism and its ethical, moral or political manifestations. I consider the dangers of cultural appropriation and other problematic ways to consume difference, and ask whether being cosmopolitan is an elite activity. Alternatively, other scholars put forward the notion of cosmopolitanism as ordinary, and as part of the day-to-day experiences of many different social groups. The idea of cosmopolitanism as banal (an almost unnoticed consequence of globalisation) is contrasted with the 'reflexive cosmopolitan', who consciously and actively engages with the Other. I then trace these themes in the literature on youth travel and gap years, highlighting work on inter-cultural relationships, including criticisms of volunteering, and how being cosmopolitanism might be employed to make status distinctions in line with individual goals of self-development.

Chapter 3 picks up the theoretical debates surrounding cultural value and identity work that are illuminated through the study of gap years. Firstly, it reviews the concept of cultural capital, and how this might operate in the field(s) of gap year travel. Secondly, the chapter introduces two influential but contrasting models of self-development. Is the self-development of gap year travel pursued on an individual basis, and do young people critically reflect on these processes? Such a position is aligned with the 'reflexive modernisation thesis'. Alternatively, is this self-development an outcome of embodied dispositions, the habitus, as described by Bourdieu (1990)? Bourdieu argues that we do not consciously choose our paths through life, but that our position in the class structure shapes what we think is appropriate, which in turn guides our dispositions to action. The chapter concludes with outlining the hypothetical figures of the 'reflexive gapper', which summarises how we can understand gap years through the lens of the reflexive modernisation thesis, and the 'habitual gapper', which explains how gap years might be understood from a Bourdieusian perspective.

Existing research into gap year travel provides valuable insights into the phenomenon through interviews with gappers, fieldwork in volunteering placements, or examining the discourses that surround the practice. However, the empirical research at the heart of this book uses a different approach by analysing unsolicited blogs written to record and communicate gap years. This method, supplemented by interviews with gappers, offers a unique insight into young people's gap year stories, generated without the influence of a researcher. Chapter 4 argues that blog analysis is an appropriate and innovative method to examine narratives and the framing of events for audiences. It outlines the pros and cons of blog analysis, including the pragmatic issue of dealing with large volumes of multimedia data; the quality of online research; and the ethical decisions that need to be made.

Chapter 5 is the first of three substantive chapters that review the gappers' blogs. It explores the representations of people and places encountered during gap years, and how difference is dealt with and framed. Travel is generally seen to 'broaden the mind', but this chapter questions whether there is evidence of a cosmopolitan attitude in the gappers' accounts. Gappers show a desire to experience authenticity, yet the framing of gap year locations is limited by structural and historical discourses surrounding difference. There are indications of a particular form of cosmopolitanism – one that is primarily concerned with telling the right story for audiences back home.

Narratives of taste in overseas gap years are discussed in Chapter 6 with reference to the concept of cultural capital and status distinctions. The adoption of 'proper travel' practices during the gap year, centred on authentic experiences, is a marker of status for gappers. This operates in opposition to mass tourism, drawing on the historical discourse of 'the tourist versus the traveller' and the kudos of a cosmopolitan attitude. Such symbolic distinctions have a moral dimension and are aimed at gaining status back home. The chapter also considers parallels between the gap year and wider trends in middle-class taste.

Central to popular understandings of gap years is that they enable self-development if conducted in the 'right' way. How do young people understand the perceived rewards of such experiences, the skills accumulated and the sorts of self-improvement enabled by gap year travel? The key argument in Chapter 7 is that gappers tend to uncritically reproduce accepted discourses regarding the benefits of taking an overseas gap year. These discourses normalise the idea that it is a young person's individual responsibility to do something worthwhile, neglecting the influence of structural factors. Value and meaning is attached to practices that are enterprising, perceived to be cosmopolitan, and that demonstrate 'good taste'. These experiences are framed using notions of worth that place cultural experiences in a moral hierarchy.

The concluding chapter summarises the key findings of the empirical study and the contribution of *A Cosmopolitan Journey?* to a number of empirical and theoretical debates. First, it considers the potential of gap years as an act of global citizenship. Secondly, it highlights how cosmopolitanism functions as a form of capital, and how cosmopolitan cultural capital is associated with good taste and is a resource in education and employment. Thirdly, the chapter criticises the view that the decision to take a gap year is related to personal choice and responsibility, because this obscures how such experiences are embedded in social contexts that shape both who has access to them, and how we understand and attach meaning to them. Fourthly, the chapter puts forward an argument for an understanding of self-development that allows for more agency than Bourdieu's model, but also recognises the structural limits to action. Finally, I consider the prospects for intervention in the gap year field and future directions for gap year research.

Chapter 2
Cultural Cosmopolitanism and Gap Year Debates

Being cosmopolitan, a 'world citizen', is usually considered to be a 'good thing'. If you are not cosmopolitan, you might be perceived as parochial, small-minded, intolerant. These are moral judgements, and we cannot separate them out from systems of power and inequality. Who decides what cosmopolitanism looks like, and who are the cosmopolitans? Cosmopolitanism is both a multi-faceted concept – with cultural, ethical, moral and political elements – and a contested one.

Much has been written about cosmopolitanism in recent years. Rovisco and Nowicka (2012) highlight the 'cosmopolitan turn' in the social sciences, driven by work that aims to understand the social, cultural and political consequences of globalisation. Overseas gap years can be placed in this wider context, in which we have much more contact with the world beyond our nation state borders. As suggested in the previous chapter, gap years are driven by these trends, and are framed by the claim that they foster cosmopolitanism among the young people who take them. This is true of independent travel that aims to provide authentic inter-cultural experiences, and volunteering placements that are seen as evidence of global citizenship. Research on gap years, and youth travel more generally, engages critically with the idea that they promote inter-cultural learning. It has been suggested that as gappers gain personal benefits, like increased employability, gap years are primarily concerned with self-interest rather than a commitment to the Other.

In this chapter, I review the debates surrounding cultural cosmopolitanism and their implications for overseas gap years. I note that cultural cosmopolitanism tends to be built on acts of consumption, such tourism, consuming global media and eating out in 'ethnic' restaurants. Consequently, scholars have questioned the relationship between cultural cosmopolitanism and ethical, political and moral commitments to openness and tolerance. The chapter then questions the progressive potential of cosmopolitanism through arguments that it is elitist, which is contrasted with work on cosmopolitan practices that are everyday and ordinary. The chapter also touches on broader debates regarding socio-cultural change and the condition of cosmopolitanism, and the implications for cultural practices leading to ethical stances. I outline work that suggests a distinction between 'banal cosmopolitanism' (the unintended consequences that arise from living in a globalising society) and 'reflexive cosmopolitanism' (an active engagement with otherness). Finally, I discuss work on cosmopolitanism in relation to gap years, youth travel, and volunteering, and consider how we might assess whether gap years engender cosmopolitan sensibilities.

Defining Cosmopolitanism

The first step is to define cosmopolitanism, a multi-dimensional concept. Vertovec and Cohen (2002) suggest the following ways 'being cosmopolitan' can be understood:

- Cosmopolitanism as a condition: processes of globalisation have resulted in hybridity and pluralism in social and cultural life.
- Cosmopolitanism as a philosophy: being a citizen of the world, where everyone shares common values.
- Cosmopolitanism as a political project for transnational institutions: building institutions such as the United Nations and social movements, such as environmentalism, which have a global perspective.
- Cosmopolitanism as a political project in recognising multiple identities: individuals have affiliations to different communities on a regional, national and global scale.
- Cosmopolitanism as an orientation: an outlook that is open to cultural difference.
- Cosmopolitanism as a practice or competence: the skills and abilities to move through different cultures.

Looking back to the discourses discussed in Chapter 1, we can think about gap years in relation to more than one of these facets of cosmopolitanism. If we are living under cosmopolitan social-cultural conditions then the benefits of developing a more global outlook are clear. Moreover, the popularity of overseas gap years can be understood as *part* of these trends, much like the internationalisation of education. Becoming a 'citizen of the world' is part and parcel of the gap year experience, centred on finding common ground and understand global conditions a little better. Cosmopolitan orientations could be the outcome of taking a gap year, or perhaps gappers are people who are more inclined to have open outlooks. Similarly, being competent in a range of cultural settings, rather than just local cultures, might be the cause or effect of taking a gap year. These last two dimensions – orientations and competences – are highlighted in the work of Hannerz, who defines cosmopolitanism as:

> an orientation, a willingness to engage with the other. It is an intellectual and aesthetic openness toward divergent cultural experiences, a search for contrasts rather than uniformity … At the same time, however, cosmopolitanism can

be a matter of competence … a personal ability to make one's way into other cultures, through listening, looking, intuiting, and reflecting. And there is cultural competence in the stricter sense of the term, a built-up skill in manoeuvring more or less expertly with a particular system of meanings and meaningful forms. (Hannerz 1990: 239)

One of the central questions in this book is whether taking a gap year is a way of developing and demonstrating this cosmopolitan openness to diversity. However, critical accounts of cultural cosmopolitanism challenge the level of genuine involvement with the Other, and are sceptical as to whether increased engagement with cultural diversity necessarily leads to an open, tolerant perspective.

Consuming Difference

As Vertovec and Cohen observe: 'A key question of our age is: can or does exposure to other cultures – from buying bits of them to learning to partake in their beliefs and practices – lead to a fundamental change in attitudes?' (Vertovec and Cohen 2002: 14). Cultural cosmopolitanism is associated with 'tolerance based on pluralism, dialogue and a recognition of difference' (Savage, Bagnall and Longhurst 2005: 181). Authors such as Beck (2002), Hannerz (1990) and Urry (2000) trace the connections between globalisation and cosmopolitanism, arguing that the flows of people, technology, capital and images enabled by globalisation provide increasing opportunities for cross-cultural interaction. These global cultural flows potentially mean we have more opportunities to learn about and engage with difference. This might lead to an increased 'awareness of the world' (Robertson 1992) and could foster cosmopolitan orientations. Following Appadurai (1990), Kendall, Woodward and Skrbis (2009) propose the idea of 'cosmoscapes', the circulation of cultural objects that carry the Other through global networks and which enable the possibility of cosmopolitan engagement. Global media, for example, offer images, views and experiences that are different to our home context on an everyday basis and develop the potential for cosmopolitan awareness (Szerszynski and Urry 2002; 2006).

According to Kendall, Woodward and Skrbis (2009), there are three dimensions to cosmopolitan dispositions to engage with different cultures. These dimensions are: mobility; cultural and symbolic competencies; and inclusivity. Mobilities include physical movement using global transportation networks but also virtual 'travel' via global media and communications. The specific cosmopolitan competencies as suggested by Kendall, Woodward and Skrbis are a kind of inter-cultural mastery, including being able to draw upon a wide range of cultural knowledge and repertoires at the right moments. Inclusivity is particularly important, as it involves not just a taste for the exotic, but a valuing of the Other (Kendall, Woodward and Skrbis 2009: 110–112).

Mobilities are therefore central to the development of cultural pluralism. This may be virtual, in the form of global media flows, but also physical, including the growth of international travel. Urry (1995) argues that a particular form of cosmopolitanism is generated in part by tourism. This 'aesthetic cosmopolitanism' contributes to contemporary social identities. According to Urry, it includes: a perceived right to travel; a curiosity about places, peoples and cultures; openness to others; a willingness to take risks; an ability to locate one's own society historically and globally; and a certain semiotic skill to interpret tourist signs (Urry 1995: 167). Such concerns resonate with desires for overseas gap years.

Germann Molz (2012a) points out that when we talk about cultural cosmopolitanism, it is often framed in a way that focuses on what people *consume*. Gap years are no exception, if we think about the purchase of flights, accommodation, tours, placements, etc.[1] For some, cosmopolitan trends in cultural consumption have arguably manifested in the growth of the cultural omnivore (Peterson 1992; Peterson and Simkus 1992; Peterson and Kern 1996). The omnivore is someone who has a taste for everything. According to this theory, high cultural tastes have changed from snobbishness to openness and tolerance. Peterson and Kern suggest this is driven by increased mobility among a 'business-administrative class':

> omnivorous inclusion seems better adapted to an increasingly global world managed by those who make their way, in part, by showing respect for the cultural expressions of others. (Peterson and Kern 1996: 906)

However, we cannot assume a 'connection between cosmoscapes and the fostering of cosmopolitan individuals' (Kendall, Woodward and Skrbis 2009: 9). As Peterson and Kern (1996) recognise, omnivorousness is associated with the cultural worlds of dominant status groups. Global cultural flows, in other words, do not necessarily result in cosmopolitan dispositions.

A number of authors suggest that simply consuming difference does not automatically result in becoming a global citizen. Calhoun argues:

---

1 Even volunteer tourism is arguably an act of consumption, especially as 'the main priority of a growing number of commercial tourism operators who provide "packaged" volunteer experiences is to make a profit and therefore to provide a commodified experience' (Lyons et al. 2012: 372). The gap year industry as a whole provides customers with a product to consume (Simpson 2004).

Food, tourism, music, literature and clothes are all easy faces of cosmopolitanism. They are indeed broadening … but they are not hard tests for the relationship between local solidarity and international civil society. (Calhoun 2002: 106)

So, travelling overseas and consuming gap year products may not necessarily result in changes in attitudes towards difference, or global political awareness. As Skey notes, there is a considerable difference between buying indigenous art and taking part in a demonstration for indigenous people's rights (Skey 2012: 467). Nowicka and Rovisco warn against conflating contemporary global phenomena, like cultural hybridity, with expressions of cosmopolitanism. This conflation is a 'thin' approach to cosmopolitanism that does not engage with hierarchies of power and material conditions (Nowicka and Rovisco 2009: 8). Essentially, the consumption of difference is something that can be viewed as superficial.

One critical issue here is that global flows are driven by commerce. Marx and Engels predicted the global reach of capitalism: the 'exploitation of the world market given a cosmopolitan character to production and consumption in every country' (cited in Calhoun 2002: 103). A taste for cultural difference might have little to do with global citizenship, but instead is a consequence of global consumerism. Difference is simply a way to open up new markets for consumption (Binnie and Skeggs 2004). These critical accounts also question the essence of cosmopolitan claims. From this perspective, gap years are better seen as products in a global marketplace that is dependent on imbalances of economic and political power. Cheah criticises the visions of a new cosmopolitan solidarity that do not adequately address the economic inequalities between the global North and the postcolonial South: 'it is unlikely that this solidarity will be directed in a concerted manner towards ending economic inequality between countries because Northern civil societies derive their prodigious strength from this inequality' (Cheah 2006: 494). Cheah's target is the concept of a global public sphere, but this criticism is equally applicable to the production of places that are 'different' in the global South for the consumption of young gappers from the global North. Similarly, Kendall, Woodward and Skrbis (2009) highlight the Anglocentric figure of the omnivore, who consumes culturally diverse products that flow from the global South to the North. The consumption of cultural diversity and difference does not necessarily mean that people are consuming in ways that are politically or ethically cosmopolitan, since such consumption tends to reproduce rather than undermine global North/South inequalities (Kendall, Woodward and Skrbis 2009: 146–147).

Germann Molz notes a paradoxical relationship when cosmopolitanism rests on acts of consumption: there is a desire to consume diversity, but difference can be 'watered down' through consumption or taken out of context through cultural appropriation (Germann Molz 2012a: 38). Commodification transforms difference into something that can be consumed without developing inter-cultural understanding. Such consumption may even perpetuate problematic views of Otherness, like exoticism, and the Other is sold to meet a consumer demand for novelty in ways that may be uncosmopolitan (Kendall, Woodward and Skrbis 2009: 127). As Beck (2006) argues:

> the glitter of cultural difference fetches a good price. Images of an in-between world, of the black body, exotic beauty, exotic music, exotic food and so on, are globally cannibalized, re-staged and consumed as products for mass markets. (cited in Germann Molz 2012a: 39)

This is encapsulated in what Hage (1997) terms 'cosmo-multiculturalism', a form of consumption grounded in power relations. Using the example of dining out in 'ethnic' restaurants by White Australians, Hage argues that such practices are markers of good taste and sophistication rather than commitments to inter-cultural interactions. Moreover, they are based on essentialised ideas about the authentic and exotic Other.

Overall, then, such debates suggest that cultural pluralism and a desire for experiencing diversity cannot be taken as evidence of cosmopolitanism in a wider sense. It is important not to collapse the differences between cultural, political and ethical forms of cosmopolitanism (Skey 2012: 467). While globalisation may mean that we have access to more diverse cultural products and images, this may not result in meaningful engagement with difference, and may in fact contribute to continuing imbalances in power relations and uncosmopolitan framings. Moreover, Skey also points out that attitudes are not fixed, so that even if the consumption of cultural difference leads to greater understanding, this can change: 'showing solidarity with an individual or a group at one moment does not preclude the utilization of cultural stereotypes or support for exclusionary practice at another' (Skey 2012: 476). What this suggests is that cosmoscapes are driven by structural and material concerns: in other words, the global movement of consumer goods. In these debates, cultural cosmopolitanism is centred on market demands rather than tolerance. Consequently, 'consumerist ideology tends to reproduce the very social divisions cosmopolitanism claims to dissolve' (Germann Molz 2012a: 39).

Similar critical concerns are raised in the second set of debates about cosmopolitanism. The figure of the cosmopolitan has often been viewed as a member of the elite, who is mobile and privileged. Viewing the consumption of cultural difference as a sophisticated competence also denotes the role of status and class, with cosmopolitan tastes functioning as a form of distinction. This is challenged by the concept of 'ordinary cosmopolitanism', which gives us a different view of cultural diversity that is grounded in day-to-day practice and everyday experience. Yet there are tangible benefits to being cosmopolitan, as exemplified in the promotion of gap years as a valuable activity for young people.

Cosmopolitanism and Elitism

Cosmopolitans are often stereotyped as 'privileged, bourgeois, and politically uncommitted' (Vertovec and Cohen 2002: 6). In addition to the challenges associated with consuming difference, cultural cosmopolitanism has been implicated in relations of symbolic exploitation and economic domination (Kendall, Woodward and Skrbis 2009: 125). A central concern is that definitions of the cosmopolitan are close to those of the elite. This is, in part, due to the fact that cultural cosmopolitanism can be viewed as a 'capitalist project', according to Calhoun, which reflects dominant class perspectives:

> imagine the world from the vantage point of frequent travellers, easily entering and exiting polities and social relations around the world, armed with visa-friendly passports and credit cards. (Calhoun 2002: 89)

Only the very privileged can engage in this; it is professionals with high status who have unrestricted movement and access to resources that *allow* them to be cosmopolitan. These inequalities lead Calhoun (2002) to question the democratic potential of cosmopolitanism. From this perspective, the cosmopolitan is an individual who is portrayed as Western, male, and part of the elite 'transnational capitalist class' (Sklair 2001). Moreover, the consumption of difference is involved in making status distinctions. As I explore in Chapter 5, to be cosmopolitan is to have 'good taste'. Being geographically and culturally mobile, and having the capacity to interpret difference, is a valuable cultural resource and one which is not open to all.

It is pointed out, for example, that Hannerz's (1990) oft-cited description of cosmopolitanism as an orientation that is open to difference both intellectually and aesthetically, and as a competence, is one of classed privilege. For Skeggs, a 'more detailed articulation of Bourdieu's (1986) analysis of class as formed through knowledge and disposition would be hard to find; as would a greater sense of entitlement' (Skeggs 2004a: 158). Being cosmopolitan is an advantageous quality, but one that needs the cultural resources of time, access and knowledge to acquire (Skeggs 2004a: 159). Being culturally omnivorous, for example, is something that reflects contemporary requirements for occupational success, like openness and flexibility (van Eijck 2000: 221). Furthermore, evidence from a study of cultural taste in the UK suggests the omnivorousness of the contemporary middle classes reflects access to scarce resources in ways that are misrecognised (Bennett et al. 2009). By showing that the middle classes are open and tolerant, Bennett et al. argue omnivorousness provides a liberal veneer to cultural consumption; sanctions access to popular activities; accords with the consumerist imperative to try everything; and provides the legitimate capital of having 'versatile repertoires' (Bennett et al 2009: 255).

So, while cosmopolitanism is predicated on openness and tolerance, it is also used as a marker of status and, as this is sanctioned as legitimate, such positions are inscribed with moral worth:

> if, in a globalizing, multi-cultural society, moral worthiness is gained through the ability to truly appreciate the cultural products and practices of 'the other', it is only logical that such worthiness is granted to those who are able to place their moral and cultural values in perspective. (van Eijck 2000: 219)

In popular frames of cosmopolitanism, to not possess such orientations and competencies is to lack moral worthiness. Hage (1998) argues cosmopolitanism is often a moralising discourse rather than critical reflection on difference. For Hage, claiming to be cosmopolitan is a status distinction, made so that people are viewed as tolerant and anti-racist. In the Australian context Hage explores, these status distinctions draw a line between those seen as racist, Anglophile, out of touch and old-fashioned; and those who are seen as urban, anti-racist, cosmopolitan and non-Anglocentric (Hage 1998: 182). The 'exposure to a certain "sophisticated internationalism"', Hage argues, enables the accumulation of 'a specific *cosmopolitan capital*' (Hage 1998: 205; my emphasis). Cosmopolitan consumption, for example dining out in 'ethnic' restaurants (Hage 1997), denotes both the sophistication of those who engage in such activities and the lack of sophistication of those do not. These status distinctions are class distinctions. What Binnie and Skeggs (2004) call the 'virtues of cosmopolitanism' are denied to dominated groups, for example the White working-classes, who are usually associated with nationalised or reactionary politics rather than cosmopolitan openness; or White working-class women who are both out of place in, and disruptive to, cosmopolitan spaces of consumption.[2]

The cosmopolitan ideal of openness and tolerance is challenged by this implication of exclusivity and class-based distinction. For some, the *definition* of cosmopolitanism that is proposed by authors like Hannerz (1990) is Euro-American, White, male and privileged (Germann Molz 2012a: 37). This means that alternative forms of cosmopolitanism may not receive the same attention or may even be dismissed. Jones and Leshkowich (2003), for example, criticise the way that the transnational practices of Nigerian women are dismissed by Hannerz as 'local' (cited in Germann Molz 2012a: 37). In other words, if the

---

2 The example Binnie and Skeggs (2004) use to illustrate this is the urban cosmopolitan space of Manchester's gay village.

very definition of 'cosmopolitan' is one which sits closely with the properties of elites, it is not surprising that cosmopolitanism is viewed as elitist. There is, however, a body of work that aims to explore alternative cosmopolitanisms, a challenge to the 'highly intellectualized, Western and elite characterisation of cosmopolitanism' (Rovisco and Nowcika 2012: 5) that excludes other forms of cross-cultural interaction.

Another critique comes from Werbner, who cites Hannerz's view of migrants and refugees as transnational (and therefore distinct from the cosmopolitan elite) as evidence of a classed and Eurocentric bias in cosmopolitan studies (Werbner 1999: 17). Werbner explores the global pathways and networks of South Asian migrants, and how they reconfigure the local and create transnational cultural worlds. She argues that it is possible for working-class migrants to be cosmopolitan, while still recognising the class dimensions of these networks. Diasporic communities connect to both the local and the global:

> Cosmopolitanism … does not necessarily imply an absence of belonging but the possibility of belonging to more than one ethnic and cultural localism simultaneously. This is as true of working class cosmopolitans as it is of third-world intellectual elites. (Werbner 1999: 34)

Lamont and Aksartova (2002) also consider cosmopolitanism among working class groups, comparing non-college educated White and Black workers in the USA with White and North African workers in France. The authors saw evidence of a cosmopolitan moral commitment to universalism (Nussbaum 1996) among their interviewees. Instead of the multiculturalism of elite forms of cosmopolitanism, Lamont and Aksartova explore the anti-racist rhetoric that ordinary people use to bridge boundaries. While different cultural resources are drawn on in different countries by different groups, they argue people tend to employ moral universalism, and recognise common humanity in the Other. The men they interviewed use 'universal criteria that can be applied to all human beings to evaluate other groups and themselves' (Lamont and Aksartova 2002: 3). Drawing on this data, Lamont and Aksartova argue for greater attention to be paid to 'ordinary cosmopolitanisms'. They call for 'a sociology of everyday practical cosmopolitanism that is less dependent on the frameworks predominant in our very distinct upper middle-class academic environments' (Lamont and Aksartova 2002: 18).

Some have questioned whether Lamont and Aksartova underplay structural factors, or indeed the complex and sometimes contradictory views that people hold (Skey 2012). However, their work represents a trend in cosmopolitan studies that puts the 'cosmopolitan and local' distinction to one side and considers how cosmopolitanism is grounded and part of everyday life. This is not an abstract project but rather one that explores 'actually existing cosmopolitanism'

(Robbins 1998). For example, Skrbis and Woodward explore cosmopolitanism as 'a set of outlooks and practices, as a disposition, increasingly available – yet not guaranteed – to individuals for the purposes of dealing with cultural diversity, hybridity and otherness' (Skrbis and Woodward 2007: 734). This enables them to consider how 'ordinary people' engage with globalisation. For Skrbis and Woodward, cosmopolitan views are not the preserve of the global elite, and awareness of other cultures and modes of living can extend more broadly. Although there are limits to this in practice, Skrbis and Woodwood suggest the proliferation of global symbols and mobilities provide the 'raw material' for cosmopolitanism (Skrbis and Woodward 2007: 733). Coming into contact other cultures through the consumption of global media, for example, means it is possible for 'understanding, empathy and, sometimes, action' to follow (Skrbis and Woodward 2007: 733).

What are the implications of these debates for researching the gap year? Gappers can hardly be said to be part of a global business elite (although they may be in the future). Yet young people who are in a position to take a gap year are a privileged group compared to their peers in the UK, and are certainly advantaged compared to most other young people in a global context. They have access to resources that enable geographical mobility in ways that are sanctioned as legitimate. In addition, acquiring omnivorous cultural tastes through gap years means that gappers can make status claims and distinguish themselves from those who do not have such experiences. In Chapter 3, I explore how the concept of cosmopolitan cultural capital can capture such taste distinctions.

Although gap years are consumption practices, they still provide opportunities for inter-cultural encounters, at least in theory. They are not quite 'everyday life' – and indeed are premised upon experiences that are out of the ordinary – but they are not solely concerned with the consumption of cultural objects. So, gap years can provide a way of exploring the links between cultural cosmopolitanism, and the claims for an ethical or moral commitment to tolerance, openness, and universalism implicit in arguments about cosmopolitan dispositions. Do gappers make sense of their identity and their cultural encounters in cosmopolitan ways? In order to consider this question, it is necessary to think through different forms of cosmopolitanism, in which reflexivity plays a greater or lesser role. In turn, this leads to wider questions about the role of reflexivity in the gap year experience.

Banal Cosmopolitanism, Reflexive Cosmopolitanism

Concerns with the everyday aspects of cosmopolitanism have led to the concept of 'banal cosmopolitanism'. Globalising processes have increased everyday encounters with diversity, so that difference is unremarkable, and consequently is not associated with overtly ethical cosmopolitan orientations. An example provided by Beck is the food available in supermarkets: 'every possible kind of food that used to be eaten on other continents and in other cultures' is available, which results in 'cosmopolitan culinary eclecticism' that is normal and taken-for-granted (Beck 2002: 28). Beck's definition of banal cosmopolitanism builds on Billig's (1995) concept of 'banal nationalism': the unnoticed use of national symbols to reinforce national identity. Beck argues that banal cosmopolitanism is becoming prevalent, as 'everyday nationalism is circumvented and undermined and we experience ourselves integrated into global processes and phenomena' (Beck 2002: 28). Similarly, Szerszynski and Urry (2002; 2006) refer to 'banal globalism' fostered through global media.

However, such concepts rest on consumption which, as we have seen, raises questions about whether cultural cosmopolitanism translates into ethical or political commitments. Germann Molz (2012a) outlines the tensions inherent in different dimensions of global citizenship, and points to debates over the difference between superficial and authentic cosmopolitan consumption. The paradoxes inherent in cosmopolitan consumer practices – commodification of Otherness, the desire for difference, exclusionary practices – problematise the idea that they may lead to genuine global awareness. 'Sociopolitical issues like human rights, migration, ethnic cleansing or global wealth inequalities are apparently not on the menu for the cosmopolitan consumer' (Germann Molz 2012a: 45). However, Szerszynski and Urry (2002; 2006) argue that what might be considered banal behaviour is still significant, and has symbolic value. Indeed, Beck (2006) suggests that even banal cosmopolitanism provides individuals with a 'new reflexivity' to navigate a globalised world (cited in Germann Molz 2012a: 46).

To establish whether gappers adopt cosmopolitan outlooks, I suggest we need to look for evidence of 'global reflexivity' in their narratives. When individuals exhibit global reflexivity they are aware of global concerns, including transnational connections and inequalities, while also being aware of their own position. Savage, Bagnall and Longhurst define global reflexivity among their respondents (living in the North West of England) as:

> an ability to look at their lives, thoughts and values from a perspective that did not take English referents as the explicit frame for judgement, but which was able to place them in some kind of broader comparative frame. (Savage, Bagnall and Longhurst 2005: 191)

Employing reflexivity in this way draws on definitions of cosmopolitanism that stress it is a '*conscious* attempt to be familiar with people, objects and places that sit outside one's local or national settings' (Skrbis and Woodward 2007: 732; my emphasis).

For example, Hannerz (1990) defines 'genuine' cosmopolitanism as not only a desire for difference but also engaging with a 'culture of critical discourse'. He contrasts this with tacit or common-sense knowledge (Hannerz 1990: 246–247). An example of genuine cosmopolitanism would be the conscious attempt to engage with the Other through travel that is not concerned with exotic, 'home plus' experiences: 'India is home plus servants, Africa is home plus elephants and lions' (Hannerz 1990: 241). Cosmopolitanism, he argues, goes *beyond* such superficial encounters to more genuine experiences of the Other. Moreover, reflexive cosmopolitanism is not just concerned with global matters, but also personal ones. According to Nowicka and Rovisco (2009), cosmopolitanism is a 'mode of self-transformation'. This involves self-scrutiny and a critical examination of the boundaries drawn between us and them, so that people are 'reflexive about their experiences of otherness' (Nowicka and Rovisco 2009: 6).

In such debates we can see cultural cosmopolitanism presented as potentially both banal and reflexive, ethical but disconnected, based on consumption but also concerned with global issues. A recent attempt to engage with cosmopolitanism as lived experience pulls all of these strands together. Kendall, Woodward and Skrbis (2009) draw on their empirical studies of cosmopolitan attitudes among 'ordinary people' in Australia to define three different types of cosmopolitanism. Firstly, they note the prevalence of 'sampling', an unreflexive position that is centred on consumption. Someone who enacts the sampling style of cosmopolitanism might take pleasure and enjoyment in being able to consume diverse goods, but does not critically engage with global interconnections (Kendall, Woodward and Skrbis 2009: 116–117). Secondly, they note immersive forms of cosmopolitanism, which are more strategic, but have a 'deeper' connection with Otherness. The immersive cosmopolitan aims to cultivate 'multicultural capital' in order achieve status and self-development. They seek out new experiences and hope to be challenged by them, like listening to 'world music' in order to broaden their horizons and develop expert knowledge (Kendall, Woodward and Skrbis 2009: 119).

Finally, in keeping with Hannerz's (1990) definition, the reflexive cosmopolitan is seen as *genuine*. They are committed to acting in cosmopolitan ways, and exhibit 'a broad willingness to step outside stable, privileged and established power categories of self-hood' (Kendall, Woodward and Skrbis 2009: 122). The reflexive cosmopolitan is looking for authenticity, and wants genuine connections with Otherness. In the context of travel experiences, for example, they dismiss tourism, the 'home plus' as described by Hannerz (1990) and instead have a desire to participate and become involved

(Kendall, Woodward and Skrbis 2009: 113). As discussed above, they are also self-reflexive, interrogating their own position in the world.

In researching these different forms, Kendall, Woodward and Skrbis (2009) find that reflexive cosmopolitanism is the least common type exhibited. People's everyday reactions to diversity are evidence of cosmopolitanism as a *possibility*, a reflection of the 'gradual and sometimes discrepant infiltration and uptake of aspects of cosmopolitanism into the practices and outlooks of everyday citizens' (Kendall, Woodward and Skrbis 2009: 123). Such work highlights how cosmopolitans are not necessarily a fixed social group. Cosmopolitan orientations and views can be employed on one occasion but not in others. Skey (2012) argues that we need to pay attention to *when* people are cosmopolitan. This would acknowledge: that people can be more or less cosmopolitan in their attitudes at different points; that local allegiances continue to matter and may be employed at certain moments; and that cosmopolitanism can be expressed for a particular purpose or to meet a particular need (Skey 2012: 476). In doing so, this recognises that cosmopolitan sentiments may be invoked in certain contexts, or as rhetorical strategies – for example, to meet perceived standards of social acceptability (Skey 2012). In this book, I highlight the importance of intersubjectivity and the relations between people in understanding gap year narratives, including what is deemed to have value and be worthwhile.

Rovisco and Nowicka summarise work (by Germann Molz, and Skribs and Woodward) on cultural cosmopolitanism as highlighting the difference between:

> authentic and reflexive cosmopolitanism, which translates into deeper forms of cross-cultural engagement with connotations of self-reflexivity, social learning and an ethico-political orientation – and certain forms of cosmopolitan consumption in which cultural openness involves little more than a positive engagement with aesthetic and sensual differences and a desire for cultural novelty. (Rovisco and Nowicka 2012: 7)

In other words, if individuals are not reflexive, their consumption is superficial. We could take this to mean that not being reflexive is the 'wrong' position. Throughout this book, I refer to global reflexivity (Savage, Bagnall and Longhurst 2005) as a way of exploring cosmopolitan engagement in gap year narratives, but I wish to note a point of caution here by returning to considerations of inequality. The idea of the 'reflexive self' is, according to Skeggs (2004a), a classed position, one that speaks from privilege and pathologises other forms of self-making. Skeggs argues that a focus on cosmopolitan reflexivity, as imagined by Beck for example, views such dispositions without considering class:

> ethics and selfhood are ... productive of, and known through, prior classification systems in which some forms of ethics and selfhood are not available to all ...

> Cosmopolitanism, like propriety, individualization and reflexivity, makes class by its *constitutive exclusion*. (Skeggs 2004a: 171)

A particular model of middle-class self-hood – the reflexive cosmopolitan – could be uncritically reproduced as the 'right' way to be. In the next chapter, I offer a fuller critique of the concept of self-reflexivity, and contrast this with Bourdieu's concept of habitus: embodied dispositions that reflect an individual's position in the social space. For Bourdieu, the dispositions of the habitus are pre-reflexive: we act in ways we think are reasonable, determined by our position in the social space. This recognises how the cosmopolitan subject exists in relation to others and is dependent on access to particular resources. I develop this by considering that the stories told about gap years involve a certain presentation of self, and consequently that we need to be aware of the intersubjective context. One of the aims here is to think about *where* critical reflection on being a global citizen might come from.

The target throughout this book is never the young gappers themselves, and I do not wish to claim they are not doing cosmopolitanism 'properly'. To do so would be guilty of reproducing the same ideas about worthwhile forms of travel which, as I highlight in Chapter 6, are tied up with processes of class distinction. Instead, this book is concerned with demonstrating that global reflexivity is not an automatic consequence of encountering difference. My argument is ultimately directed at the moralising discourses that frame gap years as a worthwhile endeavour – for example, as a way to become a global citizen – which do not question the basis for these claims. The following section engages with literature that has critically considered cosmopolitanism in the activities associated with overseas gap years: independent travel and volunteer tourism.

Gap Years and Cultural Cosmopolitanism

Engaging with Difference

Independent travel, or backpacking, is seen to have different values to 'mainstream tourism'. These are: travelling on a low budget; meeting different people; being or feeling free; being independent and open-minded; the individual and independent organisation of journeys; and travelling for as long as possible (Bradt 1995, cited in Welk 2004: 80). The values of cosmopolitanism resonate with such principles, particularly wanting to meet different people and being open-minded. Indeed, Germann Molz suggests that round-the-world travellers, who are predominantly backpackers and independent travellers, are 'emblematic of the cosmopolitan figure' in their 'mobility, tolerance and openness to difference' (Germann Molz 2006: 5). Similarly, O'Reilly (2006) suggests that backpackers are able to project the desirable qualities of aesthetic cosmopolitanism (Urry 1995). Through the backpacker's concern with authentic experiences and extended periods of time 'on the road', it is suggested they are more likely to develop cosmopolitan dispositions, engendered by 'sustained, diverse cultural interaction' (Cohen 2011: 1544). However, in a classic study of 'drifting', Cohen (1973) offers a typology of travellers as either outward-orientated or inward-orientated. Cohen suggests a distinction between 'those who seek to reach far-away locations and live with the locals, and those who seek out primarily the enclaves of their own kind' (Cohen 1973: 100). Backpackers cannot automatically be assumed to be cosmopolitan, especially as individuals may move between inward and outward conduct (Cohen 2004).

Research on youth travel presents a somewhat mixed picture of cosmopolitan orientations among backpackers. Enoch and Grossman's (2010) comparative study of Danish and Israeli backpackers suggests the former is more cosmopolitan and outward-looking as they want to interact with other backpackers and locals. The Israeli backpackers, on the other hand, are more 'provincial':

> they prefer to interact almost exclusively with backpackers from their own country with whom they can speak in their own language. They spend most of their time in selective Israeli enclaves, where they can eat Israeli food, listen to Israeli music and even see Israeli cult films. (Enoch and Grossman 2010: 529)

A recent study of long-term backpackers, or 'lifestyle travellers', finds that their 'actually-existing cosmopolitanism' is concentrated on consumer activities, and they can often be found in the same places as other 'enclavic tourists': 'Local interactions … were predominantly instrumental and commercialised. Although many sought to "go native", their participation was often imaginary' (Cohen 2011: 1544). While Germann Molz (2006) maintains that backpackers are cosmopolitan figures, their embodied practices are concerned with fitting in with a cosmopolitan 'global traveller' identity, rather than the local cultures they visit.

Volunteer tourism is often held up as a means for young people interested in travel to 'make a difference' and 'give something back' during their gap years (Butcher and Smith 2010). This is seen to by-pass concerns about inter-cultural relationships based solely on consumption. As indicated in Chapter 1, however, there is an extensive literature that criticises much of the volunteering in which young people take part (Guttentag 2009; Lyons et al. 2012; McGehee 2012; Sin 2009). Work by Simpson (2004; 2005a; 2005b) offers a critical account of volunteer placements in the 'Third World', focused on the gap year industry. Her argument centres on exploring the geography of the gap year, a space that is shaped by the legacy of colonialism and a fascination with the Other

(Simpson 2005b). The representation of gap year locations in media accounts and industry material focuses on a particular version of a 'Third World' defined by need, thus legitimating volunteering (including the gap year product of volunteer tourism). Moreover, these spaces are constructed as 'Other', providing a context for experimentation and exploration that is marketable to young people but does little for cross-cultural understanding (Simpson 2005a: 133). Consequently, Simpson questions the pedagogical benefits of gap year placements for the young people involved. Her fieldwork with young gappers in Peru shows that understandings of host communities centre on difference, and confirms what gappers already know (Simpson 2005a: 208). For example, the problematic discourse of 'poor but happy' is reproduced rather than challenged by the young people, despite their first-hand experience (Simpson 2005a: 212).

Griffin (2004) also highlights how gap year providers fail to effectively engage with such issues:

> Is it not a form of cultural imperialism to encourage unqualified youth to travel, while teaching their language to help people increase their life opportunities, because of a global system that has been influenced and ultimately dominated by colonial relations? (Griffin 2004: 44)

The potential for gap years to contribute to cosmopolitan attitudes would be limited if young people do not engage with the Other in a meaningful way, but are simply reproducing standard ideas about the people and places they encounter. In addition to this issue of problematic inter-cultural interaction, Guttentag (2009) highlights additional negative impacts of volunteer tourism: the neglect of local desire; volunteers' lack of skills affecting the work undertaken; replacing local labour; and cultural change.

Other authors are less critical of gap year volunteering. Jones (2005) shares some of Simpson's (2004) concerns, but he also aims to 'offer a counter-balance to an entirely negative interpretation of "volunteer tourism"' (Jones 2005: 89). His study of two volunteering schemes suggests they can offer cross-cultural experiences and are able to engender an understanding of cultural difference and issues of development (Jones 2005). This can help to encourage a 'global perspective' on global linkages, empowerment to make a difference, and the disposition to undertake more volunteering in the future (Jones 2005: 95–97). Such benefits are, for Jones, dependent on the quality of the placement. Raymond and Hall (2008) argue that cross-cultural understanding is not an automatic consequence of volunteer tourism, and there is an important role for 'sending organisations' in what volunteers learn. Moreover, Butcher and Smith (2010) suggest that volunteer tourism is related to trends in 'life politics', focused on individual impact rather than the macro-political. They argue we need to be less cynical about this form of volunteering, and see charity as 'commendable', although they acknowledge that volunteer tourism can offer a reductive view of development (Butcher and Smith 2010: 34).

The debate surrounding the growing gap year industry and its global impact has moved beyond academic literature and into public debate. It is not the act of volunteering itself that is seen as problematic, but rather the sorts of volunteering opportunities that are on offer. In 2007 Judith Brodie, the director of the development organisation Voluntary Service Overseas (VSO) UK spoke about concerns regarding: 'the number of badly planned and supported schemes that are spurious – ultimately benefiting no one apart from the travel companies that organise them' (Ward 2007: n.p.). In an argument analogous with those who criticise cosmopolitanism as driven by capitalism, Simpson (2004) identifies the problem as a commercialised gap year sector whose objective is offering a gap year product. Lyons et al. (2012) suggest that volunteer tourism is evidence of resistance to hegemony on the part of young people through their efforts to become global citizens, but their endeavours are hindered by a pervasive 'neoliberal ethos'. In addition to commodifcation, this can be seen in the focus on skills development and privileging processes (Lyons et al. 2012).

Status Distinctions

For Simpson (2004), linking gap years to capitalism also means we must focus on how gap years are framed around the perceived benefits for the young people involved. The gap year has become 'professionalised', turning what was once an alternative activity into an institutionalised practice, which focuses on accruing skills that will be advantageous in the employment market. Rather than volunteering being driven by concerns for justice and a critical view of structural inequalities between the global North and South, many gap year placements are now a product that can be bought and sold, and as such the spaces of the gap year have become a 'training ground for future professionals' (Simpson 2004: 143).

Much gap year research seems to agree that gap years, or at least the 'right kind' of gap year, are of some benefit to the young people who take them. In the case of gap year placements, Jones (2004) reports that employers see gap years as a way for young people to develop soft skills such as communication, and life skills such as self-discipline. In particular, it is structured schemes – those based on volunteering or work placements – that are seen as the most valuable. Jones suggests that the UK government should consider 'drawing gap year takers into spending at least part of their gap year in structured placements which accrue greater benefit' (Jones 2004: 83). For Duncan (2004), working abroad during a gap year enables young people to gain expertise and increase employability:

It adds to the personal narratives they construct through their working and travelling experiences, regaling others with work related stories and later us[ing] these same stories to construct a successful work self. (Duncan 2004: 9)

In conceptualising the value associated with gap year activities, studies often draw upon the concept of cultural capital. Simpson, for example, notes the gap year provides marketable commodities in the form of life skills and employability (Simpson 2005b: 450). Being able to accumulate cultural capital in this way draws upon the established value of authentic youth travel:

Travel has a long association with enhanced social status ... Part of the gap year product is access to the social status of being 'experienced' and of being travelled ... The idea that travel makes you a more 'interesting' person exemplifies the cultural capital embedded in travel and gap year experiences. (Simpson 2004: 152)

We can therefore start to make the links between the benefits of gap year travel and being cosmopolitan. Simpson's identification of becoming more 'interesting' through travel taps into the idea of the cosmopolitan who has accumulated life experience so that they have developed worldly knowledge and competence. Gap year products can cost thousands of pounds, so there are also economic limits to who is able to benefit. Like cosmopolitanism, taking a gap year has been criticised as an elite activity. The fact that the British Royal Princes William and Harry both took gap years is significant. Gap years are thus an experience for 'hopeful professionals and future kings' (Simpson 2005: 56). As noted by Ansell (2008), spatial difference is important for gap years, and 'Third World' places in particular are popular as they enable young people to identify themselves as cosmopolitan, and consequently gain the cultural capital of the new middle classes through their experiences in such places. The cosmopolitan mobility of young travellers is one of a particular embodied privilege: young, White, middle-class, heterosexual and able-bodied (Germann Molz 2006: 15). This is not the only version of cosmopolitanism, but it the one which is likely to have the most currency.

The implications of gap years as a privileged activity extend beyond the cultural field. To explain the growth in popularity of gap year travel, Heath (2007) locates the associated benefits in the context of expanding higher education participation in the UK. As more and more young people enter the labour market as graduates, credentials become inflated, and there is more and more competition for graduate jobs. Heath therefore suggests that gap years are indicative of middle-class strategies that aim to find 'new ways of gaining distinction' (Heath 2007: 92). To make this point, Heath draws on the work of Brown and colleagues (Brown 1995; Brown, Hesketh and Williams 2003) and the concept of the 'personality package'. According to Brown (1995) it is increasingly important for graduate job seekers to have the right personal qualities, defined as a 'charismatic' persona. Although we might think of personality as something intrinsic, and not affected by structural factors, this does not acknowledge the 'social context in which social qualities of tastes, manners, ways of knowing and personal compatibility are acquired and translated into cultural capital' (Brown, 1995: 45). Developing one's personality package through the cosmopolitan experience of taking a gap year is a way for young people to stand out from the crowd. Heath also posits a gap year hierarchy, with some types having higher status than others. Unsurprisingly, it is the relatively costly structured placements that have greater status, and in which young people from middle-class backgrounds are over-represented (Heath 2007: 94).

Cremin (2007) highlights how the official language of gap years, with its emphasis on developing skills, conflates personal attributes and what employers expect of their workers. For Cremin, the ideology of enterprise runs through gap year discourses, in which there are 'opportunities available to those who are willing' (Cremin 2007: 531). Instead of acknowledging that access to gap years is structured by social inequality, such ideologies see it as the responsibility of individuals to take charge of their advancements and self-development. Importantly, gap year scholars have highlighted that young people do not undertake gap years for the purely instrumental reasons of having a better chance of gaining graduate employment. Simpson's (2005a) ethnographic work with young gappers in Peru explores their nuanced and complex expectations of what they can gain from the experience. She argues that: 'while the gap year industry may be selling predominantly "corporate" capital, that is cultural capital specifically aimed at becoming competitive in the job market, for participants there is also status to be won amongst their peers' (Simpson 2005a: 169–170). What needs to be remembered, and what Cremin (2007) highlights, is that the 'free choice' to undertake certain activities is tied to the requirements of capital. The cultural benefits and status of becoming cosmopolitan is also about becoming an employable person, and this emphasis on self-development and personality in employability discourses leads us to think about the gap year as a form of identity work.

Identity Work

The idea that travel allows people to develop their identity or find themselves is well-established. This is a reference point in the study of youth travel, and is also drawn upon in gap year sresearch. Ansell (2008) considers gap years as a way for young people to negotiate the 'risky' terrain of late modernity. Theories of youth transitions suggest that the turning points in young people's lives – for example, leaving school – are increasingly complex and individualised.[3] This means that the pathways of progression to adulthood are less restricted by tradition or structural factors, with young people freed from prescribed routes. However, Ansell also notes the problems of individualised models of transition, such as the critique offered by Furlong and Cartmel (1997). Furlong and Cartmel (1997) argue that structural factors are of continuing significance in young people's lives. They highlight what they term the 'epistemological fallacy of late modernity', in which young people must take responsibility for the choices that they make, even though their lives are profoundly shaped by class, gender and 'race' (Furlong and Cartmel 1997: 5). Gap years occur, by definition, at a juncture in life. For Ansell (2008), gap year volunteering is a way of narrating a successful identity in the context of late modernity, which she sees as characterised by the 'postmodern desire for individuality and uncertainty, and modernity's concern for structure and risk minimisation' (Ansell 2008: 222).

Taking part in a gap year is, according to Ansell, a way for young people to negotiate these tensions. They are able to visit the 'risky' spaces of the 'Third World' via the relative safety of structured gap year placements. In the process, they generate narratives that constitute cultural capital (Ansell 2008: 226). The potential for accumulating cultural capital via gap year identity work is also put forward by Bagnoli (2009). In a comparative study of identity narratives among Italian and English young people, Bagnoli suggests that they use the experience of travel to narrate their identity at 'fateful moments' (Giddens 1991). The 'year out' is an institutionalised opportunity to produce these narratives, which 'increases cultural capital for the definition of today's young middle-class identities' (Bagnoli 2009: 342).

This focus on identity work, however, leads to a further question about gap years as a cosmopolitan endeavour. If self-development is integral to gap years, this might take priority over ethical/political cosmopolitan commitments. For example, Sin (2009) argues it is the allure of travel and the resulting gains in cultural capital that are the primary goals of volunteer tourists, rather than altruism. From this perspective, the volunteer tourist is a 'strategic cosmopolitan' (Mitchell 2003). In addition, understanding the identity work facilitated by taking a gap year as both individualised *and* as a way of accumulating cultural capital runs into some theoretical problems that are explored in more depth in the following chapter. The concept of cultural capital is part of Bourdieu's (1990) wider theory of practice, in which the hidden effects of structure shape our dispositions to action, and in which there is limited reflexivity and choice in everyday social practices. This is at odds with a model of individualised identity

---

3 Such work touches upon theories of reflexive modernity, in particular Giddens (1991) on reflexive identity work and Beck's (1992) concept of the risk society, which will be explored more fully in Chapter 3.

work in which young people are freed from the restraints of structural factors. In this book, I argue that gap year discourses may stress individual choice and responsibility to construct a cosmopolitan identity, but that structural factors profoundly shape both what 'the cosmopolitan' looks like, and also how young people understand and represent their experiences. These factors manifest in the ways that people and places are represented in gap year narratives; what counts as good taste in gap year travel; and the sort of identity work that is undertaken.

Conclusion

Cultural cosmopolitanism may indeed be informed by an interest in or openness towards the Other. However, the links between such cultural pluralism and more political or ethical forms of cosmopolitanism can be questioned. This is because many of the cultural practices held up as cosmopolitan involve consumption. As a result, they are driven as much by capitalism and commerce as by a commitment to any ideology. A prime example is the desire for exotic goods, which does little to overcome stereotypical representations of the Other, and may perpetuate them. Germann Molz argues for attention to be paid to consumption as a 'cosmopolitical terrain', where the tendency for 'consumer-based capitalism to reproduce trenchant social inequalities is countered by the political potential for consumption to serve as a more ethical form of engagement between people' (Germann Molz 2012a: 34).

Another concern is that the practices often held up as cosmopolitan are essentially those of the elite: flexible, cultivated and mobile. Only a small proportion of the world's population has access to the required resources to be cosmopolitan in this fashion. These definitions of what counts as cosmopolitanism become more problematic when cosmopolitan consumption is used as a way of demonstrating good taste. Cultural omnivorousness, for example, may be less concerned with elitist, 'snob' culture, but is still implicated in status distinctions (Bennett et al. 2009). There is a growing body of work, however, that seeks to explore actually existing or ordinary cosmopolitanism.

Distinctions are made between banal cosmopolitanism, which is an unintended consequence of globalisation, and reflexive cosmopolitanism, which involves a commitment to exploring one's global position. For some, gap years are framed as a way to enable young people to consider their place in the world and engender a sense of global awareness. I have suggested that global reflexivity (Savage, Bagnall and Longhurst 2005) is a means of establishing the link between cultural forms of cosmopolitanism, and ethical and political concerns. However, caution needs to be applied in any analysis of this, as it may also reproduce a particular form of privileged selfhood. Backpackers are sometimes held up as emblematic cosmopolitan figures, but they may be more inward-looking and concerned with meeting other young people who are like them (Cohen 1973). There are also considerable questions surrounding the global citizenship that may be fostered through volunteer tourism, which can be extended to the gap year more generally. This is linked to the (perhaps primary) rationale for gap years that sets them apart from travel pursued solely for leisure: they are viewed as a means of self-development. The cultural capital of travel contributes to claims that gappers have an advantage over their peers. Such distinctions reflect hierarchies of privilege, although they are not always recognised as such (Heath 2007). The fact that such identity work is framed as a matter of individual choice, I argue, neglects these inequalities.

As this chapter has noted, there are many different dimensions to cosmopolitanism, although I suggested there are two in particular that are relevant to exploring gap years, derived from Hannerz (1990). These are openness to diversity (a cosmopolitan orientation); and the skills to do this (a cosmopolitan competence). In this book, I draw on Bourdieu's concepts of habitus (disposition) and cultural capital (competence) to explore cosmopolitanism in gap year travel. The next chapter considers these concepts in more depth, and engages with social theories of cultural value and self-development.

Chapter 3
Theorising Good Taste and Worthwhile Experiences in Gap Year Travel

Once the preserve of the rich and well-connected … gap years are now a must for any self-respecting student. (Bennett 2008: n.p.)

Accounts of gap years in the public domain, like the one above taken from *The Times*, often suggest they are an opportunity open to all. Indeed, the gap year industry itself is keen to break away from the association with privileged, middle-class youth:

In the UK a 'gap year' was traditionally viewed as the activity of taking time out before university. The word on the street was that it involved travel for the wealthy few and pretty much nothing for the rest of us. Nowadays, however, all sorts of people are going backpacking and travelling, doing a thousand different things. The people who are out there taking gap years are of all ages, from all walks of life, but they all have one thing in common – they want to see the world! (gapyear.com 2013: n.p.)

Such a break with the connotations of privilege can be difficult to achieve in practice.[1] Nevertheless, there is an emphasis on individual identity-building in gap year discourses that encourages young people to be 'self-respecting' and take up such opportunities, freed from traditional structural constraints.

These discourses resonate with the central tenets of the 'reflexive modernisation thesis', which suggests that collective social identities have fragmented in an increasingly globalised world. Viewing gap years from this perspective, they are a way for young people to be what Giddens calls a 'cosmopolitan person', someone who carves out a distinctive identity through experience of diversity, and then integrates these experiences into a coherent narrative of the self (Giddens 1991: 190). Yet gap years are also put forward as a way of accumulating cultural capital, and thus maintaining structural advantage. Viewing gap years from this alternative position relates to Bourdieu's wider 'theory of practice' (Bourdieu 1990). Examining the gap year from

---

1 See Chapter 1 and the public response to the blogger Max Gogarty.

this perspective considers the cultural value of gap years, and how practices contribute to the 'symbolic violence' (Bourdieu and Passeron 1977) of social reproduction.

In this chapter, I develop the theoretical framework for gap years as a means of accumulating cosmopolitan cultural capital and constructing a cosmopolitan identity. The chapter begins with the definition of cultural capital as employed by Bourdieu, its applications in the sociology of education and taste, and critical developments to the concept. Next, I return to the idea of youth travel as a form of identity work, a way of telling a particular cosmopolitan story about the self. I consider how we might see gap years as a form of reflexive identity work (Giddens 1991), and then contrast this with Bourdieu's notion of habitus. Self-development from a Bourdieusian perspective is an outcome of pre-reflexive dispositions to action, which is at odds with the image of the self in the reflexive modernisation thesis, and I note the implications for reflexive cosmopolitanism. To summarise this theoretical discussion, I outline two hypothetical figures: 'the reflexive gapper' and 'the habitual gapper'.

The Concept of Cultural Capital

Defining Cultural Capital

Bourdieu's concept of cultural capital was developed in his work on education in order to explain:

> the unequal scholastic achievement of children originating from the different social classes by relating academic success, i.e., the specific profits which children from the different classes and class fractions can obtain in the academic market, to the distribution of cultural capital between the classes and class fractions. (Bourdieu 1997[1986]: 47)

For Bourdieu, this non-material form of capital contributes to domination and the reproduction of advantage because it is the culture of the dominant class that is recognised by the education system as legitimate, and consequently rewarded with educational qualifications. Bourdieu argues that cultural worth is arbitrary, but dominant culture is seen to have intrinsic value, a process he terms 'symbolic violence'. In this context, cultural capital:

> consists mainly of linguistic and cultural competence and that relationship of familiarity with culture which can only be produced by family upbringing when it transmits the dominant culture. (Bourdieu, 1973: 80)

The culture that surrounds a child as she is growing up inculcates dispositions that determine success or failure in formal education. At the time, Bourdieu was working against the common-sense view that natural aptitudes explained why children from the dominated class had lower educational achievement than those from the dominant class. Bourdieu's model looks at advantage in cultural, not just economic, terms (Bourdieu 1997 [1986]: 47–8).

In gap years taken between school and university, the skills and knowledge accumulated can be understood in terms of personal qualities, such as confidence and independence. These are advantageous at university and beyond but may be seen as 'natural' rather than dependent on social status (Heath 2007; Brown 1995; Brown, Hesketh and Williams 2003). We might see the student who is confident and contributes to seminar discussions, for example, as a 'good' student, rather than someone who is familiar with and comfortable in an academic environment.

Cultural capital also has relevance beyond the field of education, and was subsequently developed by Bourdieu as part of his wider concern with 'legitimate' culture and social reproduction. Bourdieu (1984) discusses the close relationship between cultural consumption, educational qualifications and social origins, and argues that taste is not just a marker of status, it also symbolically reproduces the cultural legitimacy of the dominant class. In *Distinction* (1984), legitimate culture is 'high culture': opera, modern art, literature. Bourdieu provides a map of the social space that is structured according to the distribution of economic, cultural and social capital. People whose capital is of similar volume and composition have similar 'conditions of existence'. They are identifiable class fractions, occupying a particular location in the social space (Bourdieu 1984: 114).

Bourdieu identifies a correlation between levels of education and the propensity to invest in and appreciate cultural goods. He argues this is not just an effect of the education system, but our past and present material conditions of existence. In other words, our place in the social structure affects how much cultural capital we possess (Bourdieu 1984: 53). When 'invested' by the family, cultural capital enables a familiarity of culture to be developed: 'The embodied cultural capital of the previous generation functions as a sort of advance … [it] enables the newcomer to start acquiring the basic elements of the legitimate culture' (Bourdieu 1984: 70). This enables Bourdieu to explain how class positions are reproduced from one generation to the next.

Bourdieu describes three forms of cultural capital: embodied, objectified and institutionalised (1997[1986]: 47). Access to economic capital is bound up with access to these forms of cultural capital; however Bourdieu argues that the relationship is concealed through the 'misrecognition' of 'being cultured' as something natural, a personal quality (1997[1986]: 54). For example, embodied cultural capital is a 'linguistic and cultural competence' that is misrecognised as legitimate as it 'combine[s] the prestige of innate property with the merits of acquisition' (Bourdieu 1997[1986]: 48). Yet the investment of time required for self-development is made possible by access to economic capital. For example, a young person who finishes compulsory schooling but stays in education can do so if they are financially supported and so do not have to enter employment straight away. The objectified form of cultural capital refers to material objects: cultural goods such as books or artworks. Obviously one needs economic capital in order to purchase material goods, but Bourdieu argues that consuming them 'properly' depends on embodied cultural capital so that their value is appreciated and recognised (Bourdieu 1997[1986]: 50). Cultural capital can also be institutionalised in educational qualifications, which can then be converted into economic capital on the labour market. The 'profit' gained depends on how scarce they are (Bourdieu 1997[1986]: 51).

We can see how these forms of cultural capital can be accumulated through gap year travel. If there is an observable shift to cosmopolitanism as legitimate culture, then cosmopolitan consumption is likely to be a classed practice. Spending money on a period of international travel or gap year programmes is a way of investing time and economic capital in self-development, but the outcomes may be understood in terms of personal competences like independence, maturity, etc. Simpson suggests two dimensions to the embodied cultural capital that is accumulated through gap years: the enhanced social status that comes with being well-travelled and the embodied qualities that are associated with employability (Simpson 2005a: 154). Gap years can also provide objectified cultural capital and evidence of travel status in material goods such as souvenirs (Simpson 2005a: 60–61). As noted in Chapter 1, young people are encouraged to draw upon their gap year experiences in job applications: they are 'something for the CV', a form of institutionalised cultural capital. There was even a period of time when a gap year 'qualification' was available, in the form of a company offering young people the chance to be awarded a City and Guilds Profile of Achievement[2] (Simpson 2005a: 154), although this no longer seems to be available. The relative scarcity of gap years offer the young people who take them a positional advantage, especially in the context of higher education expansion and increasing numbers of young people graduating from university (Heath 2007).

It seems like there is a convincing case to consider gap years as a way of acquiring cultural capital, a means of self-improvement that can be 'cashed in' for future benefits. However, the concept of cultural capital has been subject

---

2 City and Guilds is an educational organisation that offers recognised vocational qualifications. A profile of achievement is not an actual qualification but a record of activities, a way of 'showing that you've made progress doing something *worthwhile*' (City and Guilds 2013: n.p., my emphasis).

to extensive critique. One issue is that Bourdieu uses the term to 'perform different roles in ... various writings' (Lamont and Lareau 1988: 155). How the term is operationalised in both the sociology of education and studies of taste has been subject to extensive debate.

Criticisms, Definitions and Developments

The social reproduction suggested by Bourdieu's model, in which the culture of the dominant class is validated and rewarded, is challenged by Halsey, Heath and Ridge (1980). In a study of upward social mobility, Halsey, Heath and Ridge find cultural capital plays a role in how parents select secondary schools, but that it has little influence on examination results. Schools are able to create cultural capital in pupils from working class homes with little experience of education (cited in Jenkins 2002: 115). Such studies, according to Goldthorpe (2007), highlight the problems of accounting for mobility within Bourdieu's framework. Jenkins (2002) notes, however, that Halsey, Heath and Ridge use a narrow definition of cultural capital, which is only measured by educational qualifications. Already we can see the problems of competing ways of thinking about cultural capital; how does one evaluate a concept if there are competing definitions and it is operationalised in different ways?

The answer from critics such as Goldthorpe is to disregard cultural capital altogether. Goldthorpe argues that those who attempt to adapt the concept for empirical research do so in ways that are not compatible with Bourdieu's theoretical model, and those who try to remain faithful do not show how it may be used for research purposes (Goldthorpe 2007: 18). However, Atkinson (2010) suggests that Goldthorpe misreads and misunderstands Bourdieu. According to Atkinson, empirical work by Chan and Goldthorpe (2007) on music consumption, for example, actually reveals the link between education and cultural consumption. Yet Chan and Goldthorpe do not recognise these findings as the workings of cultural capital, while for Atkinson this is 'proof of class *a la* Bourdieu in action' (Atkinson 2010: 36).

Cultural capital remains an extraordinarily pervasive theoretical tool in research on educational inequality (Ball 2003; Brown 1995; Devine 2004; Reay 2004). For example, Reay (2004) draws on her own empirical work to demonstrate how a broad understanding of cultural capital can help to explain the reproduction of advantage in the education system. This goes beyond simply knowledge of 'high culture' to how the embodied resources of middle-class parents, such as a sense of entitlement and self-confidence, help them to successfully negotiate the system (Reay 2004). We need to consider that the cultural capital acquired through gap year travel does not necessarily consist of familiarity with high culture or gaining an educational qualification, but is, more broadly, a set of competences that confer future advantage.

The Cultural Omnivore

This debate has parallels in the sociology of taste and consumption, which considers the relevance of cultural capital beyond the particular social and historical context of France in the 1960s as described in *Distinction* (Bourdieu 1984). Jenkins asks if there is 'something highly specific about the relationship of the French metropolitan elite to culture' (Jenkins 2002: 148) that may not apply to other settings. The differences between France and the USA in particular have been subject to examination (Lamont 1992; Bryson 1996). This includes a debate prompted by the work of Peterson and colleagues (Peterson 1992; Peterson and Simkus 1992; Peterson and Kern 1996) on the concept of the 'cultural omnivore', who consumes a diverse range of cultural products and is more open to popular cultural forms than Bourdieu suggests. This characterises the tastes of higher status groups in the USA. Omnivorousness is 'antithetical to snobbishness, which is based fundamentally on rigid rules of exclusion' (Peterson and Kern 1996: 904). However, lower status groups have more univorous tastes (i.e. liking only a few types or genres of cultural products). Peterson and Kern conclude that new symbolic boundaries are being formed, although these are along less snobbish lines.

Alternatively, having a broad range of tastes can be indicative of new forms of exclusion, for example being a 'foodie' who has knowledge of, and consumes, ethnically-varied cuisine (Warde, Marten and Olsen 1999). More recently, Warde, Wright and Gayo-Cal (2007) argue that cultural tolerance is a sign of good taste, but there is more than one orientation to such tolerance, and that there are some fractions of the middle classes who still retain a command of consecrated culture. Bennett et al. suggest that the omnivorous orientation is dominant in contemporary British cultural tastes, although there are generational differences: 'Multi-culturalism, cosmopolitanism and an appreciation of specifically American cultural forms appear distinctive to a younger and more ethnically diverse professional-executive class today' (Bennett et al. 2009: 253). The figure of the omnivore therefore shares some similarities with the cosmopolitan, but the omnivore thesis places more of an emphasis on appreciating both high and low culture, not just diversity and difference.

Gap Years and 'Cosmopolitan Cultural Capital'

As argued thus far, the cosmopolitan gapper is flexible, mobile, self-improving and developing a taste for diversity. However, we have already seen in Chapter 2 that cosmopolitanism can be viewed as a form of social exclusiveness and elitism, and that cosmopolitan cultural capital is a subset of cultural capital (Hage 1997; 1998). To borrow from Bourdieu, the tolerance and openness associated with cosmopolitanism is misrecognised as a personal quality, rather than the possession of a valuable form of capital. The implications for gap years seem clear: they are a means of accumulating cosmopolitan cultural capital, 'saved' in demonstrable experiences and embodied in personal qualities.

What about the criticisms that have been levelled at Bourdieu's concern with high culture? This does not seem to fit the gap year experience. However, Bourdieu pre-empts such arguments, and suggests that the examination of one context does not invalidate 'drawing out universal propositions' (Bourdieu 1984: xi). This point is developed in Holt's (1997) exploration of American tastes, which finds similar processes at work, but different forms of knowledge, practices and objects as legitimated and institutionalised. In the American context, embodied cultural capital is emphasised over objectified cultural capital, and mass consumption is incorporated into good taste (Holt 1997). For Holt, cultural capital should be considered in 'a particular socio-historical setting' (Holt 1997: 99).

The content of cultural capital discussed by Bourdieu in *Distinction* (1984) may not be applicable to gap years, but the model of symbolic distinction still has some currency. In keeping with these debates, I adopt a relatively broad understanding of the concept of cultural capital in exploring the value of gap year travel. While retaining a critical view of Bourdieu's framework (explored in depth below), cultural capital is a useful way of understanding the value of gap year travel. The cosmopolitan cultural capital that is associated with gap years is potentially advantageous for young people hoping to progress to higher education and into professional careers. It is something that is institutionalised and recognised as being legitimate. Moreover, gap years happen at a point where a number of fields overlap: education, employment, and the consumption of leisure travel. What has value within these fields can be transposable *between* these fields.

The Field(s) of Overseas Gap Years: Travel, Education and Employment

In Chapter 1, I suggested that good taste in travel emphasises authentic, cosmopolitan experiences. A distance from tourism is required, and the connotations of inauthenticity associated with package holidays have resulted in more independent modes of travel becoming increasingly valued. At the same time, mass forms of leisure travel are devalued. In Chapter 6, I will explore the development of these distinctions to frame the analysis of the gappers' own views on what constitutes 'proper travel'. This is significant as the symbolic status of being well-travelled, and possessing the associated embodied qualities, has transferrable value. Cosmopolitan identities and cultural openness is a sign of good taste in other spheres of consumption, and aligns with desires to experience the 'inside' through authentic travel (MacCannell 1999). Moreover, the institutionalisation of youth travel in a product called a gap year (Simpson 2005a; 2005b) means that benefits can be transferred into the fields of education and employment.

Increasing employability through taking a gap year is not an activity available to everyone, however. There are also hierarchies within the gap year field, so that different types of gap year have different values. Heath (2007) notes that formal placements like volunteering are more likely to be seen as a way to develop employability. This would suggest that structured placements are both more expensive, and more likely to be viewed favourably by employers. However, in Chapter 7, I also suggest that hierarchies of taste in gap year travel are based on demonstrating good taste in terms of worthwhile activity and framing experiences in a certain way, not just consuming particular types of gap years. Young people require the knowledge, or embodied cultural capital, in order to legitimately consume goods, or objectified cultural capital.

The concept of employability also raises the issue of needing to work upon the self in order to be successful in contemporary job markets. In an analysis of gap year discourses, Cremin (2007) draws on a Foucauldian perspective on self-development and the practices that Foucault identified as the 'technologies (or techniques) of the self' (Foucault 1988). Work in this area (du Gay 1996; Rose 1999) argues that power is not enacted from above but by individuals on themselves. Working towards self-fulfilment – in this case, the identity work undertaken through a gap year – is a form of self-monitoring and self-regulation. For example, du Gay (1996) argues that neoliberal market economies require workers to be enterprising. To be successful, people have to display 'certain enterprising qualities – such as self-reliance, personal responsibility, boldness and a willingness to take risks in the pursuit of such goals' (du Gay 1996: 56). As will be explored in more detail in Chapter 7, Cremin (2007) views taking a gap year as a way for young people to engage in this sort of self-regulatory identity work. We can also see how the qualities of enterprising workers and the qualities associated with taking a gap year overlap. So, if a gap year is a way of working on the self in order to develop qualities that make one employable, how do young people on gap years engage with this activity? To answer this question, we need to consider two contrasting perspectives in the sociology of identity: the reflexive modernisation thesis, and Bourdieu's concept of habitus.

Gap Years as Reflexive Identity Work

In Chapter 2, I noted some studies suggest taking a gap year is a way for young people to narrate their identity (Ansell 2008; Bagnoli 2009; Deforges 2000). This work draws on theories of 'reflexive modernisation' (Giddens

1991; Beck 1992), arguing that the gap year is a way for young people to negotiate transitional moments in the contemporary period. The reflexive modernisation thesis suggests there have been fundamental changes in the organisation of social life in late modernity, and consequently structural factors (such as social class) have less of an influence on young people's lives than in the past. Instead, they have to choose their own paths. This choice, however, is accompanied by greater uncertainty and indeterminacy. In a 'risk society', 'social, political, economic and individual risks increasingly tend to escape the institutions for monitoring and protection in industrial society' (Beck 1994: 5). According to proponents of reflexive modernisation, the contemporary period has been profoundly shaped by globalisation, detraditionalisation and individualisation. This has led to increased interconnectedness through globalised communications technologies, resulting in greater access to wide-ranging experiences (Giddens 1991: 169). Technology has also brought global risks, 'dangers … that arise for all of humanity [like] nuclear fission or the storage of radioactive waste' (Beck 1992: 21).

Beck (2002) identifies the resulting changes to subjectivities as 'cosmopolitanisation', or 'internal globalization, globalization from within the national societies. This transforms everyday consciousness and identities significantly. Issues of global concern are becoming part of the everyday local experiences and the "moral life-worlds" of the people' (Beck 2002: 17). These sorts of shared global concerns lead to completing claims to knowledge (Sweetman 2003: 540). Detraditionalisation, the disembedding of traditional sources of authority, means that individuals must increasingly make their own way and must monitor their own actions (Heaphy 2007: 85). This is because social and institutional forms of legitimacy and knowledge, such as class or religion, are 'zombie categories', according to Beck (2002): they no longer have any life, but have yet to disappear due to a lack of replacement forms. Without the associated collective ties, people must monitor themselves and their actions, and make their own decisions. Society is thus increasingly individualised (Beck and Beck-Gernsheim 2002).

This has profound effects on notions of identity (Heaphy 2007: 70). To understand the nature of self-development from this perspective is to draw on the idea of reflexivity, the 'ability [of people] to reflect on the social conditions of their existence and change them accordingly' (Beck 1994: 174). For authors such as Giddens, the self is actively constructed by individual agents:

> Each of us not only has, but lives, a biography reflexively organised in terms of flows of social and psychological information about possible ways of life. Modernity is a post-traditional order, in which the question 'How shall I live?' has to be answered in day-to-day decisions. (Giddens 1991: 14)

From this perspective, it is possible to interpret young people actively engaging in identity work by taking a gap year, and choosing from a number of possible paths to gain experience that they can then draw on to tell a particular story about the self. Giddens sees this as the search for 'ontological security', a feeling of order and rootedness that was previously provided by traditional, collective sources of identity (Giddens 1991: 28–29). In order to achieve this, individuals must seek out continuity in their biographical narrative, their story of 'who they are'. They must orientate themselves to the future and weigh up the consequences of their choices of action; in other words, they must be reflexive about their identity work (Giddens 1991: 29). According to authors such as Desforges (2000) and O'Reilly (2006), travel is a way for individuals to seek coherence in their biographical narrative. In these accounts, travel provides meaningful experiences that can be used to create and represent self-identity.

Gap Years as Reflexive Identity Work

Giddens talks about heightened reflexivity at 'fateful moments' in people's lives, those transitional points that present 'new demands as well as possibilities' (Giddens 1991: 143). It is easy to see how this concept would lend itself to understanding gap years. By their very definition, they are a 'between stage', a period when we might expect young people to work on their biographical narrative. Giddens also makes specific reference to a cosmopolitan pathway as one way for individuals to negotiate the fragmentation of collective identities through experiencing different contexts:

> A person may make use of diversity in order to create a distinctive self-identity which positively incorporates elements from different settings into an integrated narrative. Thus a cosmopolitan person is one precisely who draws strength from being at home in a variety of contexts. (Giddens 1991: 190)

We can see here similarities with the cultural omnivore, which raises questions about whether this indicates the dissolution of structural boundaries or simply new forms of distinction. Nevertheless, the experiences of gappers overseas have been understood as examples of the forging of individual identities through reflexive self-narration. For example, Johan (2009) suggests that gap years enable identity work and transformation, because travel overseas provides a change of scenery and new experiences, giving young people 'time, space and place' for identity work (Johan 2009: 143). According to Johan, these cosmopolitan engagements through mobility are potentially profound and long lasting.

Similarly, Bagnoli suggests that gap years are an example of how

52

the experience of travelling can make people look at their everyday life with new eyes. What was once fate may appear very different when looked at from a distance. Fate thus becomes choice, and changing everyday realities and identities a possibility. (Bagnoli 2009: 343)

Rather than the social reproduction of a Bourdieusian analysis, Bagnoli presents a view of gap years as one of these fateful moments of reflexivity. Individual choice is emphasised in such accounts, although Ansell (2008) notes gap years provide young people with *commodified* opportunities for this identity construction. In other words, the options for young people's gap years are determined by the market. We might see the gap year as a prime example of how young people choose a particular path of self-development.

Archer and the New Cosmopolitans

An alternative theory of how reflexivity guides action is offered by Archer (2007). Although Archer sees a decline in tacit routines and embodied knowledge in late modernity, she is critical of suggestions that individuals are able to live in an unstructured environment, particularly when global inequalities are taken into account (Archer 2007: 54). However, Archer is also a critic of Bourdieu, and offers an alternative perspective on reflexivity, which she defines as 'the regular exercise of the mental ability, shared by all normal people,[3] to consider themselves in relation to their (social) contexts and vice versa'. These are our 'internal conversations' and help to determine our future action (Archer 2007: 4).

Archer suggests that there are a number of different modes of reflexivity, but there is no empirical link between an individual's structural position and the mode of reflexivity that predominates in their inner conversations (Archer 2007: 276). For example, background and socialisation do not determine the activities of a group Archer calls the 'new cosmopolitans': those who have reacted to the structural changes of globalisation in particular ways. This is a group of young people who have different trajectories than might be expected; who are disembedded from their home contexts, living abroad and following opportunities; who are working on projects; who require *reflexivity* to negotiate structural and cultural constraints; and who are remaking their social positions in a new globalised world (Archer 2007: 60–61). Are gap years an example of young people reacting to globalisation in similar ways? Atkinson argues that it is highly questionable that these new cosmopolitans follow paths which have nothing to do with their backgrounds (Atkinson 2010: 67). This is because

---

3 There is an assumption here about what is normal, which is troubling considering Skegg's critique of the moral worth of reflexivity (Skeggs 2004a; 2004b).

theorisations of identity work as individualised and creative have been subject to extensive critique.

Reflexive Identity: Critical Issues

Heaphy notes that there are some differences between Giddens and Beck's accounts, with Giddens highlighting the opportunities for empowerment, and Beck emphasising tensions and risk (Heaphy 2007: 89–90). In both models, however, social structures are weak, and it is this which is the main target for critics. If we return to the discussion of the classed nature of cosmopolitan identities discussed in Chapter 2, we need to consider the important issue of *resources*. Savage (2000) suggests it is the techniques and knowledge of a particular privileged class that can engage in reflexive self-projects. Moreover, the concept of the reflexive self favours a version of modern masculinity according to Skeggs (2004b), one that is seen to be detached from structure but in fact reproduces an advantageous position. In addition, seeing this version of identity work as universal is problematic as it pathologises other forms of self-making. A lack of reflexivity is seen as a moral and individual problem, rather than the effects of structure (Skeggs 2004a; 2004b). Alternatively, Atkinson (2010) argues that there is little evidence of reflexivity among *any* social classes. He contests the 'constant "refashioning of self"' and annulment of the past implied by the notion of reflexivity' (Atkinson 2010: 190. Furthermore, 'racial' stratification and global asymmetries of power are under-emphasised in notions of the reflexive self. This is of particular relevance to thinking about gap years, given that they are a form of self-development often located in the global South.

We can observe a number of structural factors potentially at work in gap years, which challenges individualised accounts of identity construction. Firstly, there are inequalities of access to gap year experiences. Secondly, if taking a gap year is both the outcome of possessing cultural capital and a means to accumulate additional cultural capital, the practice maintains and contributes to structural advantage. Thirdly, the ideology of enterprise and choice in gap year discourses as identified by Cremin (2007) produces employable workers of benefit to capitalism, which limits the agency involved in 'choosing' a gap year. Fourthly, the work of scholars such as Simpson (2004; 2005a; 2005b) highlights the continuing relevance of global inequality and power in understanding gap years. Finally, if we conceptualise the value that young people accumulate through taking a gap year as cultural capital, then we also need to look to Bourdieu's wider theory of practice. In particular, we need to explore the concept of habitus, which offers an alternative to the over-emphasis on agency in the view of identity work presented by the reflexive modernisation thesis.

Habitus and Identity

The habitus is 'a system of durable, transposable dispositions' (Bourdieu 1990: 52). These dispositions are shaped by the objective conditions of being located in a particular part of the social space. The habitus is a conceptual 'bridge' between the individual and the social, forming part of Bourdieu's overall theory of practice that tries to move beyond the often-presented opposition between structure and agency. He aims to demonstrate that individuals actively construct the world around them, but they are embedded in social contexts that shape this action. This vision of the world sees people's actions as neither 'mechanical reaction' nor those of a 'conscious agent' (Bourdieu and Wacquant 1992: 121). This latter point is a contrast to the image of the gapper as an individual who reflexively creates a cosmopolitan identity in a detraditionalised context. Instead, this would see gap years as the outcome of *pre-reflexive* dispositions, generated through occupying a particular position in the social structure.

The habitus is structured, but it is also structuring, as it 'organises practices and the perception of practices' (Bourdieu 1984: 170). It is how individuals attach meaning and understanding to their actions. As people share collective social positions, notably social class, they have common dispositions. Bourdieu therefore argues that social groups share 'consensus on [the] meaning of practices' (Bourdieu 1990: 56). What is seen as taken-for-granted, as legitimate and appropriate action, is a product of the habitus. It is both unique and collective. Consequently 'the individual, and even the personal, the subjective, is social, collective … a socialized subjectivity' (Bourdieu and Wacquant 1992: 126). The disposition to take a gap year, and imbue it with a particular meaning, can be viewed as an example of this 'socialised subjectivity', the outcome of young people from similar backgrounds who all value the idea of undertaking a cosmopolitan experience. Such 'corporal dispositions and cognitive templates' (King 2000: 417) are *embodied*: we carry them around with us. They influence how we think about the world and how we act, including the related concept of bodily hexis: 'the apparently most insignificant techniques of the body – ways of blowing one's nose, ways of eating or talking' (Bourdieu 1984: 466).

When individuals encounter a network of relations, or 'a field', the habitus is enacted to produce appropriate action. Bourdieu calls this a 'feel for the game', something that is shared with others in a similar social position. There is an interplay between what is out there in the world (the field) and our way of being (the habitus) (Bourdieu 1977: 214). Our experiences in the objective relations of the field shape our understandings of appropriate action, which we then pursue. What Bourdieu's theory helps to explain is the reproductive element of practice, because human agency is bounded by the field's objective requirements. The regularities of societal structure are maintained, as the external is internalised in the habitus (Bourdieu and Wacquant 1992: 17–18). Bourdieu's picture of action is very different from that of the reflexive modernisation thesis, stressing its 'social embeddedness' (Adams 2006: 513).

Bourdieu explicitly states that these processes are not rule-following, as they operate below the level of conscious thought. Rather, what we think is reasonable or appropriate in particular circumstances is the outcome of our 'embodied history' (Bourdieu 1990: 56). Rather than thinking about decisions (for example, to take a gap year) as reflexive, Bourdieu argues that social practice is guided by implicit thought:

> subjects do not, strictly speaking, know what they are doing that what they do has more meaning than they know. The habitus is the universalising mediation which causes an individual agent's practices, without either explicit reason or significant intent, to be none the less 'sensible' and 'reasonable'. (Bourdieu 1977: 79)

However, although Bourdieu places an emphasis on pre-reflexive action, he does not deny the possibility of deliberation. This might be because the 'feel for the game' might require strategic, conscious action. Also, in times of crisis, there might be a disruption in the 'routine adjustment of subjective and objective structures' (Bourdieu and Wacquant 1992: 131). If there is a lack of fit between habitus and field, our dispositions are not already adapted to appropriate action and so we cannot rely on our 'feel for the game'. Bourdieu argues that the dispositions of the habitus are relatively irreversible (Bourdieu and Wacquant 1992: 133). How we perceive and understand anything is bound up with the internalisation of our prior experience. This would suggest, for example, that previous embodied experiences guide the ways in which travellers understand and encounter the places they visit.

Gap Years and Dispositions to Action

There are some implications here for thinking about gap year identity work. From a Bourdieusian perspective, gappers do not consciously pursue a cosmopolitan pathway. Instead, taking a gap year is the result of the relational harmonisation of habitus with a structured social space. Acquiring dispositions, like 'being independent' or 'being open to difference' are not chosen, but 'tend to take place below the level of consciousness, expression, and the *reflexive distance* which these presuppose' (Bourdieu 1990: 73; my emphasis). Gappers' dispositions to action, from this perspective, are the outcome of what is considered to be appropriate so that their experiences align with official accounts of the gap year and good taste.

Bourdieu's definition of reflexivity is somewhat different to those outlined above. For Bourdieu, reflexivity is a systematic exploration of the 'unthought categories of thought which delimit the thinkable and predetermine the thought'

(Bourdieu and Wacquant 1992: 40). It is not about the self on an individual level, but an examination of an embodied collective history (McNay 2001: 142). For gappers to be reflexive using this definition, they would need to engage with their conditions of existence and be aware of how their experiences are driven by their structural position. From Bourdieu, we have a very different view of identity to that of the reflexive modernisation thesis. However, while Giddens's view of identity can be criticised for an over-emphasis on agency, critics of Bourdieu argue there is not *enough* agency in Bourdieu's model. The following section evaluates these criticisms and discusses authors who have attempted to offer a more nuanced account of reflexivity, freedom and constraint in relation to changing social structures (Adams 2006: 513).

Evaluating the Concept of Habitus

Bourdieu's vision of the social world is often criticised for being deterministic, with little possibility that objective structures can be escaped: 'Social structure and history produce the habitus. This, in turn, generates practices which serve, in the absence of external factors, to reproduce social structure. As a consequence, history tends to repeat itself' (Jenkins 2002: 97). Critics argue that the concept of habitus is too limiting in its account of individual agency, and thus it is hard to understand social change within this theory. For example, Archer (2007) argues Bourdieu does not fully investigate subjective experience. There is too much of an emphasis on homogeneity and passive agents according to Archer, and at the same time reflexivity in everyday practice is neglected (Archer 2007: 14–15). As people cannot confront their circumstances but are part of them, there is an 'ontological complicity' between habitus and field, which deprives human subjectivity of independence and the ability to reflect on these circumstances (Archer 2007: 42).

These limits to agency restrict the potential for social transformation for Bohman: 'Either agents' reflection on their own conditions is structurally determined, or agents are inevitably duped by their culture into misrecognising its culturally arbitrary and dominating character' (Bohman 1999: 141). If people are not able to take a critical standpoint on their circumstances, asks Bohman, where do alternative worldviews come from? There is an issue of elitism here, as it is only the reflexive sociologist who is able to offer any critique. This is also noted by Skeggs (2004b), who argues that Bourdieu presents a model of those resigned to their fate. This means that values outside the dominant symbolic system cannot be accounted for, such as working-class anger or feminist resistance (Skeggs 2004b: 88–89).

In addition to these questions of agency, the contemporary relevance of Bourdieu's theory has been questioned. Does this reflect a cosmopolitan outlook which is built on being open to what is new and different? Archer argues there is too much 'contextual discontinuity' in contemporary social life for habitus to be a valid concept: 'change is now too rapid and appropriate practices now too evanescent for intergenerational socialisation to take place' (Archer 2007: 41). If the trends identified by the reflexive modernisation thesis are correct, the globalisation, detraditionalisation and individualisation of the contemporary period and the associated heightened reflexivity makes a model of ongoing social reproduction problematic. Processes of globalisation are, of course, of particular relevance to gap year travel. Lash (1993) argues that a strong theory of social change is inhibited by Bourdieu's treatment of reflexivity, and the implicit claims of universality are incorrect. Calhoun (1993) suggests there is some ambiguity in Bourdieu's account regarding whether concepts such as habitus are trans-historical. We can see that the substantive claims of social stability offered by habitus and its applicability in a contemporary context have been questioned by Bourdieu's critics.

As noted in Chapter 2, one way of understanding cosmopolitanism is to view it as a disposition of openness to difference (Hannerz 1990; Vertovec and Cohen 2002). The use of the term 'disposition' suggests some similarities with the concept of habitus. Is it possible to talk of a cosmopolitan habitus? Kendall, Woodward and Skrbis (2009) suggest that it may be reductive to view cosmopolitanism as a disposition: for example, that individuals are either cosmopolitan or not. For Kendall, Woodward and Skrbis, this neglects the 'processual, reflexive and dynamic' ways that cosmopolitanism may be performed in context (Kendall, Woodward and Skrbis 2009: 107). Instead, they suggest cosmopolitanism is a type of repertoire that can be called upon, a reflexively deployed resource that is drawn in particular time and space settings (Kendall, Woodward and Skrbis 2009: 108).

In answering accusations of determinism, Bourdieu emphasises that the habitus is an open system of dispositions that is reinforced or modified by experiences (Bourdieu and Wacquant 1992: 133). The dispositions enacted by the habitus are not mechanical actions but an outcome of interaction with the field encountered, so that different fields generate variations in practice (Bourdieu and Wacquant 1992: 135). McNay (1999) develops this argument to understand the habitus as a generative structure that is enacted with objective limits. This means that it can engender 'a potentially infinite number of patterns of behaviour, thoughts and expressions that are both "relatively unpredictable" but also "limited in their diversity"' (McNay 1999: 100).

Whether contemporary social practices can be explained by Bourdieu's model is one of the key questions addressed throughout this book. While authors such as Atkinson (2010) dispute the 'heightened reflexivity' of the current period, others put forward notions of 'habitual' or 'mundane' reflexivity that address issues of social change using Bourdieu's conceptual apparatus. As will be seen in Chapter 8, these alternative perspectives offer a means of moving beyond a narrow definition of reflexivity as critical disjuncture to understanding reflection, creativity and self-awareness in gap year narratives while still recognising the constraints of structure.

Reimagining Reflexivity and Habitus

The concept of habitus, as noted by McNay (1999), provides a 'corrective' to the over-emphasis on agency in theories of reflexive modernisation. Recent social transformations are uneven: we can think back to the question 'who is able to be cosmopolitan?' explored in the previous chapter. McNay (1999) draws on Bourdieu's conceptual framework to think about occasions when there is a lack of fit between habitus and field as a driver of social change. Taking the example of increased female participation in the public sphere, women experience both the possibility of reflexive transformation due to the dissonance between gendered habitus and field, *and* the limitations of embedded systems of constraint (McNay 1999: 110). For Adkins, reflexivity does not necessarily result in social transformation, and can be a reworking of identity that maintains distinctions (Adkins 2003: 21). Reflexivity about gender has, in fact, been identified as increasingly routine by occupational research (Adkins 2003: 34).

Sweetman (2003) also suggests reflexivity is now required across many different elements of social life, including the negotiation of protracted youth transitions. This leads Sweetman to suggest the 'crises' that prompt reflexivity are more or less constant. He therefore puts forward the concept of 'reflexive habitus', in which there is a habitual adaptation to a changing social environment:

> a capacity for – and predisposition towards – reflexive engagement is characteristic of certain forms of contemporary habitus … a reflexive stance may be *unreflexively* adopted, this by no means rules out such a stance but simply renders it a more durable or stable characteristic of the individuals or groups concerned. (Sweetman 2003: 537)

Sweetman offers us an alternative model of habitus which takes account of social change and unstable conditions (Sweetman 2003: 541). However, it is not without its problems. Adams notes there is some ambiguity in Sweetman's position over whether a reflexive habitus is liberating (Adams 2006: 521). More fundamentally, Archer argues that the notion of a reflexive habitus is a paradox, as Bourdieu's theory rests upon the actions of the habitus as 'semi-conscious and quasi-automatic': 'it is hard to think of any concept less helpful for dealing with conscious deliberations and the determination of choices' (Archer 2007: 56). It is also important not to conflate individualisation and reflexivity, according to

Atkinson (2010). He does suggest, however, that the reflexive habitus may be more prevalent among more privileged groups (Atkinson 2010: 71).[4]

What are the implications for thinking about cosmopolitanism and social change? Globalising forces, as we saw in the previous chapter, mean that we increasingly engage with cultural difference. Could regular encounters with diversity be a prompt for reflexivity? Kendall, Woodward and Skrbis argue that routine cosmopolitan engagement is 'without any great reflexive consciousness or capacity to destabilize current organizations of cultural power, or interpreted unproblematically as just one component of a person's environment' (Kendall, Woodward and Skrbis 2009: 124). In other words, simply coming into contact with difference will not prompt reflexive cosmopolitanism.

Other theorists put forward cases for a more nuanced understanding of the link between habitual and reflexive action. For example, Crossley argues individuals have a 'habit of reflexivity' through the incorporation of the other as a mirror to reflect upon our own actions (Crossley 2001: 112). Sayer (2005a) also suggests that ways of thinking can be become habitual. Action is guided by tacit understandings and evaluations, including our 'internal conversations', what he refers to as 'mundane reflexivity' (Sayer 2005a: 27–28). Sayer's concern is with moral judgements that can arise from both mutual evaluation and self-monitoring of conduct. This self-monitoring may be a 'feel for the game' or more conscious deliberations (Sayer 2005a: 45). Sayer notes that for Bourdieu, judgements of the self and the other are made from within situated social relations, but that this does not adequately acknowledge how this draws on moral norms and narratives, and discourses of racism, sexism or class (Sayer 2005a: 142). It is this view of the other – this intersubjectivity – which is crucial in understanding the gap year narratives presented in this book. The moral weight of cosmopolitanism, and how this may be bound up with classed privilege, is also of relevance here. I will return to, and expand upon this point, in the final chapter.

Gap Years, Structure and Agency

Some gap year researchers propose we might fruitfully explore the interplay between the constraints of social structures and the reflexivity required in late modernity. King suggests that the identity work enabled by the gap year is both 'biographical reflexion and experimentation' and indicative of emerging social class (and adult) identities in specific contexts (King 2011: 353). Young people present a 'narrative of individuality' when describing their gap years, but

---

4 Despite putting forward this as a possibility, Atkinson (2010) finds no evidence of a reflexive habitus based on biographical interviews with people in the UK about their educational experiences, work trajectories, lifestyles, values and politics.

link their self-development to future benefits in education and employment. For King, this is a way for gappers to work through the individualisation of structural factors (King 2011: 354).

However, individualised accounts are not necessarily reflexive identity work. Atkinson (2010), for example, suggests that narratives of choice are evidence of 'faux reflexivity'. For Atkinson, the workings of capital still direct individual trajectories. 'Faux reflexivity' is simply 'mundane consciousness operating within the subjective field of possibles given class positions and dispositions but masquerading at the narrative level as action without limits or history' (Atkinson 2010: 114). There are also constraints surrounding experiences from other national contexts that are analogous with gap years. Haverig and Roberts (2011) argue that the New Zealand 'OE' (Overseas Experience) is surrounded by discourses of independence, freedom and choice, but that such activities are limited by institutionalised boundaries and regulatory frameworks. This sets out what 'freedom' should look like, so that 'even though some young people imagine themselves as freely choosing individuals, they act within clearly defined fields of opportunities' (Haverig and Roberts 2011: 601). Gap years may be built on ideas about young people choosing to follow a cosmopolitan path, but they are also encouraged and rewarded, and require access to resources in order to participate.

Conclusion

The discourses that frame gap years may stress that it is a matter of individual choice to travel overseas in productive ways. However, they are recognised as a legitimate activity and are a way to make status distinctions. Consequently, research suggests gap year experiences are a way of accumulating cultural capital. As this chapter has shown, the concept of cultural capital has been subject to extensive debate, concerning both its definition and its contemporary relevance. Nevertheless, I argue that the model of symbolic distinction offered by Bourdieu is a way of capturing the value of gap years. In Chapter 2 I outlined that cosmopolitan cultural capital can be understood as 'good taste', an embodied privilege. Overseas gap years are associated with developing these cosmopolitan competencies that can provide future benefits in education and employment.

The opposing views of identity presented in this chapter – habitus on one hand, the reflexive self on the other – returns us to the definitions of different types of cosmopolitanism from Kendall, Woodward and Skrbis (2009) in Chapter 2. We might expect someone who takes part in a form of cosmopolitanism that can be defined as 'sampling' is guided by the habitus. They may consume goods that are diverse without becoming more tolerant or open to difference in any significant way. What Kendall, Woodward and Skrbis identify as reflexive cosmopolitanism is seen to offer a more 'genuine' engagement with difference along with an understanding of one's place in the world.

In this chapter I have suggested that the debates surrounding the concept of cultural capital and competing theories of identity work offer an insight into the nature of contemporary cosmopolitanism and gap year travel. In order to summarise these perspectives, I offer two versions of young people who take gap years: the habitual gapper and the reflexive gapper. This is based on three key questions that are at the heart of this book. Firstly, how do gappers relate their encounters with people and places? Secondly, how do gappers engage with the benefits and status of travel? Finally, can the self-development associated with the gap year experience be understood as a reflexive or habitual process?

From a reflexive modernisation perspective, the figure of the gapper is a young person attempting to negotiate a range of potential courses at a 'fateful moment' (Giddens 1991: 143) in their lives, narrating their experience in a context where the distinction between themselves and the Other is effaced. Having to choose a path from the multiple options open to them, they are able to take advantage of increased global mobility to create coherence and order through undertaking experiences that define their cosmopolitan identity with fewer structural constraints than previous generations. The benefits of such activities are pursued on an individual basis with an orientation to future goals in education and employment.

This is one possible way of theorising the gap year. From a perspective influenced by Bourdieu, the gapper is a young person imbued with the orientations of others in their particular social milieu, approaching the experience with a pre-established sense of what is valuable. Given that certain manifestations of the gap year are historically associated with privilege, these gappers are likely to be those with relatively high cultural capital, and the undertaking validates their dispositions to action as they make distinctions with regards to what is appropriate (and what is inappropriate). They have omnivorous cultural tastes, consuming difference in order to make such distinctions. As this is institutionally legitimated (through government and educational establishment sanction), they will gain additional advantages – such as employability – over those from less privileged backgrounds, thus reproducing structural inequality.

How might we use these to engage with gap year narratives? In the next chapter, I explain how I put the models of the habitual gapper and the reflexive gapper to work on empirical data by drawing on Goffman's (1974) concept of framing. I suggest that blogs provide an insight into how individuals understand events through framing, and also how they draw upon shared frames in order to communicate these experiences to others. One of the central concerns of this book is whether the gappers critically reflect on the frames used to tell their gap year stories, or whether they utilise well-established frames. Chapter 4 begins by outlining the features of blogs as a medium and their narrative elements. It then discusses how blog analysis is an innovative means of studying such narratives, but also requires some careful and critical reflection on the methodological and ethical implications of adopting a novel method, particularly with regards to how 'offline' concerns may relate to an 'online' context.

Chapter 4
Researching Gap Year Narratives

The previous chapter offered two hypothetical versions of a gap year traveller: the habitual gapper and the reflexive gapper. In this chapter, I describe the methods used to analyse the narratives of young people on gap years to explore their 'cosmopolitan journeys' and the relative salience of these two models. This book explores the representations of gap year experiences in blogs written by young people during their time out, supplemented by semi-structured interviews with a sub-set of the bloggers.[1] I argue that examining the narratives presented in blogs gives us access to a different type of account than those generated through researcher interaction. My analysis is based on young people's subjective understandings of their gap year experiences and the reference points they use to communicate their stories, drawing on Goffman's (1974) concept of framing. The word 'frame' has an implicit connotation, of course, but as a concept it is used to understand the subjective ways people understand and interpret events.

This chapter introduces the features of blogs as a medium and their narrative elements, and how existing work on travel blogs can inform gap year research. Framing offers a way of asking questions about how gap years are represented in blog (and interview) narratives. I discuss different approaches to framing and compare people's active construction of frames with the idea that we have little control over the frames we use. I then outline the practicalities of generating the blog and interview data, and offer some reflections on combining data from these two sources. The chapter also includes a discussion of the opportunities and challenges of using blogs in social research. Blog analysis presents an innovative means of studying spontaneous narratives, but also requires some careful and critical reflection on the methodological implications. Finally, I consider the ethical issues that arose in the course of the study, and present a case for a contextualised approach to ethical-decision making.

---

1 See the Appendix for anonymised profiles of the bloggers. Quotations from the blogs in this book are verbatim, including any errors of spelling, grammar and punctuation (with some annotation in brackets to assist the reader). To distinguish between interview data and blog data, the suffix 'i' is used in the identifier (e.g. Lisa [3] refers to Lisa's blog; Lisa [3i] refers to Lisa's interview).

Blogs, Blogging, and Narratives

Bruns and Jacobs define 'blogging' as:

> the reverse-chronological posting of individually authored entries which include the capacity to provide hypertext links and often allow comment-based responses from readers. (Bruns and Jacobs 2006: 2–3)

A weblog or blog is the website that hosts these entries. The earliest forms of blogs from the 1990s were simple lists of links that the blogger found interesting (Blood 2004). Since then, the term has expanded to include online journals. Indeed, Herring et al. argue that blogs are decreasingly centred on links, and that a more personal style of blogging dominates (Herring et al. 2004: 9). The development of new 'genres' leads Bruns and Jacobs to suggest that the term blog no longer refers to a specific form of web content, and that a descriptive prefix is required to clarify meaning (Bruns and Jacobs 2006: 3). Examples include 'corporate blogging' or 'research blogging'. The blogs in this book can be categorised as 'travel blogs', which share similarities with the offline formats of travelogues and travel photo albums (Herring et al. 2004: 10). As such, they are not specifically concerned with providing links to other webpages, and focus on recording and communicating the authors' gap year experiences. These blogs provide *narratives* of gap year travel.

Elliott defines narratives as chronological, meaningful, and social (Elliott 2005: 4). Events are organised as a progression, so that their significance is understood in relation to the whole sequence (Elliot 2005: 3). There are similarities here with the practice of blogging. The structure of blogs is temporal, and each post adds to a sequential account. Like narratives, events are 'connected in a meaningful way for a definite audience and thus offer insights about the world and/or people's experiences of it' (Hinchman and Hinchman 1997, cited in Elliot 2005: 3). Moreover, they are 'social media', designed to be shared. Blogging the gap year provides a narrative of a significant event in young people's lives. Since the fieldwork for this book was undertaken, travel blogging and other forms of 'interactive travel', such as using social network and photo-sharing sites, have increased in popularity. Germann Molz (2012b) found that searching for the term 'round-the-world travel blog' yielded 89 million results. I have just tried these search terms myself, and received 145 million results! Germann Molz argues that the growth of interactive travel is evidence of 'new patterns of sociality that emerge when movement, communication and technology converge' (Germann Molz 2012b: 3).

Research into Travel Blogging

Social researchers are becoming increasingly interested in this rich data. One particularly prolific discipline that uses blogs to access accounts of travel experience is marketing (see Banyai and Glover 2012 for an overview). This interest has a different agenda to that of sociologists. For example, a discourse analysis by Bosangit, Dulnuan and Mena (2012) explores how tourists construct their experience in their blogs and why they blog. Some of their findings share some similarities with the research questions I examine in this book: how tourists represent places; their self-presentation and identity construction; and the 'Othering' that takes place, which highlights novelty and cultural differences. Bosangit, Dulnuan and Mena use their findings to make some suggestions for the marketing of tourist products and destinations; in other words, how to sell places to consumers. Their insights are: to pay attention to how tourists are reshaping perspectives of places through blogging; to consider how communication and marketing messages can appeal to expectations of identity work through travel; and (most worryingly) to think about the role that local people play, and whether negative accounts of difference should be acted upon or if the 'exotic' should be preserved (Bosangit, Dulnuan and Mena 2012). Here is a clear example of the complex relationship between consumption and cosmopolitanism, which exposes the potential for inter-cultural experiences to be commodified in the interests of commerce. It also suggests that blog analysis itself is part of the 'cosmopolitical terrain' (Germann Molz 2012a) of tourist consumption.

Alternative perspectives in research using online travel narratives give insights into blog audiences, cosmopolitan narratives and travel practices. Karlsson (2006) examines the narratives of Asian-American 'diasporic tourists' who present accounts of their visits to their 'homelands' for their communities in the USA. She suggests that the 'autobiographical tales of identities and homes are produced for the consumption of a specific audience' (Karlsson 2006: 310). In a comparative study of the online diaries of Danish and Israeli backpackers, Enoch and Grossman (2010) explore the audiences for these travel stories, and how encounters with other travellers and locals are described, along with the attitudes towards them. Enoch and Grossman find differences between the two nationalities, as the Israeli backpackers are more inward-looking in their encounters with the Other, and their blogs form a national 'community of strangers'. The Danish blogs, on the other hand, are more outward-looking in their accounts of travel for their audience, which consists of those already in their existing social network (Enoch and Grossman 2010: 534). Germann Molz also explores online travel journals to discuss how cosmopolitanism is an embodied state (2006) and the importance of food in cosmopolitan narratives (2007). These stories, she is careful to note, are not 'transparent representations' of the 'real world', but a way to access the cultural discourses that travellers use to imagine and make sense of their experiences (Germann Molz 2007: 79).

Travel Stories, Identity Stories

Blog research is a way to investigate how stories are told to an audience (of known or unknown others) to critically consider encounters with difference. By examining the blogs of young people taking gap years, I am able to consider if, and how, the gappers' representations of people and places are guided by pre-established ideas. Travel blogs are a useful tool to do this, given the 'narrativistic' nature of tourism (McCabe and Foster 2006); we like to tell travel tales, and a blog provides the space to record such stories for ourselves and for others. Not only do blogs have a narrative element, they also tend to involve some form of self-presentation (Rettberg 2008: 111). We might, therefore, see blogs as a way of accessing *narratives of the self*. Taking a narrative approach to understanding the self reflects a 'more active, processual view of identity that shifts over time and is more context dependent' (Elliott 2008: 131). Such a viewpoint thus recognises individual agency in self-presentation. The potential for blogs to provide the space for this reflexive self-narration seems almost obvious. Indeed, Miller sees blogs as the 'ideal environment' to 'tell one's life narrative to the world' (Miller 2011: 170). Miller draws on Giddens (1991) to suggest that blogging is an example of the reflexive identity project required in a context of individualisation: individuals are disembedded from social structures; need to create and sustain self-narratives; and establish relationships through communication and self-disclosure (Miller 2011: 170).

Despite this potential for blogs as a tool for individualised identity work, gap year research suggests there is a lack of critical engagement with issues of development in gap years and structural constraints in access to these forms of travel. Can the narrative account of an activity that is pursued to gain advantage by those in an already privileged position and is used to accumulate scarce resources be disembedded from structural constraints? Some scholars have used blogs to engage with similar questions. For example, Lynch (2011) takes a critical feminist perspective on 'beauty blogs' to explore claims that these spaces challenge preconceived ideas surrounding beauty. While the blogs in Lynch's study are interactive, there is no attempt at critical dialogue, nor does blogging seem to encourage critical self-awareness.

Conducting a blog analysis makes it possible to examine the frameworks of understanding bloggers employ without intervention or prompting. One particular benefit of using blogs is the ability to access accounts of everyday life, in which 'situated action [is] unadulterated by the scrutiny of the researcher' (Hookway 2008: 95). They are 'spontaneous' in the sense that they are not produced in relation to research goals (Arosio 2010). These travel blogs therefore offer the possibility of unobtrusive engagement with gap year narratives. In the next section, I describe the process of data generation and analysis. The first step was to construct a purposive sample of blogs that matched the research aims and objectives.

Generating Data

The sample was constructed by searching for blogs that were written by young people from the UK who were taking a gap year overseas between school and university. It seemed the best way to do this would be to look for blogs in which the author defined their experiences as a 'gap year'. To find such examples I searched for this phrase on the blog search engines 'Google Blog Search' and 'Technorati'. Based on initial results, certain hosting platforms were more popular than others, so these were also searched. Each blog viewed was recorded in a table. These efforts generated a large number of results, and in the process of data generation a total of 700 blogs were inspected and recorded. The vast majority of these were not suitable to include in the sample. A typical reason was that a blog might discuss gap years, but was not actually written by a gapper. Li and Walejko outline some common problems in blog sampling, including collecting 'spam' blogs, abandoned blogs, and access-restricted blogs (Li and Walejko 2008: 282). This would be more of a problem if probability sampling was employed, of course, and as this was a purposive sample such blogs were inconvenient but could be discarded.

The search process continued until a final sample of 39 blogs was constructed.[2] Searching was a time-consuming process, and I spent many weeks skimming through blog posts to determine if they were relevant. Some of the blogs were of considerable length with over 100 posts, and the sample as a whole contained over one million words. In order to deal with this amount of data, the blogs were converted into text files and then imported into the qualitative data analysis software Atlas.ti.[3] The blog sample is outlined in Table 4.1 below.

---

2 For an explanation of this odd number, see the section below on 'Opportunities and Challenges'

3 The use of data analysis software is subject to some debate in qualitative analysis. Some researchers consider its functions come close to the logic of variable analysis, for example by tracing relationships between codes, with the danger that the data can be dealt with as neatly packaged variables (Mason 2002: 160–161). Despite these concerns, it provided invaluable in helping to code and retrieve the data.

Table 4.1 Blog sample

	Placement only	Both placement and travel	Independent travel only	Total
Male	2	9	7	18
Female	4	12	5	21
Total	6	21	12	39

The rationale for using qualitative blog analysis was to explore the frameworks of understanding that young people use to describe their gap years. My approach was what Polkinghorne (1995) calls an 'analysis of narratives'. It examines data in the form of narrative accounts in order to identify themes and concepts (Polkingthorne 1995: 13).[4] The thematic analysis of the gap year blogs was guided by Kelle's (1997) definition of 'qualitative induction', in which specific phenomenon are described with reference to existing categories; and 'abductive inference', in which data presents new and atypical events. The guiding principle of the analysis was how the gap year bloggers told their stories with a focus on the three key themes that run throughout this book: their encounters with people and places; what they considered good taste; and how they reflected on their self-development. This drew on the concept of framing, inspired by different perspectives on frame analysis.

Framing

In *Frame Analysis*, Goffman aims to isolate some of the basic 'frameworks of understanding' in everyday life (Goffman 1974: 10). The term frame is used to refer to the 'the definitions of a situation [that] are built up in accordance with principles of organization which govern events … and our subjective involvement in them' (Goffman 1974: 10–11). They are, essentially, how we understand and attach meaning to events, the models we use to interpret the social world. Frames are employed by people to 'locate, perceive, identify and label' occurrences (Goffman 1974: 21). This attachment of meaning serves 'to organise experience and guide action' (Benford and Snow 2000: 614). Gap years are a good example of this, as calling an overseas trip a 'gap year' gives it a certain meaning, and there are also expectations about what such trips should entail. That these should be cosmopolitan journeys is a case in point.

---

4 This approach is different to 'narrative analysis', which takes 'actions, events and happenings' as data to produce stories, such as biographies (Polkinghorne 1995: 6).

Within the overarching frame of 'taking a gap year', these journeys can be framed as 'backpacking'; 'taking time out' 'volunteering'; a 'learning experience', etc. Subjective understandings are composed of frames within frames, and we engage in a process of 'frame assembly' to define a situation (Scheff 2005: 381). Individual gap years can be framed to include all, some, or just one of these associated meanings. Using the concept of framing is a means of unpacking the different ways gappers define their experiences in order to understand them and communicate this to others. However, there are different perspectives on the process of framing, centred on the agency that individuals have over the frames that they use. Frame analysis has been taken up in studies of social movements from a position that emphasises the active adoption of frames, whereas other scholars suggest we have less control.

Frame Alignment Processes

Social movement studies adopt the concept of framing to explore how people involved in collective action mobilise and counter-mobilise ideas and meanings (Benford and Snow 2000: 613). Such work analyses how social movements gain support for their goals. This includes the 'frame alignment processes' that, if successful, link individual interpretations of events with the orientations of movements (Snow et al. 1986). These strategies are 'an active, processual phenomenon that implies agency and contention at the level of reality construction' (Benford and Snow 2000: 614). According to this perspective, frameworks are not static but affected by context, including the cultural opportunities available to construct particular framings. To frame collective action, those involved in social movements have to draw upon cultural resources such as 'meanings, beliefs, ideologies, practices, values, myths [and] narratives' (Benford and Snow 2000: 628–629). If social movements can align people's understanding of such events with their own perspective, they are able to garner support for their cause. Benford and Snow (2000) suggest a number of 'core framing tasks' that such organisations employ to achieve what they call 'resonance'. An example would be 'narrative fidelity', in which the narratives that a social movement use to frame an event resonate with cultural narratives that are accepted by their audience (Benford and Snow 2000: 622). The gappers' narratives explored in this study are not aimed at gaining support for a political or social cause, as is the case with social movements. They do, however, need to make their experiences *understandable* to those who are reading them, and I suggest they utilise cultural resources that resonate. For example, in Chapter 7 I consider in detail how young people talk about what makes gap years worthwhile. Implicit in something being worthwhile is the alignment of values. Although social movement studies explore framing as an active process, other scholars suggest that frames operate at a deeper cognitive level (Fisher 1997).

Constraints on Framing

According to Swidler (1986; 1995), interpretations are constructed using a cultural 'toolkit' of tacit elements and explicit rituals. This toolkit is constrained by institutions, semiotic codes and political context, which for Swidler means that people have very little control over the associated system of meanings. In other words, to interpret events, we have to use the frameworks available, which are shaped by wider forces. Kendall, Woodward and Skrbis suggest cosmopolitanism is part of this 'toolkit', although this can be 'restrained by personal, local and national anchors which alert people to the downsides of globality' (Kendall, Woodward and Skrbis 2009: 108).

Consequently, other work focuses on the constraints that are placed on framing in a way that is analogous to discourse analysis, according to Fisher (1997). 'Deep structural frames' in the work of Donati (1992) and Triandafyllidou (1995) refer to the metaphorical tools, like narrative structures or ideologies, which organise experiences. Individuals interpret events by selectively perceiving information to fit in with what they already know (Triandafyllidou 1995, cited in Fisher 1997). This means that 'when people encounter new information or a new experience, they make sense of that experience by fitting it into an existing frame' (Fisher 1997: 4.36). Moreover, such frames operate 'metonymically', which means that they can be shared with others by referring to just one aspect for readers or listeners to recall the whole frame (Donati 1992, cited in Fisher 1997). According to Fisher (1997), these metaphorical and metonymical frames mean that people are able to share their interpretations with others. From this perspective, frames are common reference points that are not actively invoked.

Gap Year Blogging

Frames are a useful way of thinking about blog narratives. In writing a blog, young people tell their stories and describe them for others. The analysis of the frames they use, as undertaken in this book, entails an examination of both their subjective understanding of gap year experiences and the collective resources they draw on to describe them. Furthermore, an unobtrusive approach is a way of approaching the question regarding the degree of reflexivity in the adoption of frames. Do the gappers actively and reflexively employ frameworks of understanding to present their experiences? For a young person to be a reflexive cosmopolitan, we would expect that they would also be reflexive about the frames they use rather than interpret the people and places they encounter using pre-existing ideas. Alternatively, do the ways in which they describe people and places, the value of travel, and the process of self-development stick to fairly standard scripts? Throughout this book, I will argue that well-established frames tend to be employed in the telling of gap year stories. These frames include exotic or romanticised representations of the Other; the long-established discourse of travelling as superior to tourism; and institutionalised and legitimate understandings of the 'right kind' of gap year.

Objective Contexts, Subjective Understandings, Intersubjective Narratives

Blog analysis is limited in gaining an understanding of an individual's structural position and therefore the connection between cosmopolitanism and social location. However, these gap year bloggers are a relatively homogenous group of young people from the UK taking their gap year between school and university who are also relatively privileged, which means that the study is able to draw conclusions regarding dominant ideas. Their stories are not 'outsider' accounts, but instead reflect what gap years *should* be about. Blog data gives an insight into the pre-existing dispositions that guide the accounts of this particular group. What is out there 'in the world', and our location within it, interacts with our 'way of being' (the habitus), so that the discourses that surround practices are enshrined in collective and individual dispositions. As will be seen, however, I also reflect upon more critical readings of Bourdieu, which aim to capture 'habitual' or 'mundane' reflexivity without over-emphasising individual agency (Sweetman 2003; Sayer 2005a). These alternative perspectives on reflexivity, I argue, help us to understand the cosmopolitan experiences of young people on their gap years while remaining conscious of continuing structural constraints.

There are 'implicit, if not explicit, audiences' for a blog (Hookway 2008: 96). Travel blogs provide a way for family and friends to follow and interact with the traveller: they are a form of 'digital storytelling' (Germann Molz 2012b: 69). This is illustrated by the answers from the gap year interviewees when asked why they blogged about their gap year. The gappers think blogs are more convenient than group emails, and also provide a record for them of their travels. Likely readers are friends and family, or even unknown readers. These potential audiences are also evident in short introductions or 'about me' sections in the blogs that provide biographical details, which are sometimes even addressed to strangers: 'For the random readers who don't know me' (Ewan [1]). The accounts that are drawn upon in this study thus reflect a public display of overseas gap year experiences. Germann Molz (2012b: 67) argues these are 'intersubjective and social' narratives, even if they might focus on individual presentations of self. Travellers' blogs 'show and tell what they are seeing and doing and to put themselves on display as well, primarily as a mode for socializing with a distant and mobile social network' (Germann Molz 2012b: 67). The presentation of gap year narratives to a known (or unknown) audience means that we need to consider the role of mutual evaluation and understandings of value. Blogs provide a way of accessing these presentations; of gaining an insight into such dialogue, and how collective understandings and the expected view of others come into play to guide the stories that are told. This also has some relevance for the differences between the blog data and the interviews.

Blogs and Interviews

Much of the data drawn on in this book is taken from the rich narratives in unsolicited blog accounts. A series of interviews were also conducted to explore some of the themes in more depth. The bloggers were all contacted and asked if they would be willing to be interviewed. I either used the email address that they provided on the blog, the contact form on the blog, or left a comment on their latest blog post. Out of the 39 bloggers: 9 were interviewed; 6 expressed an interest but did not respond to further messages or could not commit to an interview; 1 agreed to be interviewed but did not attend; and 23 bloggers did not respond. I would have liked to have done more interviews, as even though I had plenty of blog data, it would have enriched the study to have been able to speak to additional bloggers, although conducting interviews with around a quarter of the overall sample seemed reasonable.

The interview guide was generated from themes that were identified in the course of the literature review, but also those that emerged during the blog analysis to investigate how these related to the participants' understandings of their gap year experiences, alongside some questions that were not always possible to answer using the blog data. This added a richness and depth to the analysis so that, for example, the discourses of tourism versus travel apparent in the blogs could be put to the interviewees to further explore the salience of these ideas for framing gap year travel. We could also talk about any issues not discussed in their blogs. The semi-structured approach allowed comparisons between the accounts, but still retained some flexibility so that the interviewees discussed and expanded on topics particularly important to them; for example, one interviewee talked me through her gap year scrapbook.

The interviews provide a slightly more candid account. The gappers discuss holding back some stories from the public space of their blogs (although the presentation of the experience to a 'researcher' meant that these are still, in some way, an 'official' version of their story). The existence of a variety of 'versions' of gap year narratives is noted by Francesca, [6i] who says: 'I had a written journal as well, which had a lot more in. So I had two different things, a more personal written one and a public one' (Francesca [6i]). The interviews present a way of comparing the stories that are induced through asking questions with those that are more spontaneous. In other words, asking interviewees questions *about* their experiences means they are induced to think *upon* their experiences. This of course leads to some reflection on the idea of taking a gap year, but what is notable is that the central frames are very similar, for example, cosmopolitan experiences are those with most value in both the interviews and the blogs.

The data that is generated through the uptake of new technologies such as blogging enables a means of capturing narratives without the researcher being directly involved in their generation (Hookway 2008). The issue is not just about how it may be more convenient to access accounts of the gap year through blogs, therefore, but also about how accounts of the gap year presented in blogs make it possible to consider the extent of unprompted reflexivity in narrations of experience. Such methods are not without their challenges, however. In the next section of this chapter, I consider the practical, methodological, and ethical issues associated with blog analysis.

The Opportunities and Challenges of Blog Analysis

The growth of internet communications presents a significant shift in the data available to researchers. Blogs provide access to what Beer and Burrows (2007) call an archive of everyday life. In the not too distant past, accessing the stories told by young travellers without researcher interaction would have depended on gaining access to their private correspondence or personal diaries. Of course, this raises some complicated ethical questions, which I address below. Nevertheless, scholars can now find endless personal accounts of experience online. As such, blogs are comparable with unobtrusive research using documentary sources (Lees 2000; Pauwels 2006). Blogs are like diaries in the sense that they are personal documents produced in real time, with no precise addressee, however they are also interactive and visible to anyone with online access (Arioso 2010). Blog analysis engages with the 'representational world' of individuals and groups by using these online archives (Arosio 2010). Moreover, the gap year narratives that are the heart of this study are the young people's own stories told using their own language. The issue, therefore, is not that it is 'easy' to access online data – and indeed, this would be completely inappropriate. Instead, it is possible to examine the frames of understanding employed without the intervention of a researcher. Dealing with blog data, however, can be difficult, due to the format of the text being analysed, issues of data quality, and questions over representativeness.

Blogs as 'Text'

Scott (1990) defines a document as 'an artefact which has, as its central feature, inscribed text' (Scott 1990: 5). Blog data is more complex, even though it is also a (virtual) artefact based on text. Since the first discussions of online methods, researchers have defined internet data as new forms of text. On one hand, the data are in a 'textual form that has many elements of the traditional text and is thus open to analysis with time-tested tools' (Mitra and Cohen 1999: 198–199). Converting the gap year blog posts into text files meant that they could be managed using qualitative analysis software and coded. Yet blogs do not only contain written text. A single page from the gap year blogs can also contain pictures, video clips, audio files, hyperlinks to other websites, and even adverts. Hookway suggests that blogs offer visual expression as well as textual, and that researchers need to understand how to *view* as well as read them (Hookway 2008: 101–102). Blogs are also constantly changing. New posts are added, new comments are made by readers, and previous posts can be edited or deleted. The content can even change from one audience to the next, as particular posts may be made private and available only to particular readers.

The interactive element of blogs results in meanings being negotiated, questions asked of the author and representations validated or disputed. These features make blogs a dynamic medium, but one that can be difficult to get to grips with. As a result, some pragmatic decisions had to be made during the course of the research, and this book focuses on the written text. Although the multimedia elements are also part of some young people's presentations of experience, not all of the blogs contain such content. Qualitative analysis software was, at the time of analysis, not as well-equipped to handle web data as more recent versions. To retain some ethnographic context to the textual content (and so they were viewed as well as read), I made notes on each blog as I read it online. The analysis has been informed by this reading, although only the text of the posts (including the comments) has been coded.

Data Quality

Should we 'trust' the narratives found in blogs? How can we evaluate them? One way of establishing the quality of blog data might be to consider the criteria used in assessing documentary sources. Interpreting such sources relies on assessing the quality of the evidence in terms of authenticity, credibility, representativeness and meaning (Scott 1990: 6). One key issue in evaluating an archived diary, for example, is that the author is who they claim to be. This is not always something that it easy to establish online, and there are some well-documented examples of people being misled by bloggers writing stories that turned out to be hoaxes (Rettberg 2008). For some, the uncertainty over whether these narratives are 'true' may outweigh the benefits of conducting this sort of unobtrusive online research.

Hookway (2008) questions this mistrust of online data, however. He argues that if data is not generated through researcher interaction, it is seen as problematic, but it is important to remember that we have to rely on people 'telling the truth' in any form of research method. Moreover, whether this is important depends on 'whether a researcher is looking at how blogs work to produce particular effects or whether they are looking at how blogs correspond with an "offline reality"' (Hookway 2008: 97). For this study, it is a matter of some concern, as the project is designed to explore gap years of a particular type: those taken overseas by British young people between school and university. One blog initially included in the sample was discarded (hence the odd number of 39). This is because contact was made with the author and it transpired that she was taking her gap year later in life than initially assumed. A close reading of the rest of the sample means that I am fairly confident that the remaining blogs fit the criteria, based on discussions of age, hometown, finishing school/college and starting university, etc. Moreover, it has been confirmed through the interviews that the interviewees' blogs were correctly included in the sample.

Does the potential uncertainty regarding the remaining blogs mean that the sample cannot be trusted, however? It seems very unlikely that someone would deliberately set up a gap year blog, but it is not beyond the realms of possibility. Online narratives should not be taken at face value. However, this project is concerned with the public presentation of experience rather than an offline 'true story'. With the caveat in place that it is not possible to be completely certain about the blogs' provenance, the aim of this book is not to explore exactly what happened on young people's gap years, but how their stories are framed. As in Germann Molz's study of online travel narratives, we can 'understand these stories as a rich source for examining the cultural discourses through which ... White, Western travelers imagine the world and make sense of their encounters with other cultures and their experiences on the road' (Germann Molz 2007: 79). Using interviews alongside the blog analysis enables the young people's online representations to be compared to how they articulate their experiences in an offline context. As noted above, the gappers are aware their blogs are for public consumption, and so we can see these narratives as a *version* of their gap year story.

Whose Story is Told?

An additional concern is the representativeness of the sample of bloggers. While we may tend to assume that internet use is ubiquitous, this is not the case. According to a report from the Oxford Internet Institute, 23 per cent of

Britons do not use the internet (Dutton and Blank 2011: 9). Certain groups are under-represented online:

> Some are excluded on the basis of social or economic barriers to access. Britons with lower incomes, lower socioeconomic status, and less schooling are more likely to be non-users. Medical and other physical disabilities remain barriers as well. Others are excluded by choice, such as individuals with the Internet available in their household, but which they choose not to use. (Dutton, Helsper and Gerber 2009: 6)

Conducting internet research means that groups who are under-represented online will be also under-represented in any sample. In addition, not all internet users are bloggers. As a result, the narratives of gappers who do not write blogs are not captured by this gap year study. Young people who do not blog may have a different take on the gap year experience. Moreover, this is only one form of cosmopolitan experience, which needs to be acknowledged, especially given the tendency for cosmopolitanism to be associated with privileged mobilities (as explored in Chapter 2).

These are important questions, which raise another caveat about the conclusions that can be drawn from the data. The fact that these narratives are those of bloggers restricts any comments about alternative forms of gap years, or indeed alternative cosmopolitanisms. This does not mean the research presented in this book is not 'valid', however. While the accounts analysed here may not be representative of all gap year experiences, or offer evidence about cosmopolitanism among the wider population, they do offer a unique insight into the sorts of stories that are told about gap years. These are a particular group of relatively privileged young people who are able to blog about their overseas experiences. How they tell their gap year stories gives us an insight into the cultural frames that define gap years. Blog analysis is therefore an appropriate way of engaging with these stories, although it does present some ethical challenges.

The Ethics of Blog Analysis

Making ethical decisions in internet research can be complicated, with tricky questions the 'price' for the 'wealth of data' available (Blank 2008: 541). The British Sociological Association's ethical guidelines note that 'Eliciting informed consent, negotiating access agreements, assessing the boundaries between the public and the private, and ensuring the security of data transmissions are all problematic in internet research' (British Sociological Association 2002: 5). It can be difficult to get to grips with the frequently changing environment online, with new phenomena emerging and different forms of communication becoming more or less popular (Eynon, Fry and Schroeder 2008). So, while the fundamental principles of ethical social research remain unchanged, advice from the Association of Internet Researchers (AoIR) and other internet scholars is that these need to be tailored to the specific research context (Lomborg 2013; Markham and Buchanan 2012). In this study, there are two key questions to address, building on central tensions in internet research ethics: Are the gap year blogs public or private? And are the bloggers human subjects or authors?

Establishing the Boundary between Public and Private

Firstly, the nature of online communication means that the distinction between public and private is much more 'fuzzy': 'Internet users seem to be airing much of their "private" lives in the "public" realm of the internet' (Ford 2011: 557). We could argue that these blogs are technically public because they are not password-protected. Blogs allow their authors to restrict access to content, so there is an argument to be made that if access is not restricted, it is in the public arena. This does not necessarily mean that such content is 'ethically available' (Hine 2011: 3), however. Furthermore, bloggers' perceptions may be different. There is evidence to suggest that people may act as if their online communications are private, and may, for example, object to conversations being read even if they are technically open (Hudson and Bruckman 2005: 298). When using online data, we need to consider what might be reasonable expectations of privacy, and our responsibilities towards the producers of such content (Wilkinson and Thelwall 2011).

Personhood and Authorship

Secondly, research ethics are designed to protect human subjects from harm. However, the internet 'complicates the fundamental research question of personhood' (Markham and Buchanan 2012: 7). Are the traces we leave online, for example our social network profiles, part of 'who we are'? The issue for the gap year is whether the blogs should be considered as representations of the bloggers, or as documents. Here, another boundary is blurred, between subject and text. This is a crucial question, as it determines whether informed consent is required to use this material as data, and whether the identity of the bloggers needs to be protected. It can be difficult to anonymise internet communications as they can be traced using search engines (Beaulieu and Estalella 2012). On the other hand, if we view the gap year bloggers as authors, we might deem it necessary to cite their material and we would not need to gain consent to use it (Bassett and O'Riordan 2002: 244). An analogy would be analysing a document such as a newspaper article. We could quote from this without the journalist's permission, but we would need to provide a reference to the article. Researchers conducting blog analysis therefore need to decide whether to preserve the anonymity of the blogger or credit them for their work (Hookway 2008: 106).

A Contextual Approach to Research Ethics

Negotiating these tensions has been difficult, and in writing this book (and other outputs from this research) I have deliberated on the most appropriate way forward. Human subjects can be defined as 'a living individual about whom an investigator … conducting research obtains data through intervention or interaction with the individual, or identifiable private information' (Frankel and Siang 1999: 16). The blogs have not been produced as a result of interaction with me; they are accounts of experience produced for both a known and potentially unknown audience. Moreover, it is these public representations that are the object of study, not the gappers themselves. So, a case can be made that informed consent is not required. In my dealings with the young people who *were* interviewed, I obtained informed consent for both the interviews and their blog postings. This is important as the interview data has been generated through interaction.[5] Interestingly, the interviewees did not show any particular concerns about their use of their narratives in an academic study. Rather, they expressed a mild curiosity about how I had found them.

The blogs are consequently treated as online documents, which, while personal, are not private (Hookway 2008). If I were to follow the principle of treating the blogs as public documents to the letter, I would provide direct links to the blogs used.[6] Yet although the young people writing the gap year blogs may have been aware that their blogs are in the public domain, they would not expect that this would result in a sociologist exploring issues of cosmopolitanism, class and identity through their stories. The gappers often provide their names, photographs, and contact details on their blogs. I feel some responsibility towards the bloggers, and have endeavoured to provide some protection when writing up this research. A helpful resource has been Bruckman's (2002) 'continuum of possibilities' of reporting internet research. I have adopted 'moderate disguise' (Bruckman 2002), and changed identifiable details, while still quoting from the blogs. I have not provided links to the blogs themselves to avoid directly connecting the research to the gappers' representations. In doing so, I have followed the example set by Hookway, who privileges the identity of bloggers over providing credit to them as authors (Hookway 2008: 106). Of crucial importance here, and which is worth repeating, is that context is very

---

5 All of the bloggers were contacted, of course, which does challenge the status of this project as wholly unobtrusive research.

6 I have acknowledged the host website in the Appendix.

important in making these decisions. Had the blogs contained very sensitive material, I would not have taken this approach, for example.[7]

Conclusion

The advent of blogging provides scholars with innovative ways of engaging with accounts of experience. Travel blogs allow researchers with an interest in cosmopolitanism the means to consider the stories that people tell about their encounters with the Other. Blogs also allow us access to what is valued in such experiences, and the ways in which these are also forms of self-presentation. However, we need to critically reflect on the idea that blogging itself is always a reflexive endeavour. Bloggers might *reflect* on their experiences, but may not be reflexive about them. In adopting the concept of framing, I suggest that instead we need to assess the extent of reflexivity in these accounts. How 'cosmopolitan' encounters and experiences are framed tells us about something about the relative salience of the habitual gapper and the reflexive gapper outlined in Chapter 3.

Drawing on blogs to explore gap year narratives has some clear practical advantages, but it is exceptionally important not to undertake online research because it is seen to be easy, or to allow the availability of data to steer the research. In fact, as can be seen from this project, blog analysis is not straightforward, and there are some tricky methodological and ethical hurdles to overcome. Yet the rich narratives provided in these online accounts are an appropriate way of engaging with how stories are told. Blog narratives are unprompted by interaction with a researcher, and are what young people themselves want an audience to know about their gap year journeys. Investigating the framing of these stories considers both their subjective understanding, and the use of collective resources, or shared frames, to describe them. In reading the blogs, I have asked: what are the key frames that are employed? As will be discussed in the chapters that follow, historical legacies and classed identities influence the frames that are used. This is not intended to be a criticism of the young people who have produced these accounts, but rather that some standard 'scripts' are used to describe people and places, good taste and the sorts of identity work that count as being worthwhile.

Moreover, combining the blog data with interviews means that these dominant framings can be explored further. Throughout this book I examine points where more critical reflection on the gap year experience may emerge, and the dialogue of an interview situation is one place where this can happen.

---

7 For further critical reflection on the ethical approach taken, and whether this was the 'right thing to do', see Snee (2013).

The interviews also provide an indication of the gappers' rationale for blogging. I also do not want to suggest these young people are completely devoid of agency, unthinkingly and unwittingly making their way through the world, but we need to consider the limitations of the frames to which they have access.

I have argued that using blogs provides access to gap year narratives without interaction, but no data are 'untouched by the researcher's hands' (Silverman 2001: 159). For example, my interest in gap years as a field of study is driven, in part, by my own experiences of independent travel. This is useful in many ways, and helps me to understand some of the reference points within the blogs, but it will have undoubtedly impacted upon my interpretation of the gappers' accounts. Other critical issues include the huge amount of data collected, along with data quality. However, as the research is driven by gaining an insight into the framing of gap year narratives, rather than 'accurate' presentations of experience, offline concerns with the authenticity of documentary sources are less relevant. Future research into the narratives presented in blogs would benefit from integrating the multimedia aspects into the analysis to more faithfully capture these presentations. It is also very important to restate that the sample excludes gappers who do not blog about their gap year, or those who may undertake their gap years in the UK. This is significant, given the hierarchy of gap year experiences (Heath 2007) and the critique of cosmopolitan experiences as elitist as explored in Chapter 2.

Innovative methods such as blog analysis present a number of ethical challenges. A particular concern for this study is defining whether the blogs are publicly available data. Although the blogs are available in the public domain, the ethical decisions have not been straightforward, and any researcher interested in blog analysis should consider this carefully. A contextualised approach to the ethics of blog research is particularly important. I have presented a case for negotiating the tensions between public and private, and subject and author in a particular way, but ongoing critical reflection is required in this sort of work to ensure that social research engages with these new narrative forms in responsible ways.

Gap Year Stories

In the next three chapters, I move on to present the findings from the empirical study into these rich gap year narratives, drawing mainly on the blog data but also the interview dialogues. Chapters 5, 6 and 7 take each of the key themes in turn to explore the framing of gap years in terms of the representation of people and places; the benefits of travel; and ideas about self-development. Throughout, I reflect on the implications for gap years as cosmopolitan journeys: in how gappers engage with difference; the references to cosmopolitan good taste; and the place of cosmopolitanism in a moral hierarchy of self-development. To begin, Chapter 5 deals with the fundamental issue of how the gap year bloggers frame their encounters with difference. It considers the dominant framing of 'the exotic' while also noting some incidences of critical reflection, and a continuum between 'globally reproductive' and 'globally reflexive' accounts.

Chapter 5
Encountering Difference: Gap Year Narratives of People and Places

As the previous chapters suggest, taking a gap year overseas is often framed as a cosmopolitan endeavour, a 'conscious attempt to be familiar with people, objects and places that sit outside one's local national settings' (Skrbis and Woodward 2007: 732). After all, this is the rationale for going 'away' rather than staying at home. This chapter focuses on the representation of people and places in gap year narratives. The gappers' stories construct a context for their gap year experiences: the stage on which they are set and the characters that are present. The analysis that follows explores the framing of encounters with difference, and considers if the gappers reproduce common ideas or if their representations are 'globally reflexive' (Savage, Bagnall and Longhurst 2005). The dominant framings in these gap year narratives tend to reproduce discourses of the Other that reflect both historical legacies, such as colonial narratives, and current global inequalities.

In this chapter, I introduce some critical perspectives on representations of the Other, and note the ways people and places are constructed as exotic in the gappers' stories. This is followed by reflections from the gappers on what happens when they interact with the local. Next, I explore how gap year locations are framed as different from 'home'. The gappers' accounts can be placed on a continuum from globally reproductive framing that presents an authentic, exotic Other, towards the globally reflexive, in which these young people reflect on their place in the world. I suggest their framings are a form of 'self-referential cosmopolitanism' (Savage, Bagnall and Longhurst 2005). These gap year stories are more about gaining status 'back home', and less about reflexively engaging with difference while away.

Representing the Other

The *desire* of young people to go beyond tourism is well documented among gappers, backpackers and other independent travellers (Desforges 2000; Huxley 2004; Germann Molz 2006; Loker-Murphy and Pearce 1995). What becomes potentially problematic is how other cultures are represented and understood, particularly when it is the global North that is framing the South. Viewing the Other as more 'authentic', according to Wang (2000), is a driver for international tourism to the 'Third World'. Yet this 'ritual respect for difference', or what we might call cosmopolitan attitudes, can actually distort the Other through romanticised, exotic framings (Wang 2000: 140–141). For Wang (2000), this is a nostalgic idealisation of more 'primitive' ways of living. Such concerns are particularly relevant for gap year travel, as they are associated with volunteering and budget travel in the global South. Indeed, a considerable amount of gap year literature focuses on volunteering placements in such communities, and how these schemes are implicated in transnational inequalities of power and wealth (Guttentag 2009; Lyons et al 2012; McGehee 2012; Simpson 2004; 2005a; 2005b; Sin 2009). Such work considers how providers of gap year placements often do not engage with these issues and tend to present simplistic models of development. We have already seen in Chapter 1 that controversies over volunteer tourism also crop up in public debates from time to time.

In these critical accounts, the relationship between gappers and their hosts is naïve and ill-informed at best. At worst, it sells young people the experience of encountering difference in the hopes of developing their CVs while offering little real benefit to (or even damaging) the people and places they visit. Such arguments mirror criticisms of cosmopolitanism consumption as superficial, as cultural appropriation, or as exploitation. Inequalities also manifest in how gappers' mobilities are categorised and framed as not all movement has the same value. Backpackers visiting Australia are welcome, for example, while the movement of 'illegal immigrants' is criminalised (Allon 2004: 61). Similarly, migrant workers are not 'travellers' as they are restricted by their 'race' and class positions (Galani-Moutafi 2000: 204). 'Western travellers' have a status that is not afforded to others who are mobile. Young people's gap year narratives need to be situated in this context, in which the experience is part of wider mobilities, and images of gap years circulate in 'cosmoscapes' of value (Kendall, Woodward and Skrbis 2009). Their framing of people and places are shaped, in part, by inequalities and reproduce certain ways of thinking about the Other.

In *Orientalism*, Said (1978) argues that 'the Orient' is a historical invention of colonial Europe, a place of otherness that is constructed as a mirror for the west. Portraying the Other in a particular way provides a framework for 'dealing with it by making statements about it, authorising views of it, describing it, by teaching it, settling it, ruling over it' (Said 1978: 3). Research on independent travel notes the endurance of these discourses and their significance for understanding the meaning attached to travel practices. Although Desforges (1998) does not suggest that the projects of young travellers are those of colonialists, the framing of locations for their backpacking stories marks them as 'different'. Places are seen to contain novel experiences that can be incorporated into identity narratives (Desforges 1998: 175). This incorporation is an ideological process in which locations are shaped, 'part of the complex power relations between the West and its global Others in the "Third World"' (Desforges 1998: 176).

The construction of gap year spaces is informed by historical legacies, according to Simpson (2005b): European colonialism; the Grand Tour; and missionary and volunteer work. The narratives of these processes and perspectives remain 'evocative and powerful' in contemporary gap years (Simpson 2005b: 457). While less critical accounts of gap year experiences suggest some contribution to global understanding (Jones 2005), this is tangled up in enduring ideas about difference. The Other often features in travel narratives in ways that confirm rather than question established images (Galani-Moutafi 2000: 215). Being able to understand what gap year locations and the people who inhabit them are 'really like' is hindered by these dubious inheritances. They surface in the framing of gap year experiences. It is worth noting here that the majority of the blogs in this study document at least some time spent in the global South, so such questions are particularly appropriate. However, even in 'developed' nations like Japan and the USA, representations of difference emerge that are drawn along lines of 'race' and class.

Exotic Places and Exotic People

An Exotic Landscape

In their blogs, the gappers highlight they are somewhere different by drawing on popular representations of exotic places. One environment that is synonymous with the exotic is the 'perfect beach'. Places in the global South can be literally transformed by Northern tastes so that they fit these images, such as the illicit movement of sand to change beaches into an 'ideal tropical paradise' (Duffy 2004: 41). The bloggers who talk about beaches describe them in comparison to such imagined, idyllic locations; they are a powerful frame. Both Bryn [2] and Jo [18], for example, highlight the 'white sand and blue sea' of Australian beaches. Bryn thinks the view before him is 'just like the ones you see in films', whereas Jo's beach is 'just like the ones on the postcards'. These places are so perfect that Sian [39] expresses disbelief: 'the sort of Sandy beach that you see in postcards and never in real life'. Exotic beaches are therefore out of the ordinary and almost unreal, like fiction come to life. Indeed, a number of gappers make reference the Alex Garland (1997) novel and Danny Boyle (2000) film *The Beach*.[1]

---

1 Garland's novel (1997) follows a young backpacker who tires of the 'mainstream' backpacker circuit in Thailand and finds his way to a seemingly idyllic secret island

This ideal of a secret perfect place that *The Beach* represents is used as a frame that recalls a tropical paradise:

> One day we hiked 2 hours through the coastal rainforest to get to the remotest beach on the Island – the whitest, untouched sand you could possibly imagine, beaten by the clear, empty seas of Brazil. We took a small packed lunch for the day and just chilled on this virgin beach in what reminded me of a scene from my book 'The Beach'. (Adam [28])

The Beach deals with a setting that is part of backpacker mythology, of a special location that only those 'in the know' can access. Yet describing places in this way has certain connotations. Tickell (2001) analyses the endurance of colonial travel narratives in contemporary fiction, including *The Beach*. These new stories draw on Victorian literature, in which picturesque landscapes were 'a way of neutralising the threat of difference inherent in the tropical landscape' (Tickell 2001: 45). These views of idyllic landscapes indirectly draw upon ongoing Western fascination and domination, according to Tickell, and we can see the echoes of these tropes in the gappers' narratives.

'Perfect beaches' are also places of seclusion. These locations resonate with representations in popular culture, for example the beautiful but inaccessible 'desert island'. Indeed, the backpacker ideal of exploring the unknown is the central plot device for *The Beach*. Adventure travel narratives, according to Tickell (2001), are another legacy of colonial expansion. Tickell highlights three elements of such narratives: 'going native'; the invasion of civilisation; and the lack of opportunities for adventure in modern life (Tickell 2001: 50). A driver of contemporary tourism is to discover places outside of history with 'unspoiled nature and savagery' (MacCannell 1992, cited in Tickell 2001: 51). We can see these ideas in the excerpts from Adam's blog above: 'remotest', 'untouched', 'empty', 'virgin'. Likewise, Bryn's fantasy beach was 'nice' because it 'wasn't busy'.

The frame of the 'perfect beach' evokes undiscovered lands and places that are far away from home. The presence of tourists would disrupt the idea of places that are remote, just waiting to be discovered by the adventurer. Framing places in this way casts them as exotic and unknown to 'the West'. As discussed in the previous chapter, frames can operate metonymically, so that a reference to *The Beach* means that readers can recall a wider frame of 'exotic'. Popular culture references are consequently a useful resource for gappers to describe

---

community of other travellers. The gappers' reference to *The Beach* is somewhat ironic, given that it satirically charts the dissolution of a 'backpacker paradise'. Moreover, Boyle's (2000) film is a Hollywood adaptation of the novel that caused controversy when the natural beach locations in Thailand were altered by the production team, an example of the transformations discussed by Duffy (2004).

places and highlight their connotations of adventure. Other examples include New Zealand described with reference to *The Lord of the Rings* trilogy and its fantasy landscapes;[2] and gappers who tour the ruins of Angkor[3] in Cambodia mention the film *Tomb Raider*,[4] specifically the temple visited by the central female character – an adventurous explorer.

At other times the gappers make more explicit comparisons between their gap year locations and their home. Chris, for example, reflects upon his surroundings in Tanzania as follows:

> Tanzania is much more inspiring than England as a natural wonder, a chameleon falling on you when you're eating dinner is a bit cooler than looking at the sheep from your bedroom window. (Chris [15])

Here, the context is somewhere that is *better than home* due to its novelty. Similarly, Lucy finishes the description of her day white-water rafting in Ecuador with the statement that it 'Beats [Home Town] any day!' (Lucy [30]). Andy's blog post on a visit to some Japanese gardens notes that 'We just don't have this sort of thing in England' (Andy [26]). For Urry (2002) such escapes from the everyday are at the heart of tourist motivations: 'Tourist experiences involve some aspect or element that induces pleasurable experiences, which, by comparison with the everyday, are out of the ordinary' (Urry 2002: 12). As we will see in the next chapter, the gappers distance themselves from tourists, and are more likely to see themselves as travellers. Yet their narratives of viewing the landscape share some similarities with Urry's description of the 'tourist gaze': how difference is seen and contrasted with home.

One example of how tourists 'read' a landscape is to look for signs of pre-established notions of places (Urry 2002: 13). Such pre-conceptions are apparent in how Paul describes his arrival in Uganda. He talks about leaving the 'western' world behind, and reflects on his pre-conceptions of 'Africa'; would there:

> be mud-huts everywhere or would all the towns and cities feel just [like] western ones? Seeing orange roads criss-crossing hinted at the former but really I knew it would be somewhere in-between. (Paul [32])

Paul both challenges and reinforces images of Africa in the popular imagination. The references to mud huts and dusty roads conjure up a vision of a less

---

2 New Zealand provided the locations for a series of films based on J.R. Tolkien's *The Lord of the Rings* novels.

3 Angkor is the remains of a Khmer city near Siem Reap in Cambodia, popular with tourists due to the hundreds of ruined temples, and is a UNESCO World Heritage Site.

4 A film based on a computer game that features a female adventurer.

developed place, a process of Othering that homogenises a continent. Paul is on the lookout for these signifiers, although he shows some cosmopolitan awareness of the presence of cities. His way of describing this encounter with landscape gives a clear sense that he is arriving somewhere that is *away*.

A key element of the gappers' narratives of experience, then, is looking around at the settings to note that they are coming into contact with something Other. These draw upon, and are bound up with, established ideas about exotic locations: ideal beaches, fantastical scenery, unusual animals, material evidence of a 'non-Western' way of life. On the surface we might interpret these as cosmopolitan engagements with difference, but a critical reading questions these representations. For Simpson, such discourses are perpetuated by the gap year industry that frames the 'Third World' as a place for experimentation (Simpson 2005a: 111).

Exotic Food

As well as their surroundings, the bloggers articulate their encounters with exotic food as a means of highlighting difference. Francesca [6] recounts how her Russian friends tease her because she has just eaten horse meat without realising. Horse meat is something so different that Francesca cannot recognise it. When Francesca tells the story in her blog, however, she is quite careful to mention that it was 'extraordinarily delicious' and 'tasty'. This is a way of presenting a cosmopolitan identity, of being open to difference. Similar encounters crop up throughout the blogs. Helen [27] finds Mongolian dumplings full of 'strange meat' and 'reeeaaally strange!', but she stresses they are 'nice' and recommends them to her readers. Ewan also describes his Thai breakfast as extraordinary but something he enjoys:

> One more thing: vegetarians please stop reading at this point and skip to the next paragraph. For breakfast this morning [Friend] and I had a bowl of rice and a dish of pig bits. There were lumps of pork, liver, kidneys and tripe in it. Surprisingly – it tasted good. (Ewan [1])

These ingredients are used in European cuisine, yet the meat and offal is presented as almost gruesome.

Food that is not consumed in the UK is described by the bloggers as a source of entertainment:

> It was here that i picked up a "variety bag" of deep fried ... all sorts. These ranged from Scorpions- (shown below) to cockroaches and locusts. Sadly (i think) any flavour that may have survived the intensive frying process was

90

masked by the soy sauce and chilly [chilli] powder but none the less it was a good laugh. (Owen [37])

The spectacle of these snacks, available at a Thai market, highlight how food is central to 'the Western cosmopolitan's search for "novel" tastes – for consuming difference literally, alimentarily' (Duruz 2004: 248). Food is part of the performance of a cosmopolitan identity (Germann Molz 2007). For Duruz, this is cultural appropriation, a result of a 'colonizing eye' searching for meanings that can be drawn from 'ethnic' food. The gappers are able to tell a story of adventurous travel by framing their consumption of food as the consumption of the exotic. Keeping an 'open mind' gives them a level of cosmopolitan sophistication, yet again the bloggers reproduce certain discourses about difference. bell hooks (1992) argues that 'ethnicity becomes spice, seasoning that can liven up a dull dish that is mainstream white culture' (cited in Duruz 2004: 248). Ethnic differences as symbolized by exotic food lend the bloggers' stories this spice, making their accounts interesting and worth telling. Germann Molz (2007) argues these embodied performances of openness and consumption of difference result in the framing of White/ middle-class/First World as the norm, with the Other as exotic and strange.

Not all of the gappers enjoy the local food. A notable example here is Tim, who works in France for the ski season. He moans about the staff meals:

> The food was awful, and to give you an example, the first evening meal was horse which was as bloody as … a very bloody thing. I've never eaten such shit in my life! (Tim [23])

Tim isn't happy until an English chef arrives; he *wants* to consume the familiar, not difference. This account could be held up as an example of the 'home plus', non-cosmopolitan experience as described by Hannerz (1990). Tim is something of an exception to the rest of the bloggers, however. His main trip is taken in Europe and he is concerned with constructing a successful career narrative. For Tim, it seems that demonstrating cosmopolitanism through stories of the exotic is not particularly important. Instead, he discusses how working in a ski lodge will give him 'a good step up the career ladder'. Clearly, Tim has different concerns.

Exotic People

The blogs also document the people encountered in these exotic places. Francesca pays a visit to Siberia towards the end of her gap year, and her account shows some interesting tensions:

Alongside a few Orthodox Chruches [churches] are also Buddhist temples, and of course the ethnic diversity is totally different – a good 40% of the people if not more are ethnic Buryats or Mongolians. If I squint my eyes I really feel as if I'm in China (or what I think parts of China feel like anyway). (Francesca [6])

This is a fascinating excerpt. Francesca demonstrates some local knowledge and an awareness of ethnic and religious diversity, but then her statement about physical appearance homogenises the peoples of Asia as 'Chinese'.

Francesca's comments show that when describing their gap year experiences, the young people look around at who they can see and talk about perceived physical differences. Ewan, for example, is conscious of standing out in Thailand:

The road itself was a sea of Thais (with my head bobbing along above them – I mean nigh on 6 foot 2 I'm pretty damn conspicious [conspicuous]). (Ewan [1])

Ewan's description suggests his appearance is very distinctive among an anonymous mass of Thai people. Yet this is taken from a night out with a group of other gappers, when he is walking down one of the most infamous backpacker destinations, the Khao San Road in Bangkok, a veritable hub of hostels, shops and cafes catering to Western travellers. This trope – of the tall Westerner in Asia – often surfaces in popular culture, such as the film *Lost in Translation*, as a metaphor for being an outsider.[5]

If we consider that gappers are in pursuit of authentic experiences as part of their cosmopolitan journeys, then it is important to gain access to the 'inside' of a culture (MacCannell 1999). Feeling like you stand out in a prominent way would hinder getting inside. Highlighting physical differences can frame an experience as taking place somewhere exotic, but may also be a way of talking about not fitting in. Dave [7], as 'the white guy', feels like he was 'the exhibit' at a museum in Tanzania. A similar feeling is described by Kevin [34] when he talks about being an 'attraction' while on a train in India. In these accounts, skin colour is a signifier of difference, such as the references throughout Andy's blog [26] that his pale skin and blond hair make him stand out in Japan. Ethnicity is a marker of insider/outsider status, something that is clear even in the 'West' when Hugo arrives in New York:

---

5 *Lost in Translation* (Coppola 2003) is an American comedy-drama set in Japan. There are a number of scenes in which the central male character visibly stands out due to his height, such as being a taller than a group of people in an elevator or not being able to fit into his hotel shower. The film was criticised at the time for its stereotypical depictions.

We were slightly nervour [nervous] about travelling on teh [the] subway esp[ecially] later in the evening. However it wasnt too bad despite getting a few looks adn [and] for a whi;e [while] travelling in a carriage where we were the only white people out of 20 or so people. (Hugo [33])

In describing feeling out of place in this way, the gappers once again frame these locations as exotic. When Ewan and Dave explicitly say that being tall, or having pale skin, makes them stand out, this is an implicit statement that local people are not tall, or not White. Encounters with Otherness permeate these gap year discourses, which according to Simpson (2005a) do not critically engage with difference. In the blogs, there was little reflection upon the 'exoticness' of local people:

Although we got hassled by a zillion school trips there, all these Japenese [Japanese] and Vietnamese school trips were loving us. Non stop requesting photos and even individual ones with all of us, I felt actually famous! A tad creepy though! (Travel Buddies [20])

This blog is written by a group of four young women who backpack together during their gap year. Like other gappers, they feel uncomfortable being 'on display' at a tourist attraction in Vietnam. They recount a number of times they are photographed by local people. The young women are exotic themselves, but they do not welcome this attention, and there is little reflexive examination of why such interest in difference might be reciprocal. An exception is Adam's blog [28], in which he thinks about the attention his skin receives in South East Asia. Adam criticises the 'ideaology' [ideology] of Whiteness as attractive, prompted by coming across skin whitening cosmetics in a local shop. The politics of Whiteness is recognised by Adam, but such considerations are limited in most of the gappers' accounts.

'Cultural Differences'

Difference can also be marked by cultural knowledge, or lack of it. Jason [9] describes, with some embarrassment, being brought a knife and fork in a Hong Kong restaurant. This is his first meal in Asia, and it is not just the food that is exotic but the whole cultural experience of dining. Jason, however, frames this as a cosmopolitan encounter, and negotiates this awkwardness through his existing knowledge. He goes on to say that the knife and fork is unnecessary, as he can use chopsticks. By stating this, Jason asserts he is a cosmopolitan traveller as he has the expertise to deal with difference. Another story of cultural difference comes from Christina, who spent her gap year teaching at a school in Uganda. One day, she and her friend get into trouble with over body language:

[Friend] and I were told yesterday that we were not standing appropriately! We had our arms crossed which is a sign of disrespect, instead you must stand to attention! If you do not do this and an important head of state is present you can get arrested! At least we know now. (Christina [10])

Christina spends a full year in Uganda, and this is just one of the examples of when she talks about how her extended stay means she can learn to avoid such faux pas. In these narratives, Jason and Christina are presenting themselves as successful travellers. Jason draws upon his established knowledge to deal with not fitting in, while Christina talks about developing understanding through prolonged access to local knowledge.

The gappers worry about such encounters, and are concerned that they might cause offence. Harri [36] is self-conscious when she is the only woman not wearing a headscarf in a Russian Orthodox church, and Andy [26] feels bad about breaking the 'rules' of a Japanese tea ceremony. Paul reflects on how he felt when he first arrived in Uganda:

I could not help but feel out of place. I was still heavily culture shocked and I think the root of it was a great uncertainty of how the people around me would react. I knew that the Ugandan people I was surrounded by had a life very different to mine, what could I say to them? How would they react to my prescence [presence]? What if I do something to offend them? (Paul [32])

Paul goes on to state that he learns to get over this, so exposure to difference can help to deal with these feelings. Interacting with difference in this way is important in order to be able to demonstrate cosmopolitan competence, the 'personal ability to make one's way into other cultures, through listening, looking, intuiting and reflecting' (Hannerz 1990: 239). This can enable the gappers to negotiate not fitting in, and consequently move beyond touristic relationships.

Fitting In

Feeling comfortable or uncomfortable in a social setting can be understood using Bourdieu's concepts of habitus and field. The habitus provides individuals with a feel for the game, so they know how to act without thinking about it. If these dispositions do not fit, it can result in bodily discomfort and unease (Savage, Bagnall and Longhurst 2005: 9). This can help to explain why the young people feel out of place, as their dispositions to action – their body language, for example – may not be the most appropriate in a given situation. Bourdieu's theory is an account of practice in social space, but feeling comfortable also helps to engender a sense of belonging to geographical locations (Savage, Bagnall and Longhurst 2005). There is also some space for reflexivity in this model, as this emerges when there is a disjuncture between habitus and field. Later in this chapter, I discuss how some of the gappers reflect on their place in the world, in part prompted by the experience of not fitting in.

Stereotypes

Yet alongside instances of critical reflection are instances of very stereotypical representation. Here the exotic is represented in its crudest form, again framed by popular culture references. Comments about 'ladyboys' in Thailand are not uncommon, for example, with male bloggers receiving warnings from their readers not to get 'confused'. The following comment from Neil's blog [17], for example, draws upon this framing, combined with ideas about Korea and the consumption of dog meat:

> [Comment] You say you had a drink in a petrol station well what were you drinking Gasoline!!!! If you drink too much of that stuff the Ladyboys of Bangkok will get to you. Look for the adams apples that is a sure sign!!!! I am curious the web site has sponsors of Dog Beds and Pet Supplies etc. Surely when you get to Korea they sponsor dogs heads!!!! (Neil [17])

These are not Neil's own words, but he does not contradict them.

Other gappers, and their readers, joke about mistranslations of English in East Asia, and describe them as 'Engrish'. Stereotypical representations of 'developed' countries like Australia also occur. These may even be *recognised* as stereotypes, like Kevin's [34] description of a 'sterotypical [stereotypical] outback oz bloke' who is 'remarkably like crocodile Dundee'.[6] Viewing gap years as a way to help young people become more cosmopolitan and knowledgeable about the world cannot be maintained if their stories make fun of the people and places encountered in these ways. For Simpson (2005a), there is a strategic advantage for the gap year industry in stereotypical representations. The product offered to young people is the cultural experience of coming into contact with the Other, so these stereotypical images circulate in how gap years are marketed (Simpson 2005a: 111).

Gap years are acts of consumption which, as we saw in Chapter 2, have a complex relationship with cosmopolitanism. As already suggested above, however, the gappers do not always resort to stereotypes, and they reflect upon the practice and outcomes of their interactions with local people. Rapport (1995) argues that stereotypes can be a useful frame to deal with diversity because they contextualise both the person who is 'out of place' and the people encountered.

---

6 *Crocodile Dundee* (1986) is a successful film comedy, in which the eponymous protagonist is a tough Australian from 'the outback'.

While Rapport notes that stereotypes are personalised by individuals, I suggest that collective framing occurs at these moments, as it also enables the benefits of interaction with local people and places to be understood by those at home. To tell a cosmopolitan story, the locations and actors need to be exotic, with local people leading 'very different' lives.

Cosmopolitan Encounters

'Meeting the People'

Engaging in local interaction is often put forward as a key advantage of independent travel, a way of going beyond the tourist experience. Twenty-five years ago, the backpackers in Riley's research cited 'meeting the people' as their primary goal of travel (Riley 1988: 325). Such interactions were a way of distinguishing themselves from 'tourists'. These preferences surface time and time again in studies on youth travel, for example in Huxley's (2004) work with Western backpackers. Huxley notes, however, that such engagement can be constrained by economic asymmetries; imbalanced roles and relationships; limited time spent in a place; and encountering other backpackers (Huxley 2004: 40). Gap year placements are appealing in this context as they seem to mitigate these constraints. Working and volunteering are activities marketed by gap year providers as a way of developing 'real' knowledge, rather than passing through a place as a tourist. However, this does not meant that cosmopolitan concerns are not important to those young people who backpack on their gap year. The narrative of getting inside is simply something that is more easily told by those who stay in one place for an extended period of time. One perceived outcome of a longer visit is being able to demonstrate an understanding of the host community. As with the description of places as exotic and different, a tension emerges as the result of the frames that are available.

Learning about the Other

In a discussion of the standard of living in Uganda, Christina [10] reflects thoughtfully on the idea that the children she teaches should be pitied. She talks about how local people grow their own food and, inspired by this, plants her own vegetable patch:

> If you live by subsistence farming you will have a very stress free life (providing you can grow enough!) Compare this to England; how many people pay to go to yoga classes or therapists, or just permanently feel tiered [tired]? (Christina [10])

How can we interpret Christina's reflections? Gap year programmes are criticised by Simpson (2005a) for the paternalistic view they perpetuate of 'Third World' countries. In this blog post, Christina is thinking beyond the idea of 'poor people who need the help of the West', and feels she has learned something about quality of life from interacting with the people around her. By comparing Uganda and British cultures in this way, we might see this as an example of the 'global perspective' as suggested by Jones (2005). Jones suggests young people may not develop a *sophisticated* understanding of development needs through going on volunteering placements, but gap years may induce reflection on different cultures. Yet if we think about how Christina's discussion is framed, there are references to Ugandan life as less stressful, simpler and more traditional with strong family ties. Framing the comparison in this way invokes a romanticised view of the Other.

This is not to say that the gappers do not learn anything. During her time in South Africa, Anna [29] reflects on the legacy of Apartheid. In her blog, she talks about being able to understand the political situation by being exposed to difference:

> Africa is amazing. The weather is fantastic, the culture is so different from home and the people are friendly. But only when you come here do you relaise [realise] that there is still so much to be done. Aparthied [Apartheid] is still very recent and I've even heard some people say it still exists. (Anna [29])

Here we can see the frame of 'being there' as a way of developing understanding. However, Anna's account suggests that outside help is needed in 'Africa' (there is a tendency for the bloggers to use nation state names and 'Africa' interchangeably).

As well as politics, the gappers are exposed to differences in personal relationships. This leads Kevin to change his opinion about arranged marriages in India:

> what really interested me was that at the start i thought the whole thing was a really bad way of working but i can kind of so that if it's done by the right people for the right reasons it can work really well. ... . [group leader] said that in the west we start with love and work on commitment and here thay [they] do it the other way around. and it seems to work ... think i'm happy doing it the western way but it's really interesting to see. (Kevin [34])

This exposure to situations, traditions, and practices in situ means that the gappers can present their reflections as authoritative. In the next chapter, I will discuss how this insider position gives the bloggers a certain cosmopolitan status of being worldly.

This view is exemplified in Libby's [8] blog post about Shanghai. Libby spends the majority of her gap year at a Christian organisation in New Zealand that offers a 'discipleship training camp'. As part of an outreach project, she travels to China for five weeks and undertakes missionary work in Shanghai. In writing about this experience, Libby criticises the inequalities she sees, the suppression of unofficial religion and internet censorship. Much of her time is spent interacting with people and talking about Christianity, and this helps her to critically reflect upon the local context. Seeing these issues first hand lends Libby a level of authority in her observations: she is 'there' and able to comment. There are some troubling elements to Libby's relationship to the local, however. It is focused on missionary work through the organisation she travels with, an echo of historical attempts to convert the Other to Christianity. While sympathetic and well-intentioned, Libby does not question the value of what her organisation is trying to do. It is not my attention to criticise Libby herself, but her case highlights how inter-cultural encounters are structured by existing frameworks.

Other gappers are also concerned with inequalities, and demonstrate some awareness of potentially exploitative relationships. Ewan [1] teaches during his gap year in Thailand, and rather than move on as planned, he decides to extend his placement. When discussing his decision, he is keen to stress he is not doing it for the money but because he enjoys it and he wants to contribute. Ewan uses the Thai word for 'Westerner', *farang*, to describe those who teach English for inflated wages. In doing so, he creates a distinction between himself and the foreigners who take advantage of the country's resources.

There were also instances of gappers attempting to show sensitivity to local culture, such as behaving respectfully in a place of worship. On Harri's blog [36], her boyfriend recounts their rationale for not climbing 'Ayers Rock' (Uluru), which he links to a wider reflection on the impact of tourism:

> Me and [H] decided not to out of respect for the culture, but so many people did and that really bothered me how so many of us demand respect for our own cultures, yet arent prepared to give it to such a sacred place ... . its just its hard to enjoy it when you see what its done to the aboriginal culture that surrounds it (a lot of aboriginals havent adapted to this 'new' way of life at all, and have developed bad drinking problems among other things). (Harri [36])

Climbing Uluru becomes a symbol of the damage inflicted by colonialism upon indigenous populations. At the same time, the idea of an unspoilt, original Other is invoked, and the larger systems of dominance are not discussed. Moreover, this also enables Harri and her boyfriend to distance themselves from the practices of tourists through their cultural sensitivity. This sort of cosmopolitan expression is complex, with narratives framed by existing ideas about difference but also articulating critical reflections on local issues.

Personal Relationships

By interacting with local people, the bloggers are able to present their gap year as a cosmopolitan experience, and thus such relationships are generally seen as something positive. The closer these relationships are, the better. The main part of Bryn's gap year is spent in Japan, and his placement involves working in a kindergarten. He is accommodated in a community care home, something he sees as mutually beneficial: 'The idea is that we're not all isolated and living in an apartment somewhere on our own, but we're integrated into a community' (Bryn [2]). Just by 'being there' and developing these relationships with the staff and residents of the care home is seen by Bryn as a 'winning' situation. This connection with people and places is portrayed as a key benefit of structured placements. Valuing such closeness can be observed in the eagerness of the bloggers to talk about making friends with local people. Andy [26] posts some photographs of his gap year in Japan to his blog and points out a young man he identifies as his friend:

> The Japanese guy (bottom left, second photo) is my buddy [Name]. We meet up and he teaches me Japanese and I teach him English and then we drink too much and forget everything and the beautiful cycle restarts, like the seasons. (Andy [26])

This is the only reference to the young man on Andy's blog, but their relationship in this instance is framed as mutually beneficial.

These sorts of connections are important to the bloggers. When Lucy [30] finishes her placement in Ecuador, she finds it difficult to say goodbye to her hosts. She emphasises that volunteering work is valuable, as evidenced by the appreciation shown by the community to her and her fellow gappers. In describing these moments, she is also able to demonstrate her knowledge of local customs. When the local pastor's wife washes her team's feet, she says 'it is a huge display of thanks and love here in Ecuador' (Lucy [30]). There are some uncomfortable connotations here, in a narrative of grateful locals showing deference to outside help. From Lucy's perspective, she has done something good and feels that this is evidence of a 'real relationship'. Similarly, Huxley (2004) found that the young travellers in her study placed great value on feeling part of a community as it is a more authentic experience:

> By being accepted into the local community by staying with friends or locals, backpackers thought that they were able to penetrate the façade of the places

they were visiting and experience a more valid host-guest relationship. (Huxley 2004: 41)

Thus, by making friends with local people, the gappers are able to narrate a move beyond touristic relationships.

These feelings of authenticity are particularly apparent in a blog post from Katy, in response to a hostile comment from a reader that raises a number of the criticisms levelled at the development benefits of gap years. While she acknowledge that her actions may not have 'made a difference', Katy defends her teaching placement in Nepal on the basis of her relationships with local people:

> no one can begin to imagen [imagine] the warmth with which we've been greeted by everyone we've met. the children at the school all wrote us letters, drew pictures, sang songs, and wished up 'a sweet and safe journey'. the teachers i consider as genuine friends. (Katy [5])

Katy defends her decision to volunteer and argues that the charity who organises the placement does valuable work. Her experiences prompt some thinking about the world and have engendered a 'global perspective' (Jones 2005). Again, however, local people and places are described with reference to the differences between life in Nepal and the UK with the latter missing the 'simple things'. Like Christina in Uganda, she reflects on difference, but in ways that see the gap year location framed as more 'authentic'.

Negative Interactions

So far, I have discussed positive interactions between gap year bloggers and the local people they meet, those that are focused on broadly cosmopolitan desires to encounter, embrace and understand difference. There are also instances where discomfort and unease are felt, cases in which the gappers cannot tell stories of successfully meeting the Other. One common complaint is being on the receiving end of 'hassle' from local people. We can compare Katy's discussion regarding authentic relationships with a post detailing her frustrations:

> still loving nepal, but the hassleing [hassling] and staring is starting to get to us. we've begun to shout at guys if they stare, and just shout ' hoina'[7] at any street trader who hassles us. think some of the westerners who have only just arroved [arrived] in ktm [Kathmandu] think were crazy, but you cant walk down the street without someone wanting your money. for a while its bearable and now its just too much. (Katy [5])

---

7 Nepali word for 'no'.

Although these are not successful encounters with difference, Katy is still able to frame them as evidence of her experienced traveller status. She can deal with it like an insider, unlike the 'westerners' who have just arrived.

Dave [7] also experiences what he calls 'hassle', and he writes about an arduous journey in Indonesia when he and his female friend are followed, feel threatened and are repeatedly asked for money. Reading Dave's post, it is clear that he and his friend were intimidated and feared that they would be robbed or hurt. It is difficult to find cosmopolitan sensibilities in this vitriolic account, in which local people are described as 'weasely', 'little' and 'sweaty'. His outburst of 'fuck Indonesians!' is an unusual expression of hostility among the bloggers, but the idea that their experiences are being spoiled by the actions of local people is not. Adam, who thoughtfully discusses Whiteness and beauty in South-East Asia, has a less reflective response to hassle in the Philippines. He sees this as 'an unfortunate parasite on a would-be ideal destination' (Adam [28]). He wants to go scuba diving and view the exotic scenery in peace. In such accounts, gap year locations would be perfect – if only there were no local people there!

For some of the female travellers, these negative interactions have an additional dimension in the form of sexual harassment. Jenny talks about her discomfort with the behaviour of local men in Guyana:

> The men in Georgetown are pretty intense as well. They seem to think that calling us "white meat" and asking us "to marriage them" will win a special place in our hearts. It's so romantic ... (Jenny [13])

Jenny presents this with a light-hearted, wry tone, but the use of the phrase 'white meat' marks these encounters as racialised as well as sexualised. Germann Molz (2006) argues that female travellers can be treated differently, and are more likely to be sexually harassed. Gender has an impact on the ability to fit in (Germann Molz 2006: 15). Moreover, Germann Molz notes how non-White travellers experience the 'contingencies of fit' differently. Bryony [35] is the only non-White British gapper in the sample. She is of British Chinese heritage, and thinks that her appearance sets her apart from both locals and non-locals:

> But yes ... It is staring [starting] to get to the point where I just want to turn around and, proper Townie style, yell "HEY, what the HELL are you LOOKIN' AT" or possibly, in response to "Hellomadamwhatisyournaaaaaame??" maybe just "Oh, SOD OFF". Though maybe it'll calm down again once we get out of Jodhpur. I am finding the whole monoculture thing abit [a bit] weird here. You know, there are local Indians and there are white/sometimes oriental tourists and THAT'S IT (Bryony [35]).

As Germann Molz argues, cosmopolitanism can be 'physically constrained or enabled' (Germann Molz 2006: 18).

Other irritations for the gappers include being scammed: 'They also try and rip you off the whole time just because you're western' (Hugo [33]); and seen as a source of money: 'I no longer feel like a walking dollar sign' (Owen [37]). The solution, according to Zoe [38], is to 'get inside' a place:

> many Indians are really very nice, once you get past the language barrier. And succeed in finding someone who isn't just interested in selling you something. (Zoe [38])

In the next chapter, we will see that by avoiding being ripped off, the gappers are involved in 'proper travel' away from 'tourist traps'. Negative interactions with local people may be incorporated into some familiar frames: a desire for 'real' and 'exotic' locations, for example. These criticisms are based on idealised versions of people and places. Again, critical reflections are often absent, such as thinking through *why* privileged visitors may be responded to in particular ways. The gappers' narratives also suggest that fitting in is 'contingent on the body' (Germann Molz 2006: 17). Physical markers of ethnicity or gender make some interactions with the local difficult, and these affect the gappers in different ways dependent on how their bodies are 'read'. In the next section their accounts construct gap year places with reference to poverty, tradition, disorder and risk, as opposed to more idealised, exotic framings.

'Us' and 'Them'

Visiting the Global South

Out of the 39 gap year stories explored in this book, 28 document at least some time spent in the global South. Such countries are popular with gappers as the sites of volunteering placements or inexpensive places for long-term travel. Simpson argues that organised gap year programmes 'produce and reproduce particular notions of the "Third World", of the Other and of development' (Simpson 2004: 682). The way volunteering is framed, according to Simpson, creates binary oppositions between 'us' and 'them'. For example, poverty is something that is experienced by a foreign Other, without reference to global structural inequalities (Simpson 2004: 687). On one hand, these framings undermine the cosmopolitan ideal. Yet on the other, they are part and parcel of the cosmopolitan's search for diversity. The gappers' description of their host countries often draw attention to 'cultural' differences to home related to the discourse of being 'less developed'.

The gappers who work in schools as part of their gap year often complain that these institutions are 'disorganised'. According to Jenny [13], 'half the teachers don't even go to their classes' at her placement in Guyana. Charlotte [12] explicitly refers to an example of 'Otherness' from her host school in Thailand:

> Later walked past classrooms to find chaos and children everywhere but no teachers, went to find a one, all were in a meeting during the day about the inspection happening at that moment! Its so different from home and a constant reminder of the culture difference. (Charlotte [12])

Complaints such as these not only highlight difference as something the gappers have to deal with, but also implicitly justify the presence of volunteering schemes. Discourses of the gap year industry perpetuate the 'need' for intervention in 'Third World' countries (Simpson 2004: 686). The fact that these schools are disorganised means that they need help.

Another common complaint is that the host communities have a different temporal orientation to the gappers' home cultures. Harri [36] becomes 'fed up' with people being late and 'Mongolian time'. A similar phrase is used by Duncan when he tries to arrange a meeting:

> When I asked him when he would be swinging by he firstly looked confused, he then explained to me the philosophy of 'Ghana time'. Ghana time is fundamentally 'whenever it happens, it happens'. (Duncan [21])

As well as these discussions of tardiness, the relative work ethics of Batswana and Zimbabwean people are discussed by Daniel [31] during his time in Botswana. He suggests that the former are 'lazy' while the latter are 'often illegal' (referring to their immigration status) and thus work harder. These characterisations of the Other – the disorder, unreliability and even laziness – are positioned in opposition to models of modern Western rationality. These are not limited to gappers on organised placements. Indeed, these discourses are interwoven with travel narratives. Galani-Moutafi notes that the traveller's journey of self-discovery is located in the 'inverse image of home' that the Other provides (Galani-Moutafi 2000: 215). These contrasts are a way of highlighting a cosmopolitan engagement with difference, yet rely on problematic framings that are linked to issues of power.

These discussions of chaos and disorder are entangled with the visions of the exotic place. According to Wang (2000), Western Europe has a paradoxical relationship towards modern life that is encapsulated in tourism and travel. The framings of place represent self-confidence – home is superior – but also discontent – home nations have lost their authenticity and the simple way of life (Wang 2000: 138–139). These seem like 'big issues' to draw upon when discussing the gap year stories of young people with good intentions: colonialism, modernity, exoticism. Yet how young people talk about the people and places they encounter draws upon these framings of difference, and as such unsettle claims for cosmopolitan encounters. Moreover, the paradoxical relationship that Wang (2000) describes can be seen in their frustrations with host communities and also their nostalgic portrayals of authenticity.

Tradition and Authenticity

On a number of occasions, the gappers present their encounters with local cultures in ways that frame places as 'traditional'. Peter's [16] description of his arrival in a Maori village (as part of an organised tour) is very suggestive of the intrepid traveller meeting the 'primitive':

> On arrival we were challenged at the gates to the village by the chief and some warriors. This was to determine wether [whether] we came in peace or to make war. After one of the chiefs had taken the peace offering we were allowed into the village to see the dirrerent [different] huts and how the maori lived before the European settlers came. (Peter [16])

This continues with 'traditional song and dance' and 'the traditional meal'. Displays such as these, like the Maori haka,[8] are cultural signifiers that can become the dominant perception of a nation, defined by gender and ethnicity and based on an idea of 'naturalness' (Urry 2002: 156). Of course, Peter's experience is part of a display especially put on for visitors: 'staged authenticity' in MacCannell's (1999) terms. This does not detract from the idea that the haka is an insight into an original way of life, a way of reconnecting with what has been lost. Wang (2000) notes that staged authenticity can be seen as a product of the impact of modernisation on local cultures. Both the recreation of the 'authentic original', like Peter's Maori village, and rejections of staged settings, are a wish for the exotic to remain 'frozen in time' (Wang 2000: 143). Furthermore, the idea there is a traditional, authentic Other who can be encountered – and consumed – is a feature of other gappers' stories.

An example of this is the consumption of 'homestays' with local families, an activity a number of the bloggers describe. The benefits of interacting with local people are a clearly defined product in these activities. What is being consumed is essentially an encounter with a traditional way of life by lodging with families marketed as 'ethnic' or 'tribal'. An industry has emerged in regions that are

---

8 A form of dance made famous by the displays of New Zealand's Rugby Union team before their matches.

popular with backpackers, notably South East Asia, which is based on offering these experiences along with 'hill tribe' treks. Hill tribes are 'ethnically, culturally and linguistically different' tribal groups (Cohen 1989: 34). Treks and homestays developed in Thailand from the 1970s onwards in order to meet the demands of independent travellers seeking adventure and authenticity, something to be found through interactions with 'primitive' and 'remote' places (Cohen 1989: 36). As Cohen points out, these alternative experiences are still staged to meet travellers' expectations. The industry has continued to grow, and travellers can book their encounters online, including 'ethnic minority trekking adventures' in Vietnam (Footprint Adventures 2013), homestays with the Karen tribe in Thailand (Responsible Travel 2013), and volunteer work on building and development projects for 'rural minority groups' (Kaya Volunteer 2013).

The gappers who engage in homestays and treks see these activities as a way to connect with tradition. Helen [27] looks forward to her homestay in Sapa, Vietnam, with an 'ethnic minority family that have sustained their way of life'. These encounters are framed as a means to engage with an Other that is unchanged. Adam [28] describes this as getting 'back to basics' in 'the remotest parts of the north'. The exotic, traditional, authentic Other is positioned as the opposite of 'civilisation' in Owen's blog:

A few miles away from the town all civilisation seems to disperse and all you have are a few rather traditional people living an extremely simplistic life. (Owen [37])

In these accounts, local people enable stories of adventure into the unknown. None of the gappers who undertake these encounters question their value.

There are other examples of the authenticity of local culture compared to life in the UK. This is particularly apparent when encountering ethnic minority peoples. For example, Libby [8] mentions that she find the Maori greeting of touching noses 'really humbling' compared to the stiff conventions around physical contact at home. This discourse of the humble, simple, basic Other as more 'real' informs good taste in travel, as will be seen in the following chapter. In evaluating these as cosmopolitan encounters, we need to think about what kind of engagement with difference is being presented in the gappers' blogs. O'Reilly argues there are enduring tropes of European expansion and colonialism in contemporary travel narratives:

These tropes and fantasies include the 'natural' native who has never set eyes on a white person; a nostalgic and naïve view of the 'traditional' life found outside the West, untouched by modernity but rapidly disappearing; and the simple, 'happy' native who gets by with very little and appears not to mind living in poverty. (O'Reilly 2006: 1003)

Again, it may seem unnecessarily critical to refer to the history of colonialism here. However, the gappers' narratives are framed by these tropes. They are powerful and enduring ways of thinking about difference that are difficult to escape, and in many cases, it seems that the gap year experience does not always provide the means to critically reflect upon them.

Poverty and Inequality

Being away from home is also reflected on when the gappers encounter poverty. Charlotte is shocked by the lack of possessions of the children at the school she works at in Thailand:

> Some kids didnt have shoes and so were running arround [around] on the floor, their feet got badly burnt. (Charlotte [12])

Such encounters also happen in gap year locations like the USA, where the bloggers still experience difference. Lisa works at a private boarding school in New York State during her gap year, which runs volunteering programmes in the local area and in New York City. As part of her placement, Lisa joins in with these projects, encountering less fortunate Americans than her boarding school students. These Others are defined by class and ethnicity. In one post, she describes a project that she finds particularly difficult, which involves boys and young men from poor, Black, inner-city backgrounds:

> After school today, it was my first time at [Community Project]. I was a bit nervous, I didn't know what to expect. [It] is an interesting sort of place. It's for boys aged 5 – 20 who have had to leave home because their household is not safe, or they can't live with their parents anymore, or they don't have parents etc. And because of this some of the boys are very unruly, a lot of them haven't had a great education, and some of them don't have very good social skills or manners. (Lisa [3])

Engaging with the Other can be hard, and the gappers describe feelings of 'culture shock'.

One way that the gappers frame and understand such inequalities is through drawing comparisons between rich and poor. Anna [29] writes a blog post about the differences between the standard of living in a South African town centre and the townships. She reflects upon the effects of poverty and wants to share this with her readers:

> Many of the people living in the townships have HIV and other diseases. Although the government is trying to improve their living conditions, it is

hard to do this. In this one township alone, there are over 1 million people. Unemployment is high and the p[o]verty is blantant [blatant]. (Anna [29])

Are such reflections evidence of a 'global perspective' (Jones 2005)? In Anna's account, it is presented as a localised problem. My argument is not that the gappers are indifferent or not empathetic, but that for the most part their accounts do not consider *global* inequalities.

In Simpson's (2004) study of gap year volunteers, young people speak about poverty as the result of a kind of global lottery. The privilege of being born in the UK is a matter of luck, and consequently the roots and causes of poverty are not questioned (Simpson 2004: 689). These discourses also frame the gappers' stories. For example, Owen [37] describes a visit to a local textile manufacturer in India where young people work:

> These guys, or so the management claim, take half of the profit directly into their wages. Never the less it made me shuffle out guiltily as we realised just how lucky we are, being the same age as many of the workers. (Owen [37])

Poverty is observed through comparison with Owen's own life, but he is not able to engage with the 'bigger picture' of *why* he is lucky.

The final notable example of difference in the blogs is the framing of places as risky and dangerous. These frames are required for the narratives of adventure explored in Chapter 6. This calls upon other elements of difference, such as physically standing out in unknown spaces. Jenny [13] thinks the local city centre in Guyana is dangerous because she is young, White and alone. Similarly, Alicia [14] is uncomfortable in Brazil because Rio de Janeiro is 'hot, unfamiliar and pretty scary'. Embodied feelings of discomfort and the risk of bodily harm run throughout the blog narratives, and these frames can be employed even before the gappers leave home. Paul [32] has to 'break the news' to his mother that he will be going to Uganda on his gap year. His research on the BBC News website 'scares' him. Exoticism is also employed as a frame to highlight risk and danger, particularly in the context of dangerous animals and diseases:

> Geesh there's so many things to kill me in the jungle you'd think it weren't natural for us humans to live there! :O[9] I have to take loads of tablets (expensive!) and cover myself in insect repellent to prevent getting malaria. Great. (Will [40])

Will's description of the 'jungle' in South America sets the scene as somewhere adventurous.

---

9 This is an 'emoticon', a representation of an emotion using text characters. In this case, Will is referring to an open-mouthed expression of alarm.

Other references to danger overlap with the discourse of 'unorganised cultures', such as perilous traffic. There are numerous stories in the blogs detailing the horrors of being 'on the road', but also the gappers' insider knowledge about such conditions. This means that Jessica and Celia [19] are able to offer advice in their blogs, warning their readers 'don't ever drive in delhi! No-one cares about lanes, other people, speed'. For Harri [26], the traffic in Mongolia is 'mad', and crossing the street is 'hell'. Another reference point is the 'health and safety' culture of the UK compared to the gap year locations. Lucy draws on this to highlight cultural differences when she climbs the tower of a local attraction:

> I am pretty sure that Ecuadorian Health and Safety standards are no way as high as their English equivalents; we ended up climbing up ridiculously steep metal ladders which had hand rails each side and nothing else to stop you falling off/ through the bottom of them to the crowded city below. (Lucy [30])

The frame of disorder runs through Lucy's post, including in the reference to a 'crowded city'. Constructing these locations as dangerous and risky puts them in opposition to the relative safety of 'the West', something which Elsrud (2001) argues gives independent travellers status, which I explore further in Chapter 6. Throughout the gappers' narratives, then, we can see the bloggers engaging in the tension between difference as something alluring, and difference as something inferior (but potentially exciting). In both cases, gap year places are clearly marked as places that are not 'home', allowing narratives of cosmopolitan adventure to be told.

Reflecting on Difference: Interviewing Gap Year Bloggers

Narratives of difference are also apparent in the interviews with the gappers. They talk about taking a gap year to gain an understanding of local contexts. However, this desire is held in tension with the tendency to stress they travelled to somewhere away from home. For example, Francesca [6i] thinks her experiences in Russia help her to understand that 'culturally it is pretty different'. Francesca is interested in Russian history, and feels that she experienced a place 'you don't get anywhere else'. This is clearly a cosmopolitan framing: of encountering difference and appreciating it. Christina [10i] talks about how this is complicated, and gives rise to mixed feelings. She feels she has learned about the history and economics of Uganda during her gap year, but stresses that the 'cultural stuff' is very different. Christina felt alienated from the female teachers at her placement in a school, because she thinks 'it's hard to find things in common with people, women in Uganda have a very different role and different expectations' (Christina [10i]). These feelings of not fitting in can be unpleasant, but such encounters are also seen as developing understanding. Christina is able to talk authoritatively about gender roles, for example.

Encountering people and places that are different is not just limited to the gappers who visited the global South. Lisa [3i] suggests one of the best things about her gap year in the USA was coming into contact with people from different ethnic backgrounds. This diversity is not something she is used to in her home town: 'I go to America and I'm surrounded by Black people and Asians, I'm sharing a house, a bathroom, with people who don't look like me' (Lisa [3i]). Encounters with difference are a key part of the gap year experience, and something that Libby [8i] deliberately set out to achieve. When asked about her motivations for taking a gap year in New Zealand, she says 'If I'm leaving home, I might as well do it well and good, and go to the other side of the world!' (Libby [8i]). Similarly, Peter [16i] gives his rationale for his gap year in Australia and New Zealand as:

I was out there for a year out of my choice to see something different. Australia and New Zealand are both different enough to be foreign yet have very British qualities which ease any homesickness. (Peter [16i])

Owen [37i] gives comparable reasons for spending his gap year backpacking in Thailand. He thinks it has enough of a travel infrastructure so that it is 'easy to get around' but not so much 'to be in your face'. Owen suggests Thailand can provide an authentic experience of difference while remaining convenient. However, he suggests he would like to move beyond such relatively 'safe' places in the future. Gap year spaces, therefore, provide a place to experiment with difference (Simpson 2005a).

The gappers talk about their genuine cosmopolitan aims, and that they took gap years because they wanted to engage with their host communities and learn something about countries they visited. Although they reflect upon and evaluate the success of this, they do so in ways that are complex and contradictory. Daniel [31i] thinks that during his gap year in Botswana:

I learnt what Africa's like, obviously I can't talk about the entire continent but I've met people who travelled there and I used to think of it as a continent. But now I see it as different countries with different situations and people and cultures as well. (Daniel [31i])

Daniel has developed an understanding that helps him to think beyond Botswana as part of a homogenous continent. He contrasts this with how he thought of 'Africa' when he was planning his trip: 'the idea of AIDS, people starving'. Despite Daniel's discussion of developing understanding in this way, he does not place the local inequalities he witnessed in a *global* context of disparities between nations. Daniel also still finds some amusement in crass stereotypes, such as the warnings from his friends who said 'watch out for cauldrons full of water and onions!' (Daniel [31i]). It does seem remarkable that a young man who has spent time in a Batswana medical clinic would still make jokes about cannibalism. As in the blog narratives, the interviewees suggest gappers negotiate a tension between challenging and reproducing dominant representations of the Other.

Conclusion: Representing Difference in Gap Year Narratives

The people and places that young people encounter during their gap years are often framed as different. After all, for an experience to be cosmopolitan, this difference has to be established. The overseas gap year is ascribed a certain status because it *does not take place at home*. What is up for debate is how this difference is constructed and the implications for thinking about cultural cosmopolitanism. The gappers tend to use popular representations of the exotic, for example, and idealised versions of places. Interacting with local people can result in reflection on global issues, but also frustration and critique. Running throughout the accounts are ideas about the Otherness of these people and places, and making comparisons between 'us and them'. A common theme is that the Other may live a more 'authentic life'. A concern for getting to know what 'real life' is like features strongly, but this co-exists with an exoticisation of the environment, people and culture.

This raises some problematic issues for the ways in which host communities are represented, and questions for the gap year industry as a whole, not just those responsible for volunteering placements. Much of the literature on gap year travel focuses on volunteering: that these projects do not challenge paternalistic views and lack a critical engagement with development issues. This is clearly a matter that needs to be addressed. What this chapter shows are the common ideas about the Other that cuts across different types of overseas gap year experiences, be they structured or unstructured, in the global South or not.

Once again, the gappers themselves are *not* the subject of criticism here. Their stories show some genuine desires to learn about the countries they visit. Yet the gap year industry claims they help the host communities (in the case of volunteering) and/or help young people arrive at a greater understanding of the world (in all cases). As suggested in Chapter 2, to establish a link between the cultural dimensions of cosmopolitanism and ethical and political concerns, we need to address the issue of reflexivity. A sense of being out of place does lead some of the gappers to think about their global position, especially those who spend an extended among of time in one location. In this way, they exhibit a certain 'global reflexivity' (Savage, Bagnall and Longhurst 2005) or a more 'global perspective' (Jones 2005). We can begin to see that gap years may offer a form of cosmopolitan experience. It is difficult, however, to get away from preconceived ideas, such as the exotic Other who leads a more authentic life. There is a tension in these representations of place, where a genuine engagement with difference is desired, but in which people and places tend to be framed in terms that reproduce standard discourses. This tension can be understood as 'globally reflexive' versus 'globally reproductive' framing. Skey (2012) suggests a similar continuum of progressive to regressive forms of cosmopolitanism. There are also parallels here with research into student volunteering based in the UK. Holdsworth and Quinn (2012) argue such activities are often 'reproductive' in terms of existing power relations and inequalities, rather than 'deconstructive', which would allow young people to develop an awareness of (and critically engage with) social conditions.

Being able to reflexively engage with the Other during a gap year is limited by the existing frameworks that young people use in their blogs to narrate and understand such encounters. The picture of the reflexive gapper does not hold up well, given that structural and historical legacies are reproduced in the young people's understanding and representation of people and places. Yet the habitual dispositions in Bourdieu's theory of practice do not account for some of the nuanced reflections on being 'out of place' in these gap year stories. Bourdieu locates reflexivity only at 'times of crisis' (Bourdieu and Wacquant 1992: 131). These do not seem to be crises, but moments of comparison between the self and the Other. Indeed, at crisis points – for example, feeling threatened by hassle – the narratives often retreat to stereotypical representations. The gappers' stories of being open to the Other are held in tension between globally reproductive and globally reflexive tendencies. We can see gap years as part of what Germann Molz (2012a) calls the 'cosmopolitical terrain' where gappers both consume difference and attempt to engage with Others in a meaningful way.

The narratives of the gap year experience presented in the blogs are directed at an audience 'back home'. As noted in Chapter 4, the interviews suggest gappers write their blogs to have their own record of their gap year, but also as a way of communicating with friends and family, and sharing their stories. The other people involved in these stories are not just those encountered in exotic places, but those readers – real or imagined – who are following the narrative online. The stories are framed using references from home contexts. In this way, these encounters with difference are analogous with a self-referential cosmopolitanism, in which individuals may claim a cosmopolitan identity and 'are attracted to the idea of appreciating global cultures' but 'in which people seek security through identifying with other similar places' (Savage, Bagnall and Longhurst 2005: 206). Consequently, we need to think about *when* 'being cosmopolitan' is invoked (Skey 2012). As will be discussed in Chapter 7, gap year narratives emerge in an intersubjective context – in other words, in the relations between people.

In the next chapter, I explore how gap year stories help young people to align themselves with other cosmopolitans. The status distinctions made by participants to define 'good taste' in travel centre on the *idea* of openness towards and understanding of difference. Representations of gap year experiences are implicated in gaining status back home and demonstrating cosmopolitan cultural capital. I argue we can see both explicit articulations and tacit understandings of 'proper travel' in gap year narratives that draw on classed ideas of value.

Chapter 6
A Traveller not a Tourist: The Value of Cosmopolitan Experiences

To be cosmopolitan is to have 'good' taste. The social status of 'independent travel' is derived from being viewed as an alternative to mass tourism, and these ideas have been incorporated into the gap year phenomenon. This chapter explores the influence of wider trends in travel practices and the significance of middle-class taste for the gappers' narratives. Authentic experiences and a cosmopolitan attitude are central to the notion of 'proper travel', and are markers of status for young people taking gap years. Despite the limitations to the cosmopolitan encounters described in the previous chapter, a genuine engagement with the local is desired. However, attaching value to these forms of travel demonstrates how the exercise of taste, as Bourdieu (1984) suggests, is a form of 'symbolic violence'. This reproduces and asserts the legitimacy of the dominant class by claiming intrinsic value and worth. Classed expressions of good taste and value judgement are central to the framing of gap year stories.

In this chapter, I outline how young people's gap year narratives are framed by these class-based distinctions, which are centred on the long-standing distinction between 'the tourist' and 'the traveller'. What they consider to be good taste draws a line between proper travel and mass tourism. Throughout their stories, tourists and tourist practices are portrayed as non-cosmopolitan. This reproduces the dominant idea that being cosmopolitan has intrinsic value. Their definitions of proper travel resonate with documented tastes in independent travel, including the status afforded to being cosmopolitan and 'being inside' a place. The final section of the chapter suggests that insider knowledge is a form of cosmopolitan cultural capital and that gap years enable young people to accumulate this, as long as they travel in the 'right' way. For example, the stories stress the difficulties of gap years to their readers back home, whereas being a tourist is easy but inauthentic. Value is attached to scarce resources, and this is how status claims can be made: not everyone has the good taste to take a gap year. I suggest the gappers draw on established frames of a particular form of travel as superior, which obscures the structural forces at work.

A Historical Distinction

There is a historical dichotomy between tourists and travellers. This distinction rests upon travel as a cosmopolitan activity as opposed to tourism as 'home plus' the exotic (Hannerz 1990). Boorstin (1961) provides an influential critique of mass tourism, which is summarised by Wang (2000) as a division between the 'high taste of travel' and the 'low taste of tourism'. These opposing figures – the traveller and the tourist – resonate with the gappers' narratives of good and bad taste. High taste is concerned with: simple means; hardship; risk and adventure; active discovery; self-reliance; contact with the local; genuine experiences; exploration; authentic attractions; and independence. This is in contrast to low taste in travel, like being concerned with comfort and ease (Wang 2000: 180–181). We have already seen elements of this in the gappers' stories of encountering the Other, such as risky gap year spaces and desires to connect with local people. These distinctions demonstrate the superiority of the traveller over the tourist through more authentic experiences and the acquisition of insider knowledge. There is a history to these frames which is founded on class difference. Gappers' stories feature 'another other' – those who have poor taste.

The idea that the 'art of travel' is superior to tourism can be traced back to the growth of the bourgeoisie, and later the advent of mass tourism, in the nineteenth century. Being in a position to travel was historically reserved for the elite. This meant that it was a marker of status, like the rite of passage Grand Tour for the British aristocracy. With the industrial revolution came the growth of modern transport infrastructures. It also led to the new industrial bourgeoisie encroaching on upper-class travel practices, which generated criticisms of the expansion of touring (Butcher 2003: 34–35). The exclusivity of travel was further threatened by the development of the package tour by Thomas Cook in the 1840s. This democratisation resulted in intellectual condemnations of tourists, the uncultured masses who were uncouth and unrefined: 'Tourists are vulgar, vulgar, vulgar' (Henry James, cited in Urry 1995: 129). At the time, good taste in travel was based on the Romantic ideal of individual contemplation. Cook's tours were at odds with this, as they utilised mass transportation and collective itineraries. Travel was seen to have been stripped of a 'spirit of adventure' (Wang 2000: 178). Package tours continued to expand throughout the twentieth century and travel was progressively opened up to the masses.

The democratisation of leisure travel has resulted in class-based distinctions. As noted by Urry (2002), differences in where we go on holiday, and *how* we travel, reflect symbolic struggles between classes. In *Distinction* (1984), Bourdieu highlights the different travel practices of intellectuals on one hand and employers on the other as an example of the tension between the two poles of dominant class taste: 'On the one side ... camping, mountaineering or walking;

on the other ... three-star hotels and spas' (Bourdieu 1984: 283). The former relates to possessing relatively more cultural capital, the latter more economic capital. Such differences can be seen today, although the ways in which this manifests reflects differences in the social structure, as suggested in Chapter 1. Urry notes that the 'consumption of tourist services cannot be separated off from the social relations in which they are embedded' (Urry 1995: 129). As the service class and the 'new petite bourgeoisie' grew in the latter half of the twentieth century, so did tastes in travel that saw these groups distinguishing themselves from elitist bourgeois culture and the coarseness of working-class tourism (Urry 2002: 85). Consequently, Munt (1994) argues that the rise of 'independent travel' is linked to the rise of the new middle classes. The distinctions they make draw upon the classed tourist/traveller discourse, and the 'high taste' of travel that Boorstin decried as lost (Wang 2000). Moreover, the ability to engage with difference, as explored in Chapter 2, is an important resource in an 'increasingly interconnected and open world' (Skrbis and Woodward 2007: 746). This historical distinction between travel and tourism is a significant frame in the gappers' blogs.

Defining Tourists, Defining Gappers

Tourists as Inauthentic

The gappers' stories make frequent references to the deficiencies of being a tourist instead of a traveller. Adam [28] is disappointed when he reaches Machu Picchu,[1] because it is like 'Disney Land' full of 'chubby americans' who wear branded sportswear and souvenir t-shirts. These figures typify the problems associated with tourism. Tourists' bodies are laden with the trappings of Western culture: obesity and consumer goods. Adam goes on to talk about how he appreciates the 'remoter' parts of Peru that have not been ruined by a mass influx. The presence of lots of tourists at a location is a problem for other gappers as well. Bryony [35] complains that tourists at an Indian temple nearly spoil her visit, and she wants to go back when it is quiet. When Kevin [34] arrives in Sydney, Australia, he is disappointed at the prevalence of English accents. The trouble with encountering tourists is that the gappers are *not* encountering the Other, thwarting their cosmopolitan ambitions. According to Desforges, 'The presence of other travellers ... interferes with the Otherness and difference of places' (Desforges 1998: 182). The gappers want their locations to be distinct from home. Tourists like Adam's 'chubby Americans' encroach upon this.

---

1 An ancient Incan city in Peru.

It is not just the presence of tourists that is criticised, but also how these visitors approach experiences. For example, the 'Travel Buddies' align themselves with the practices of 'Asian' tourists who are visiting Angkor Wat in Cambodia, distinguishing themselves from the less authentic 'Westerners':

> We watched the sunrise over Angkor Wat with the other early birds – japenese [Japanese] only, proving all other westerners were hungover in bed. (Travel Buddies [20])

Another blogger, Ewan [1] is also disparaging of 'Westerners' who do not leave the beaten track at Angkor, unlike the 'local' tourists and, importantly, like him. In both instances, the bloggers show they have a more authentic encounter with destinations, and contrast this to an inauthentic Western experience. In this way, the gappers are able to maintain a narrative of cosmopolitan travel, even when visiting popular tourist sights/sites.

Not all young people are able to maintain this narrative of cosmopolitanism, however. Dave [7] has a difficult time in Eastern Africa. His blog documents his frustrations and unhappiness with a perceived lack of tourist infrastructure and he feels isolated and alone. It is not until he reaches the backpacker resorts and the company of other 'Westerners' in Thailand that he really begins to enjoy his gap year. His story highlights some of the contradictions at work in such journeys: they are dependent on the provision of tourist services to facilitate independent travel, but too much tourism is undesirable. The backpacker enclaves like the Khao San Road in Bangkok have long operated on the distinctions between travel and tourism as a result. In an early study of backpacker culture, Riley defines 'budget traveler ghettos' which function as foci of communication networks to enable proper travel to be conducted: 'the "best" places to visit and the "best" (i.e., cheapest) places to eat, sleep and so forth' (Riley 1988: 322). These established meeting points are key for travellers who are keen to distance themselves from the 'tourist' label.

The bloggers talk about how certain places and activities are fake and in contrast to what 'real' places are like: 'thamel is a bit scummy, not very nepali, made for tourists etc.' (Katy [5]). So although Thamel is *in* Nepal, it's not 'Nepali'. Tourism leads to commercialisation, making gap year locations less authentic. Helen [27] finds one city less friendly and more 'touristy' than others in Vietnam. She speculates that it is the presence of 'Westerners' that is behind this: 'There are Westerners everywhere!! think it's become corrupted by tourism'. Again, cosmopolitan encounters are dependent on an image of an unspoilt, original local that can be ruined. Wang (2000) argues that tourism needs to be understood within the frame of modernity, yet the relationship between the two is ambivalent. Technological and social advances make travel possible, but the key motivations for 'getting away' are feelings of dissatisfaction and alienation with the modern way of life (Wang 2000: 216–217). For MacCannell, tourism is driven by the inauthenticity of modern life:

> Modern man has been condemned to look elsewhere, everywhere, for his authenticity, to see if he can catch a glimpse of it reflected in the simplicity, poverty, chastity or purity of others. (MacCannell 1999: 41)

Western tourists and their effect on places disrupt the gappers' search for this authenticity.

It should be noted again that not all travel may be concerned with the authentic. Some may actively search out inauthentic experiences, playfully engaging with tacky and artificial tourist practices. Feifer (1985) refers to this as 'post-tourism' (Urry 2002: 12). In the gappers' stories, however, there is little evidence of post-tourist concerns. Their narratives are framed by notions of authenticity as good taste, and critical accounts of the intrusion of the West. As noted by Urry (1995), places can be literally consumed, so that what is significant about them, their 'goods', are depleted. Too much modernity (or too many non-locals) means that the gappers cannot have genuine cosmopolitan encounters. Of course, this is somewhat contradictory, because the gappers themselves are part of the problem. Owen makes some interesting comments about something he calls the 'tourism beast' and its destructive influence when he visits the Thai lagoon where *The Beach* was filmed:

> Number 3 on Thailand's most beautiful lagoons is a memory that i will cherish in its movie debut, as the reality was a sharp reminder that the beautiful untouched is fast becoming the hideously groped! (Owen [37])

Owen frames places that are unsullied and pure as more valuable. What is fascinating is that he prefers the fictional idyll he saw on film to the real thing. Concerns about the environmental impact of tourism, while distancing oneself from the transformation of places, has been described by Duffy (2004) as 'ego-tourism'. New distinctions of taste have arisen based on 'being thought of as an environmentally aware traveller' (Duffy 2004: 34). Such distinctions do not consider how local development policies that cater to the tourist market may be problematic, according to Duffy, but are primarily concerned with distancing oneself from the masses. There are elements of this at work in Owen's comment, of not wanting to be part of the negative impact of tourism even though it is driven by the desires of other people like himself who wish to visit such exotic places. Owen does struggle with this, noting that his comments are also 'hypocritical'.

Gap Year Travel as an Alternative to Tourism

Employing the tourist/traveller discourse means the gappers can distance themselves from such negative influences on place. The blogs often describe 'Western tourists' in ways that highlight the gappers are not the same, for example: 'An annoying British tourist just came into the post office' (Francesca [6]). The bloggers also use local words for White foreigners, like *farang* in Thailand and *mgunzu* in Uganda. Tourist services are thought to be over-priced, and the best experiences are found by avoiding 'tourist traps'. Being a tourist is associated with naivety and inexperience, of not being 'in the know', or the embarrassment of not fitting in. Lisa [3] discusses how she 'appeared' to be a tourist when she navigates her way around New York with her map and an expression of apprehension. Duncan would rather get very lost in Ghana (which is what happens) than stand out:

> I emerged 10 minutes later from a strange, station-side market and appeared to be at a large, busy cross road. Afraid to look at the map section of the book, for fear of looking like a tourist … (Duncan [21])

Here, Duncan rejects the label of tourist very strongly.

The gappers employ a variety of frames in order to disidentify with tourists. Those who are on gap year placements are able to frame their activities as working or volunteering in another country. Christina [10], for example, describes what happens when she and her friend arrive at a local resort lake in Uganda to teach swimming lessons. They are 'greeted as tourists' but they are quick to point out that they are volunteers. Other strategies involve talking about distinctive activities or ways of approaching them:

> We just got back from staying in a Ger² camp. Was sehr [very] luxury. We even went horseriding in the Mongolian countryside. It's really good having a guide who knows the area and can take you to the interesting places that normal tourists wouldn't know about. (Helen [27])

Helen is not a *normal* tourist, but someone who has a connection to the local context and so can make these distinctions. Chris [15] wryly reflects on such attitudes when he joins a tour in Thailand: 'Bunch of frigging tourists. Glad I'm not one'. Perhaps Chris is comfortable adopting this attitude as he volunteers in Tanzania at the start of his gap year, and he is only a tourist temporarily. As will be seen later in this chapter, being a tourist is not necessarily something that you *are*, but something that you *do*.

---

2 A camp of 'traditional' Mongolian nomadic dwellings.

The interviews with the bloggers provide an additional perspective on the tourism versus travel debate. All but one of the interviewees reject the label of tourism. The gapper who acknowledges he was a tourist during his gap year, Owen [37i], is also the only interviewee not to undertake some kind of placement. It might be easier for those who volunteer during their gap year to draw these sorts of distinctions. However, Owen still utilises the tourist/ traveller discourse to make a distinction between him and other, 'normal' backpackers. He emphasises his concern to have a cosmopolitan, cultured, mature experience:

> We were actively more trying to interact with the local people than, I think other people [who] were just cruising out there for a party. Especially in Thailand, they were heading out for a teen holiday to go and get drunk on the islands. It's great, I had a lot of fun doing that but it's not what I wanted to do the whole trip. (Owen [37i])

The majority of the interviewees state that the main purpose of their trip was neither tourism nor travelling. They talk about 'living' (Francesca [6i]; Lucy [30i]) or 'working' (Christina [10i]; Daniel [31i]; Peter [16i]) in their host countries. For periods of mobility, they prefer the term travelling, although are also a little reluctant to use this term as well, due to its association with the negative sides of backpacking: 'it just seems really pointless to go to another country and just to get drunk … They just hang out with other travellers' (Kevin [34i]).

'Tourism' and 'tourists' are used by the interviewees as derogatory terms. Lucy [30i] compares her placement in Ecuador, where she felt she was 'living with the people' to a period of travel in Peru where she wasn't working on a project and where she and her companions 'just felt like tourists'. Similarly, Daniel [31i] refers to how he was able to spot 'White tourists' during his time in Botswana. Rather than standing out like a 'White tourist', Daniel is able to frame his story as one of integration into the local context. This is a common benefit ascribed to gap year placements. For example, Francesca [6i] talks about tourism as 'being on the outskirts and I wasn't on the outskirts, you were in the whole society'. Lisa's [3i] knowledge of New York City through her time on her placement in New York State meant that when she went back to the City, she 'wasn't a tourist because [she] knew where [she] was going'. Christina's [10i] definition of her experience extensively draws on the idea of local knowledge and more difficult conditions to make her distinctions:

> You don't live like a tourist, you don't act like a tourist. Like, you speak a little bit of the local language, you barter for stuff you don't just hand over 5 or 10 times the amount what it's worth! You have living conditions which aren't anything

like a tourist would probably expect. And, I think people are probably more honest with you than they are with tourists. (Christina [10i])

Christina's thoughts encapsulate the benefits of gap year placements as a way to have a truly authentic experience: language skills, knowing how to act, experiencing real life. Throughout these stories, both online and offline, the gappers draw on the tourist/traveller divide to frame their accounts in similar ways. Some go one stage further and disassociate their experiences from both inauthentic tourism and inauthentic travelling.

The Backpacker as a Spoiled Identity

While many of the gappers independently travel for some or all of their gap year, the presence of individuals they identify as 'backpackers' can also ruin the authenticity of a place. There are criticisms of independent travel infrastructures and services in some of the blogs. The gappers' discussion of the *Lonely Planet* series of guidebooks exemplifies this. *Lonely Planet* began life in the 1970s as an independently-produced guide to overland travel across Asia, put together on a kitchen table. It is now a global brand that has printed over 100 million guidebooks (Lonely Planet 2013). One blogger, Bryony [35], relies on her 'beloved *Lonely Planet*' as an authoritative source. Most of the other gappers' references to the guidebook are more critical, for a number of reasons. Firstly, the effect of recommending a destination can create a 'tourist hotspot' where commodities are 'ridiculously overpriced' (Ewan [1]). Secondly, according to Katy [5], those travellers who follow it word-for-word are 'boring as hell'. Expense and a lack of spontaneity are seen as antithetical to proper travel.

The *Lonely Planet* guidebooks are also thought to be unreliable compared to local knowledge. Indeed, some gappers state that they know more about their locations than the guides. One of Harri's [36] friends, for example, 'couldnt believe that *Lonely Planet* ... had lied to us'. Instead, there is more value in acquiring local knowledge first-hand. Butcher notes that *Lonely Planet* is emblematic of a growing backpacking culture that has been extensively criticised in what he calls the discourse of 'new moral tourism': 'the guides are deemed to have "institutionalised" travel, making it similar to, and as damaging as, package tourism' (Butcher 2003: 45). The accounts of the gappers reflect such debates. They do not want to be package tourists, but they also do not wish to be associated with the unthinking masses of backpackers that follow the advice of the guidebooks uncritically. What constitutes good taste is not fixed, but shifts and changes.

Temporary Tourism

The gappers are antipathetic towards tourism, but they also talk about behaving 'like a tourist'. Being a tourist is something that young people on gap years want to avoid, but their relationship with tourism is complex. One tourist activity they undertake is sight-seeing. Ingrid [4] goes sight-seeing when she only has a short period of time in Melbourne, Australia, something she describes as 'the touristy thing'. Although intimate, cosmopolitan encounters are those which are most prized, the blogs also indicate that there are some places that need to just be 'seen':

> However I think I am going to manage to at least get most of the touristy stuff done before I leave: we did the Sugarloaf and the Christ today (as you can see) and we are doing a favela³ tour tomorrow, which apparently is great. (Alicia [14])

Despite its association with tourism, sight-seeing remains a key activity when visiting a place. Urry argues that the division between the ordinary and the extraordinary at the centre of tourist practices is established or sustained by seeing a unique object or particular symbolic representation of a place (Urry 2002: 12). From reading the blogs, each gap year location seems to have a list of 'must-see' places, just as guidebooks often have a list of essential things to see and do. One of the must-dos for Alicia, the *favela* tour, exemplifies the commodification of poverty as an authentic tourist attraction. This cosmopolitan encounter is a product to be bought and sold.

One interesting consequence of wider trends in the cosmopolitanisation of culture is that sometimes the bloggers are underwhelmed by iconic sights. Visual media has resulted in an 'upward shift' in what is extraordinary (Urry 2002: 92). Rojek notes that tourists are sometimes disappointed with the 'real thing' as they do not match the representations already viewed in guidebooks or media:

> sights are often anti-climactic experiences. Standing before the Sphinx in Cairo, or the Sydney Opera House, one may feel that the sight is not as breathtaking as one had been led to believe. (Rojek 1997: 54)

One of the sights that Rojek refers to here is mentioned by Jo:

---

3 Alicia is referring to Sugarloaf Mountain and the statue of *Christ the Redeemer* in Rio de Janeiro, Brazil. A *favela* is a Brazilian 'shanty town'.

> Next day, I got up early and went exploring Sydney harbor, saw the bridge and
> opera house, it's a creamy colour and tiled. Was slight[ly] disappointed but still
> unbelievable that I was final[ly] here! (Jo [18])

Jo's viewing of the Sydney Opera House means she can claim the status of
seeing it in real life because she is there, even though the building itself is not
what she was expecting. Rojek (1997) argues that the dynamic movement on to
new sights, as part of a widespread 'cult of distraction' is an important element
in contemporary travel practices. As discussed below, being on the move is
something that is important to gappers during periods of travel (as opposed
to the time taken to get inside during a placement). So, while the bloggers'
narratives are concerned with creating distance between the gappers and
tourists, their forays into sight-seeing enable a place to be 'done' quickly. A
'touristy' version of a place is constructed in the gappers' accounts, but this
does not have as much value as the authentic inside when even the real sight
lacks merit in comparison with its representation.

Another advantage of adopting tourist practices is that they are a break
from proper travel. The 'Travel Buddies' [20] describe Surfer's Paradise in
Australia as 'very touristy', but they welcome the change from the 'many remote
areas' they have previously visited. Unlike a 'post-tourist' (Feifer 1985), they do
not do this playfully but provide a pragmatic rationale. For example, Andy [26]
acknowledges the inauthenticity of a shopping trip and justifies it as saving
time:

> We decided to check out a few of the souveniour [souvenir] shops along the
> main street. I realise that this is a very touristy thing to do, but we were pressed
> for time and very rather hungry, so rather than search out the traditional shops
> we gave into quick advertising. (Andy [26])

Implicit in this statement is that proper travel is hard, and that being touristy is
an easier, quicker option. It is possible to temporarily 'do' tourism, and adopt
tourist practices, without actually becoming a tourist. Inauthenticity can be
justified as a temporary strategy that does not threaten their overall claims to
proper travel.

Indeed, being touristy is a treat for some of the gappers. Gap year travel is
rarely luxurious. This means that the convenience and comfort of 'Western' life
are a respite, for example going to a tourist hotel for the day and using their
pool. Framing this as an occasional luxury maintains distinctions from normal
tourists. When there is a disruption to her tour in Australia, Ingrid [4] and her
fellow 'smelly backpackers' get a simple but appreciated stay in a 4-star hotel
for one night:

we all had huge baths, stole all the free tea and coffee. Then ate tim tams[4] and pot noodles in bed, while watching TV. Honestly nothing has ever felt so luxurious in my life. (Ingrid [4])

Even though Ingrid is on an organised tour at this stage, she still aims to align herself with alternative forms of travel. When tourist breaks are planned, they often involve having a break from local food. We have already seen how authenticity can rest on being able to consume the exotic successfully. Charlotte [12] talks about how excited her friend was to eat pizza for 'the first time in ages'. While in China, Harri [36] thinks it is 'awful' that she loves going to a French restaurant, 'but after [eating] chinese after chinese you apreciate [appreciate] Western food so much!'

Ritzer and Liska (1997) suggest there has been a 'McDisneyization' of the tourist industry. This applies Ritzer's 'McDonaldization of Society' thesis to trends in travel practices, drawing on the sorts of experiences provided for visitors to Disneyland. These trends reflect how the world is 'increasingly efficient, calculable, predictable and dominated by controlling non-human technologies' (Ritzer and Liska 1997: 97). The overall desire of gappers to disidentify from tourists suggests that they are resistant to McDisneyization. Yet it is the familiarity of home comforts that are sought in their tourist breaks: hot water, familiar food, comfortable beds, television, easily accessible consumer goods, and so on. This chimes with Rizter and Liska's argument, as they suggest 'for many of those who desire to see the extraordinary, there is also a desire to have McDonaldized stops along the way' (Ritzer and Liska 1997: 101). As will be shown in the next section, proper travel is hard, and these stops offer a retreat. We can also see elements of 'McDisneyization' in the standardised list of tourist sites/sights that should be visited.

Framing these tourist breaks as only temporary actually reinforces the gappers' claims to status. Their tastes, for the most part, are for authentic, simpler experiences. This juxtaposition is clear in Jenny's discussion of how she finds it difficult to adjust to the trappings of 'modern life' upon her return home:

Hot running water was another strange one as well as flushing the toilet. Oh and one thing that I am trying to stay strong about (and slowly failing) is owning a mobile phone. I don't have & I really don't want to get a new one. It is much easier said than done though because everybody seems to own a watch & obey the rules of time here whereas in Guyana we sometimes waited over 6 hours for a truck to pick us up. Yes there was no way you could have been contacted but you still got your lift in the end so what did you have to complain about? (Jenny [13])

---

4 A brand of chocolate biscuit.

Jenny's cosmopolitan experiences of another way of life draw out the differences between being at home and being away. For the most part, the gappers' narratives indicate a desire to travel in ways that are 'proper'.

Proper Travel

Munt (1994) outlines how the discourse of independent travel defines itself in opposition to tourism, even though this is also a commodified experience offered by industry providers. In listing adjectives from independent travel brochures, Munt identifies the key principles: 'adventurous, broad-minded, discerning, energetic, experience, keen, imaginative, independent, intrepid, "modern", real and true' (Munt 1994: 116). For Munt, this classificatory system is based on social and spatial struggles for status. These values also resonate with the principles of cultural cosmopolitanism: being broad-minded, engaging with difference and what is real. Proper travel is identified as important to backpackers in travel research (although, as already noted, the backpacker may be becoming a spoiled identity). To travel 'properly' is to: spend an extended period of time on the road; use low budget transport and subsistence; and embrace serendipity (O'Reilly 2006: 999). The blogs suggest that the gappers also share these ideas, especially (but not exclusively) during periods of being 'on the road'. In the gap year narratives we can see the influence of youth travel and the wider cultural value of new middle-class travel practices. Their blogs detail their lack of comfort, how little they spend, adventure and exploration, and the challenges faced.

'Roughing It'

While the principles of proper travel are recognised by the gappers, it might not be something they are able to maintain. For example, Jenny [13] often calls herself a 'bad traveller'. Jenny thinks that she and her friends 'really are the worst travellers in the world. The amount of luggage us girls have is just stupid -we can't even lift it, it's that heavy'. For Jenny, there is a right and wrong way to travel, and not embracing a minimal 'back to basics' approach is not right.[5] In contrast to their views of tourist experiences, the bloggers document what they see as a basic standard of living, particularly in their sleeping arrangements. This may due to conditions in hostels, or even occasionally verging on sleeping rough. Bryn [2] recommends sleeping in internet cafes as 'a pretty good way to

---

5 The implications of 'girls' who are not 'good travellers' is discussed again in Chapter 7.

save money whilst travelling around Japan'. Rich [22], Ingrid [4] and Jo [18] all mention nights spent sleeping in cars.

Another influence on the development of youth travel is the history of 'tramping' and the journeyman wanderings of the working classes (Adler 1985). Initially driven by economic necessity (although they did contain elements of pleasure), they were romanticised by middle-class authors in the nineteenth and twentieth centuries, for example in the work of George Orwell (Adler 1985: 350). The romantic vision of the wanderer still resonates with young travellers. Adler notes that it can be particularly powerful for young people in transitional moments as 'travel in a poor mode may be one way of attempting to establish an inalienable, rock-bottom sense of self' (Alder 1985: 351). In contrast to the luxury and comfort of normal tourism, the gappers experience difficult conditions and a lack of possessions. Hugo [33] describes in his blog what it is like 'to live out of a suitcase'. The status of experiencing a 'poor life' is not only for those who are on the move, however, but also the gappers on placements. For those gappers visiting the global South, not having access to hot water or electricity is frequently discussed, but they are able to 'handle it':

> Our "running" water turned out to be not so "running", which means that we have to "shower" outside by chucking buckets of freezing water over us … Our previous 2 months' practice of this procedure is serving us well though :)[6] (Lucy [30])

For Christina [10], such conditions are novel and fun: 'cold baths and candlelight' are 'cool'. While bloggers might complain, they also feel a sense of achievement.

Being Frugal

As well as the romance or status of 'roughing it', the gappers are young and have limited funds. Consequently, the discourse of travelling on a budget runs throughout the gappers' stories. In an early piece of work on backpackers, Riley (1988) notes the almost obsessive focus on budget: 'Status among travelers is closely tied to living cheaply and obtaining the best "bargains" which serve as indicators that one is an experienced traveler' (Riley 1988: 320). Roughing it therefore has a symbolic value and, for those travelling in more expensive countries like Japan and Australia, is a necessity. Rather than spend two weeks in relative luxury on a package tour, they aim to eke out their budgets to stay overseas as long as possible, or at least not run out of money before their placement finishes. In poorer countries, the bloggers are delighted at 'ridiculously cheap' commodities, a phrase used by both Charlotte [12] and Alicia [14]. Other talk about how they are able to 'live it up' for a small sum. During one of their tourist

---

6 This is the emoticon for a smiling face.

breaks from the hardship of travel, the 'Travel Buddies' [20] stay at a resort in Vietnam but are careful to point out they are 'living the high life' without spending a lot of money: 'We never stop until we know we have the best … for the cheapest!'. A key marker of proper travel is getting a good deal, as well as being frugal. Those who pay over the odds are inexperienced and naïve, or inauthentic tourists. In some ways, this is part and parcel of their cosmopolitan concerns: of experiencing real life and living as 'the locals do'. Yet if we think about this critically, this is a temporary engagement with poverty. The gappers still have the means to return home to a more comfortable life. None of the blogs link the low cost of travel to global inequalities, apart from references to food being cheap as countries are 'poor'. It is difficult to make the case for gap years engendering a sense of 'global perspective' in such discussions.

Travel and Adventure

Gap years are a break from the norm, so as well as experiencing 'simpler' ways of life, gappers are also concerned with doing something adventurous. As Simmel states, 'the most general form of adventure is its dropping out of the continuity of life' (Simmel 1971, cited in Elsrud 2001: 603). The term 'adventure' is often used in the blogs, both with reference to the whole period of time out:

> The adventure begins. (Anna [29])
> globetrotting adventures. (Bryn [2])

and individual events:

> I go for a little adventure on my own. (Molly [24])
> My last and final adventure. (Louise [11])

Readers of the blogs also use these frames when commenting, such as Tim's [23] friend who says it 'sounds like you're having extreme adventures!'.

Specific events are framed as adventurous when the gappers are faced with unfamiliarity. When Francesca [6] catches the wrong bus during her teaching placement in Russia, she calls it 'silly' but also an 'adventure'. Getting on the wrong bus, something that would be annoying back home, is recast by Francesca as part of a narrative of encountering the unknown. The everyday can be redefined as out of the ordinary, like when Lisa gets lost in the local mall near her placement in New York State:

> I decided to try and find my way out. I got lost. Lost! In a shopping centre. Oh my. However, I got out and lived to tell the tale! Hurrah! (Lisa [3])

In addition to reframing the everyday, many of the bloggers talk about taking part in adventure sports, including bungee jumping, parachuting, rafting, climbing and mountain-biking. These sports highlight the embodied aspects of travel, involving 'intense bodily arousal' that demarcates experiences from normal life (Urry 2002: 155). The tradition of youthful, adventurous travel is also evoked by the gappers who hitch-hike: Bryn [2], Libby [8] and Kevin [34] all do this potentially risky activity. The romance of being 'on the road' still has some status despite gap year organisations and other advisory bodies specifically counselling against hitch-hiking.

Gap Years and Risk

Hitch-hiking and adventure sports are risky activities. As discussed in the previous chapter, gap year locations themselves are often defined as dangerous, and the intertwined themes of adventure and risk run through the bloggers' stories. Dealing with risk has even been incorporated into the gap year industry. A BBC News story from 2004 on 'backpacker murders' quotes an ex-Army officer who offers a one-day safety course for gap year travellers. He comments: 'The very nature of a gap year student who travels is that they are adventurous, so perhaps they will not always be fully aware of the dangers' (Bates 2004: n.p.).

Elsrud (2001) argues that much of the identity-building status of independent travel is derived from a perception that it is more 'dangerous' than package tourism. This is one of the ways that proper travel can be distinguished. Furthermore, encountering difference – the cosmopolitan experience – plays a role in the narrative of risk-taking. Harri [36] goes to the black market with her camera in Mongolia even though it is 'risky' because her insider knowledge enables her to weigh up the potential danger: 'it was ok like last time'. Other gappers find themselves in risky situations by accident, like Jessica & Celia, who are 'saved' by a local woman when they are stuck in a town at night:

> The idea of what might have happened if she hadn't been there or if she'd had some other agenda is enough to give our mothers nightmares. (Jessica & Celia [19])

Some deliberately seek out risk, like Adam [28] and his friends who mountain-bike down 'the Worlds Most Dangerous Road'. This is simultaneously a risky, 'alternative' pursuit but also commercialised. Adam emphasises:

> how dangerous it is, last week an Israeli man fell off and died. Unperturbed by that, we gonna do it and get the T-shirt that only the survivors get. (Adam [28])

Many of the blog posts have a cheery 'Don't worry, I'm still alive!' message for their readers. Gap years are something to 'survive'. They are the endeavours of cosmopolitan explorers venturing into the unknown.

Negotiating risk is consequently central to gap year travel. Ansell (2008) suggests these experiences enable young people to deal with the tension between modern risk-avoidance and postmodern uncertainty. This experimentation means that sometimes young people are scared or uneasy on their gap year. Charlotte [12] describes her apprehension of seeing sharks on a dive in Thailand, although she is an experienced diver. Even if there is not a specific incident to be afraid of, there are moments of general unease. Paul's encounters with the exotic in Uganda are unpleasant for him at first:

> I woke the next morning pretty unhappy, I [a] short walk into the centre of Entebbe the evening before had left me feeling slightly more confident but I was culture shocked. The thought of going into Kampala was terrifying and travelling elsewhere in the country on my own was unimaginable. (Paul [32])

Being cosmopolitan and embracing the unknown leads to feelings of fear for Paul. His blog notes that he eventually overcomes this, and the 'culture shock' clears so that he enjoys his time in Uganda. He therefore tells the story of a successful traveller who can deal with it. As we have seen, this comes up time and time again in how the gap year blogs are framed.

Exploring the Unknown

Adventure narratives are also developed through references to searching. In such descriptions, the gappers are framed as explorers. One of Bryn's [2] aims in a particular post is to 'try to find a beach somewhere'; Simon [16] refers to being 'on the road'; and Andy [26] thinks what he does best is 'exploring and eating'. These stories are told using the language of adventure travel: 'a group of six of us intrepidly set off for Rwanda, not really know what to expect or exactly what would be there' (Christina [10]). This is proper travel, setting off to encounter the exotic in ways that are unplanned and exciting. Referring to exploration brings to mind the tropes of European colonial expansion, of explorers setting out to 'discover' unknown lands. This is not uncommon in discourses about travel (O'Reilly 2006: 1003). The 'Travel Buddies' tell a story about exploring 'the jungle' in Malaysia that uses this frame:

> We decided to journey off on our own without a guide, taking a wander down signposted paths to the canopy walkways. Here we walked over the wobbly wooden and rope bridges that spanned across the canopies. It was pretty darn scary, but a lot of fun! Afterwards we took a more challenging trek into the

jungle. At some points we were worried we'd ventured off the paths! ... In the afternoon we ventured to the Gua Telinga caves. The entrance was TINY but surprisingly we were allowed to crawl in and clamber down the rocks to a large cavern at the end that was filled with bats! It was ace! Haha. I really enjoyed that day, as did everyone I think. (Travel Buddies [20])

This moment is adventurous, scary, risky and dangerous: a challenge, but also something that is enjoyable and fun.

Sometimes these adventurous encounters with the unknown are described as surreal or bizarre, rather than risky. Andy's blog [26] contains extensive posts that document his humorous take on the differences between English and Japanese culture. He describes a school sports day as involving 'a host of bizarre games that focus less on physical prowess and more on, well, hitting other people'. Kevin [34] is also amused by his encounters with difference, such as finding 'hard core [N]irvana[7] fans' in 'remote' Malaysian villages.

Indeed, exploration runs throughout the bloggers' overarching narratives. The gap year as a period of exploration is an especially dominant frame for those who travel extensively rather than stay on a single long-term placement. Such 'explorers' talk about having 'itchy feet' and do not want to stay in one place for too long: 'I loved Thailand, but I needed a new adventure, a new place to get to know and to explore. And I was here. Cambodia. Bring it on' (Chris [15]). Chris's story is framed by the desire for the new, as difference can become familiar, after all. Similarly, Owen [37] talks about wanting to move on from the backpacker centres of Thailand to Cambodia and Laos, and also describes his drive to find somewhere 'new'. This is fuelled by the networks of information provided by other travellers on the South-East Asia circuit, but Owen does not want to spend too long in more 'mainstream' traveller places.

According to Boorstin, the traveller 'was active; he [sic] went strenuously in search of people, of adventure, of experience. The tourist is passive; he expects interesting things to happen to him' (Boorstin 1961, cited in MacCannell 1999: 104).[8] This discourse of travel's superiority over tourism frames the gappers' narratives, and spontaneity in the decision to move is valued. Dave loves the fact that he only has a rough idea of where he's going in Australia, and what he's doing:

The plan now is ... there is no plan, but hopefully I'll get a couple of trips booked in the next couple of days, and have a damn good time on [F]riday (St. Patricks day) before heading up north to Cairns and the barrier reef. (Dave [7])

---

7 An American 'grunge' band from the 1990s.

8 MacCannell (1999) notes that this attitude is actually fairly commonplace amongst tourists themselves.

Other gappers drastically change their plans after they start their gap year. Kevin [34] undertakes an unplanned three-month Bible study course while in New Zealand, and Ewan [1] cancels his original round-the-world air ticket to stay on longer in Thailand then travel around South-East Asia. Alicia [14] simply plans to travel 'wherever I feel like going'. When describing this spontaneous mobility, the gappers place themselves, once again, in opposition to tourists:

> Anyway, determined not to be a tourist and just see everything that everyone else has taken a million photos of and written a million books about, I decided to leave the guidebook at home for one day, hop on my bike, and go where the wind decided to take me. (Andy [26])

Following impulses and not planning too much are a way of making distinctions between proper travel and the prescriptive nature of package tourism. While moving around in this way is not always possible for the gappers on structured placements, they still embrace these values when they describe how they spend their time when not volunteering or working. An element of 'randomness' guides their action, such as Jenny's [13] decision to 'randomly' visit Brazil on her day off from her placement in Guyana.

The Difficulties of Adventure

Unfortunately, undertaking adventurous travel can be unpleasant. The gappers tend to complain about the length of journeys, or local transport:

> i think the people who made the roads tho[u]ght that they'd make as many loops and curves as they could (and chuck in alot [a lot] of bumps too) just for a laugh. then make the cliff roads single track. needless to say i felt quite sick and spent most of the journey panting and looking green out the back of the jeep (which did i mention contained 9 people.). (Kevin [34])

Sometimes, being on the road is not a positive experience. Journeys are variously described as 'hairy' (Ewan [1]); 'miserable' (Dave [7]); 'a bit of a challenge' (Katy [5]); 'torture' (Travel Buddies [20]); 'pain' (Adam [28]); 'nightmare' (Hugo [33]); and 'awful' (Harri [36]). There is a different emphasis here to the thrill of living cheaply. Proper travel using local transport, can be very uncomfortable:

> We got what's known as hard seat's . This is pretty much the lowest class you can get, and we were on there for 26 hours. On a seat that was straight up and down and barely enough room to face forward. Was tiring to say the least. (Helen [27])

Yet as with other examples of roughing it, enduring such travel has a certain kudos. It makes the experiences worth talking about. Travelling in this way is 'character-building'; the self-development opportunities it offers will be explored in detail in Chapter 7.

'Disasters' are often central to travellers' tales, and are used to impress peers (Duffy 2004: 35). Things that are difficult and challenging make for a good story. Certain experiences, such as when Bryn [2] is accused of stealing a bike by undercover Japanese police officers, or when Ewan [1] is chased by dogs down a dark alley, are described in a way that makes these dangerous or difficult stories worth telling. Even Chris's encounter with armed bandits in Tanzania is seen as something that can be talked about in a jokey manner and as something to be prized:

> You might be shocked, scared for us, or just relieved that we are OK, but we all had the experience of a lifetime, and it in turn brought us closer together. On the plus side, I wasn't shot, stabbed or gang raped. [Male friend] was a little disappointed on the last. Just kidding. (Chris [15])

It is a shocking story, but it is framed in such a way that it thrilling, a 'true adventure'. This is an extreme example of how the gappers tell stories about overcoming challenges and encountering risk. Through these narratives of adventure, they make claims to undertaking proper travel, and in doing to, they set themselves apart from tourists. An additional way to mark this difference can be seen in the gappers' accounts of being inside a place and their claims to cosmopolitanism.

'Being inside'

The benefit of proper travel is that it enables the gappers to frame their accounts as the real experience of place. In the previous chapter, I noted how the blogs construct a version of gap year locations as places that are authentic. In order to experience this authenticity, gappers need to 'be inside'. One of the reasons that proper travel has such status is that it enables claims to local connections. Using public transport, staying in basic accommodation and eating in local cafes are more authentic, cosmopolitan experiences than the commodifed, 'home plus' comforts of tourism. MacCannell (1999) draws on Goffman's division of social establishments into 'front' and 'back' areas to discuss this desire to be on the inside. Those in search of real life experiences want to access the back, 'an authentic and demystified experience of an aspect of some other society or person' (MacCannell 1999: 94). This is a cosmopolitan desire to consume cultural difference rather than experiences that are similar to home.

Experiencing Real Life

'Roughing it' means the gappers can talk about how they are able to experience real life without 'Western' trappings. This is framed by a discourse that tends to romanticise certain aspects of life in the global South, seeing it as simpler and less complicated. Charlotte [12], for example, refers to how the lack of air conditioning in her Thai accommodation is 'a wake up call to real life [f]or Gap Year students'. The value attached to this realness is a point of distinction, a way of distancing experiences from those of tourists. Daniel reflects on this when he discusses his trip on safari in South Africa. He finds the artificial environment of a lodge a stark contrast to his experience of everyday life in Botswana, where he is on a placement:

> It was a very different Africa that I saw in that 5 star lodge (one night was more than a month's budget ...), and one that I think most of us want to see when we come over on holiday. But, it is a very different place to what most Africans live with. For example, I think half of these guys have never seen a lion, yet we have it on our 'must see' list. Don't get me wrong, I loved my time there, not having to worry about food (fridge still broken), getting shown everything in great comfort, but I am also enjoying my tim[e] in the real world, with friends and a routine. (Daniel [31])

Here, Daniel criticises the 'home plus lions' experience of luxury safaris, invoking Hannerz's (1990) concept of the 'true' cosmopolitan. He refers to the differences in price, comfort and authenticity between the 'real world' that he has become a part of, and the artificiality of a place dedicated to recreating the game hunt for wealthy foreigners. Similarly, Harri [36] compares camel rides with local people in Mongolia with the 'touristy' ones on a family holiday in Egypt. Harri is able to draw on the existing cultural capital of previous travel in order to evaluate new and more valuable experiences on her gap year.

Interestingly, such reflections on real life are also possible in countries like the USA. Ingrid [4] volunteers as a counsellor at a summer camp in Oregon during her gap year. The camp's lack of facilities leads her to consider this time as enabling more intimate connections:

> When you strip away everything else; TV, electronics, make up, showers(most of the time) you end up meeting real people and you form such strong relationships with these people so quickly because nothing else gets in the way. (Ingrid [4])

Although Ingrid is in 'the West', this is still an experience that is different to home, drawing on the same discourse: the simple life is an authentic way of life.

Ingrid is framing her interactions in similar ways to the gappers in the global South.

Local Connections

We have already seen that the gappers are uneasy when they do not fit in. They also seek to develop their narratives as proper travellers who can think or act like a local. Like true cosmopolitans, Bryn [2] thinks he has 'got into the Australian frame of mind' and Francesca [6] states she is 'thinking like a Russian now'. Having a more authentic experience is associated with making local connections, and again the extended period of time afforded by gap year placements can be an advantage here. The gappers who spend time on structured projects talk about feeling settled. Libby [8] discusses how she feels integrated with the local community during an outreach project in China:

> We also celebrated New Years with them … the place became a home away from home and such a huge blessing to us. Saying goodbye was definately [definitely] not easy. (Libby [8])

Such connections to the local are indicators of success in gap years. Places are different from home, but become like home when cultural differences are overcome. Other gappers refer to being part of a family (Jenny [13]), or how life on a placement becomes normal with friends who drop by to say hello (Lucy [30]).

The embodied cultural capital of language skills can be a sign of being inside (and conversely, not possessing these skills can mark outsider status). Learning the language may contribute to the future goals for some of the bloggers. Francesca [6] intends to study Russian at university, and both Bryn [2] and Andy [26] have places on Japanese degrees. Gaining language skills are also talked about as a way of improving local interaction, and being able to talk in the local language is a significant marker of status. Ewan [1] attributes the ability to learn language skills to his position 'inside' Thailand:

> We stop and ask him (in Thai – we've all become sponges in the sense that Thai seems really easy to pick up here due to total submersion into the language. We're still crap at it but we keep practising! (Ewan [1])

The bloggers share and demonstrate these language skills, using local words in their posts, or starting an entry with a greeting in the host language. Some discuss wanting to impress local people, and being able to converse 'naturally' is prized. Sian is very enthusiastic about her Spanish lessons in Guatemala:

> I am begining [beginning] to understand what people are saying and can ask stuff ... I am totally loving it though, and thought it was awesome when I actually thought "peligroso" instead of "dangerous" without trying to!!! (Sian [39]

It is telling, of course, that the word she refers to is dangerous. Language skills are a cosmopolitan competence, the ability to move through and encounter difference and interact with it meaningfully. In addition, the gappers talk about the benefits of ordering in restaurants, booking transport and other such practical issues, another way to distinguish themselves from normal tourists and get a 'good deal'.

Alternatively, the gappers discuss the problems associated with the 'language barrier'. They become frustrated when they cannot understand, or make themselves understood. This, of course, challenges their cosmopolitan status; lacking language skills makes them feel like an outsider. Some of this frustration is framed as being excluded by local people in some way. Katy complains: 'also went to the "peace programme". it was all in damm nepali! so hardly understood what was going on all day' (Katy [5]). They make negative comments that the local people do not speak English, or that they are less willing to talk to them. Christina [10] finds it difficult when she goes to her placement school without her fellow English volunteer for company, because the Ugandan teachers may answer her questions in English, but speak Bantu among themselves. Similarly, Harri [36] doesn't like the fact that she cannot communicate with her workers when she is on a short volunteering placement in Mongolia. She feels like she is 'wasting time'. As will be discussed in the following chapter, doing something 'worthwhile' is important to many, if not all, of the gappers. It is crucial to have an authentic experience and to get to know places, yet they are often unreflexive about this. The irony that they complain about local people speaking local languages seems to be lost on them.

Food plays a key role in constructing this narrative of being inside (food is, in fact, a common talking point in the blogs – see Chapter 5). Knowledge about authentic food is gained through local interaction. The bloggers want to pass on this wisdom to their readers, such as when Chris [15] is able to give the '3 golden rules of Thai food'. Authentic food is defined as where local people eat, which is usually small cafes and street vendors. These places are described as 'healthy', 'fresh' and 'traditional':

> As it was Saturday night we headed out for a night on the town, starting with a nice meal in a waterfall restaurant with traditional [T]hai food. Still so cheap and the quality was amazing, although all the food cooked fresh on the street seems to be healthy and clean. (Travel Buddies [20])

Andy [26] demonstrates his insider knowledge in his blog post on how to get the best out of eating seafood in Japan, through where to buy it from ('street vendors') to speaking to the vendor in Japanese. Yet again, the gappers are making status distinctions between their practices and those of tourists, via this connection with local knowledge, and there are lots of examples of this throughout the blogs. Ewan [1] claims that the 'backstreet' venue he visits is 'known to Thais only'. He is able to enter this 'backstage' area because he has become acquainted with a Thai man. There is value in being taken to restaurants by local people, or eating with a local family, because this involves the consumption of what is proper and real. Both Helen [27] and Zoe [38] talk about getting used to 'spicy' food, which for Helen is 'proper [C]hinese food'. Jessica & Celia [19] write a blog post about having Mexican food with 'true' Mexicans (this is a strange turn of phrase, suggesting the existence of 'fake' Mexicans!). Food and its consumption thus reflect the gappers' attempt to engage with the local and be cosmopolitan. They make claims for having authentic tastes (literally for food, but also for a type of experience). Such narratives of being inside a place mean that gappers acquire a form of cultural capital that consists of expert travel knowledge.

Demonstrating Cosmopolitan Knowledge

Local Information

Writing a blog is a way of imparting cosmopolitan knowledge to an audience. The gappers can give authoritative accounts of the places they visit, predominantly facts about local culture and sites/sights. This might include a history of the host town, like Francesca's [6] blog post about the setting for her teaching placement, or discussions about what television is like in Japan (Bryn [2]; Andy [26]). These blog posts tend to be rich in detail, and the gappers recommend places to visit. These parts of their stories are reminiscent of travel guides. Lisa [3] suggests places for her readers to visit in New York, like:

> the Metropolitan Museum of Art. The place is HUGE! There are art displays from all around the world and from all time periods. If you're really into your art then it's fab! (Lisa [3])

The gappers who visit the same places tend to recount similar information. For example, the popular gap year destination of Australia has a number of common places for gappers to visit, and the bloggers who go there write about the same facts. They explain the name of the Blue Mountains in New South

Wales; that Fraser Island (off the coast of Queensland) is the largest sand island in the world; or blog about the threatened status of a particular lake:

> lake wabby (it won't exist in 10 years dontcha know. it's being eaten by the sand dunes!! which are a bitch to climb by the by). (Molly [24])

> Also a Lake called Lake Wabby which you had to walk across about 1km of sand (like a desert) and then the dune just dropped away into the lake so we rolled into the lake. they say the lake is going to be gone in like 5 years cos the sand is going into it and filling it up. (Hugo [33])

This is not privileged information, as anyone who tours or reads about Lake Wabby is likely to come across this fact, but visiting a place lends a certain authority to the gappers' accounts. Even in the briefest descriptions of places, facts add additional levity, particularly when they refer to a 'world ranking' of sites/sights. When Peter [16] goes to see the 'steepest street in the world', or Jo [18] travels across 'the 3rd longest bridge in the world', they evoke their first-hand encounters with global places.

Collecting Places and Becoming Experienced

In a study of independent travel narratives, Desforges (1998) finds that young people often see places as containing knowledge that can be collected. Through exploration, places are 'done', ticked off the list, and recorded in an itinerary. Blogs offer a way of documenting this knowledge accumulation. Christina [10] lists the attractions of Kenya which has 'everything' that a traveller could want, noting that she and her friend have 'done' them all. Some blogs, like Helen's [27], use maps that display the countries visited. Passports are another way of objectifying and saving experiences. The gappers discuss comparing stamps and visas with fellow travellers. More stamps mean more knowledge gained, a signifier of status:

> I got up at 6am the next morning ready to catch a coach to Kuala Lum[p]ur and got tow [two] more stamps in my passport. (Jo [18])

Passports are a way to verify something ephemeral and objectify the cultural capital accumulated. They are a 'record of achievement and experience' (Munt 1994: 112).

Collecting places like this provides gappers with a 'good story'. Daniel [31] plans an excursion to Zimbabwe from Botswana, and contemplates the kudos such a trip would provide:

Also, I get to say 'Zimbabwe? Oh yes, I've been there. Nice place' That alone
might be worth the p2000 (200 pounds) I'm budgeting for it. I mean, when will
I get the chance to do it again? (Daniel [31])

Daniel wants to make the most of this 'once-in-a-lifetime' opportunity to
become as experienced as possible. The gappers improve their travel skills
through these experiences. The 'Travel Buddies' [20] state they are 'all getting
much better at the travelling thing now', defining such skills as bargaining and
being able to navigate around unfamiliar places. Similarly, when Jessica & Celia
[19] encounter the 'hectic' traffic in Mexico City, they are able to deal with it
as 'after India, we have (nearly) no fear'. Duncan [21] is able to cope with the
'ridiculous' nature of African travel taking it in his 'now experienced stride'.

To demonstrate their knowledge, the gappers sometimes give advice to
others. Writing a blog means that readers can get in touch and ask them for
help. Some posts answer specific questions or are directed at people they know
are reading. For example, Bryony [35] addresses her friends directly to share her
knowledge and assist them in planning their own future travel:

You may wish to consider Nepal because it also has loads of wikkid [wicked]
adventure sports. From the beginner's to the ohhmygodi'mgonnadieeeeee … .
Lots of white water n' STUFF. (Bryony [35])

Of course, simply visiting places is associated with mainstream tourism as
well. Consequently the gappers try to show that they *understand* the places they
visit. The status of being inside a place means that gappers are able to talk
about local culture and are able to make authoritative statements about what
their host country and its people are like. Using words like 'typical' and 'usual'
is a common way for the participants to evidence their status as experienced
travellers and their knowledge of the inside:

This was real Africa. (Dave [7])
It was a very typical Ugandan market. (Paul [32])
typical Australian! (Zoe [38])

In some cases, this goes beyond simply presenting knowledge, to reflecting on it.

Reflecting on Knowledge

There are some instances in which the gappers adopt a critical eye on a country's
history, for example when Duncan talks about the colonial history of Namibia:

Swakopmund had a large white population and the white ascendancy and colonialism was apparent. We got played some German folk by two weird German girls from a youth movement which followed the path of some Kaiser who colonised Namibia. (Duncan [21])

In this passage, Duncan both acknowledges the European legacy in southern Africa, but distances himself from past and present White involvement. His liberal and worldly critique of colonising influence is like reportage. Other gappers compare the differences and similarities between countries. Both Bryony [35] and Owen [37] offer an analysis of the changes they see when they visit different countries in Asia. Owen suggests that Thais' 'dealings with foreigners' are guided by the influence of Buddhism, whereas religion in India has less of an impact on attitudes to visitors. An adage about India and Nepal is considered by Bryony, and she is able to interpret this from the perspective of someone who has visited both places and can provide a global comparison:

There's this saying about India and Nepal "Same, same. But different". and whilst I can see similarities it is like the difference between, I don't know, England and Southern Ireland. Nepal is cooler, much less populated. (Bryony [35])

As argued in the previous chapter, the gappers' stories can be understood as existing in the tension between global reflexivity and global reproduction, with some adopting a more critical stance than others. One such example of this is Bryn [2], who reflects on the 'standard' descriptions of Japan that are often used to describe its culture. His thoughts are prompted by a photograph he takes of a Buddhist monk next to a hi-tech telephone box. Bryn gives the reason for having such ideas are because he is 'in Japan'. Interestingly, Bryn also examines his own preconceptions of his host country, and mentions his reference to such 'tired' representations in his UCAS personal statement.[9] In these discussions of politics, culture and history, there is some evidence that the gap year experience may encourage greater 'global understanding' (Jones 2005). This is not limited to those who undertake a structured placement, as both Owen [37] and Bryony [35] spend their gap year 'just backpacking'. Yet again, this understanding is limited, and not all of the blogs engage in such reflections. What is at work here is the display of insider knowledge, something that can be gained from engaging with the local through proper travel as well as extended periods of time spent in one place. Describing local contexts in this way builds a narrative of the experienced, cosmopolitan traveller, demonstrating their cultural capital.

---

9 A section of the application form to enter higher education in the UK, in which prospective students write about their interests, skills and abilities.

Conclusion: Making Distinctions in Gap Year Narratives

Young people on gap years share some of the values of independent travellers, whether they are on the move, or getting to know a place through a structured placement. They make distinctions between themselves and tourists; they value authentic experiences; they define proper travel as difficult, adventurous, risky, active and challenging; and they want to show a cosmopolitan openness to the people and places they encounter. Their tastes demonstrate the cosmopolitan cultural capital that is utilised and accumulated through travel: the embodied knowledge gained through being inside a place is achieved by travelling properly. Understanding the right way to travel distinguishes the gappers from 'normal tourists'. In this chapter, I have argued that this discourse – of the tourist versus the traveller – has a classed history, one of symbolic violence in which the democratisation of mobility (at least in the global North) has led to conventional tourism being devalued. Consequently, the gappers' preferences highlight the value attached to scarce resources, like travel experiences that are more difficult and challenging than the ease of tourism.

The cultural capital that is accumulated through taking a gap year can be saved in the blogs, which provide a medium for the display of insider knowledge, alongside more conventional 'records of achievement' like passports (Munt 1994). While the gappers sometimes undertake tourist activities, they are able to do so because certain practices, like sight-seeing, are justifiable if time is limited. Sometimes temporary tourism actually reinforces the difficult nature of proper travel because it provides a break. Gap year locations are ideally authentic, and can be uncovered through being inside, a position enabled through both extended placements and proper travel. These signifiers of status also reflect trends in wider contemporary middle-class tastes.

Firstly, and most importantly, openness to the Other and wanting to engage with the authentic inside reflects the cosmopolitan desire at the heart of gap year experiences. We can think of Hage's definition of cosmopolitan (cultural) capital as accumulated through 'sophisticated internationalism' (Hage 1998: 205). Secondly, knowing when it is acceptable to consume inauthentic tourist experiences is similar to an 'omnivorous' sensibility (Peterson 1992; Peterson and Simkus 1992; Peterson and Kern 1996), rather than a 'post-tourist' scepticism about authenticity. This is not anti-snobbery, however, as the gappers define themselves against the mass of tourists who do not travel in the right way. As Chapters 2 and 3 noted, omnivorousness is a form of distinction in itself. Thirdly, the tastes of the gappers show evidence of contemporary trends in 'alternative living' and the popularity amongst certain sections of the middle classes for products such as health food, real ale, non-Western medicine and natural materials (Urry 2002: 86). These wider consumption trends also associate value with authenticity and what is real.

A concern with realness attaches a moral value to a particular way to encounter the Other. In *The Moralisation of Tourism* (2003), Butcher argues that ethical tourism is an indication of changing attitudes towards the concept of leisure travel, in which mass tourism is seen inherently destructive for the environment and for local cultures. The gappers do not want to be these kinds of destructive tourists; they want to be culturally-sensitive travellers. While Butcher importantly raises this moral dimension, his argument that contemporary criticisms of tourism lack the snobbishness and elitism of the past do not fit with the gappers' travel narratives. The discourses that frame the bloggers' stories have their origins in an intellectual condemnation of the vulgarity of the masses; the practices themselves are drawn along class boundaries (as the rise in the middle classes is tied to the rise in independent travel); and, perhaps most importantly, employing notions of morality is bound up with notions of worth, value and class. The ways in which the gappers frame the legitimacy of their experiences have an implicit classed dimension, as they are defined against the 'uncultured' masses. Furthermore, such representations of the gap year in the blogs are framed by tacit assumptions of the moral worth that readers back home may ascribe to them.

It is this final point that is dealt with in the next chapter. What distinguishes gap years from other forms of independent travel is the notion that they need to be worthwhile. Gap years involve self-development through cosmopolitan experiences and the acquisition of cosmopolitan cultural capital. So far, the gappers have exhibited limited reflexivity about their experiences. They tend to reproduce standard discourses about the Other, and about good taste in travel. There is little evidence of the reflexive gapper described in Chapter 3. Rather, Bourdieu's concept of habitus explains the reproductive nature of gap year practices, particularly as the gappers make reference to well-established, classed, notions of worth. The judgements they make about value, about what makes a gap year worthwhile, have a moral dimension. As such, we need to consider the role of mutual evaluations of these journeys (Sayer 2005a). This is particularly relevant for the blogs, which present the story of the gap year to an audience. The expected views of others shape gappers' narratives of self-development as cosmopolitan travellers.

Chapter 7
Gap Year Identity Work: Doing Something 'Worthwhile'

The debates that surround gap year travel centre on whether they are 'worthwhile':

> Gap years have an image problem. It is so bad that the head of one of the oldest organisations to offer them won't use the phrase … only a quarter of those who take a gap year 'do something worthwhile', according to Richard Oliver, chief executive of Year Out, the industry group. 'The others may say they are on a gap year, but this usually means they are taking a year off, rather than a year out'. (Rowley 2013)

> Today's priorities are different. Organisations and individuals have distanced themselves from the 'gap yah' idea – a chance for affluent brats to 'do India' – and design worthwhile and beneficial experiences. (Moore 2013)

> By spending the year doing something worthwhile and at the same time gaining independence you not only boost your university application but could improve your future employment prospects too. (Gordon 2009)

In these debates, the most valuable gap years are not just concerned with leisure, but involve young people in a process of self-development. This chapter considers how we can understand this gap year identity work.

The encounters at the heart of gap years enable claims for a cosmopolitan identity, and the hypothetical reflexive gapper outlined in Chapter 3 is a young person narrating a coherent story about their self through an active, reflexive orientation to future goals (Giddens 1991). The evidence from the participants' accounts so far suggests a *reproductive* element to the gappers' representations, with little critical engagement with the framing of their stories. We have already seen that difference is framed to construct a particular version of Otherness, and that classed notions of good taste are used to draw lines of distinction. As this chapter shows, the bloggers also tend to reproduce standard narratives regarding the self-development benefits of a gap year. They may be reflecting on their experiences, but they are rarely being reflexive about them. Moreover, if gap year travel is a way of accumulating cosmopolitan cultural capital, it will provide structural benefits.

This chapter maps out what the bloggers see as the rewards of gap year travel; the skills they think they have accrued; and their reflections on self-improvement. As in the previous two chapters, there is little evidence of reflexivity in the gappers' accounts of self-development, and the discourses of being enterprising and doing something worthwhile are reproduced. In examining this notion of worth, the gappers' narratives are framed by discourses of morality, normalising a particular, privileged version of cosmopolitanism. Identifying what makes a gap year worthwhile engages with the moral dimensions of class (Sayer 2005a; 2005b; Skeggs 2004a). Young people's gap year stories are not produced in isolation, but in specific contexts, with boundaries surrounding what does and does not have value. This may not be explicitly stated, but involve inner reflections on the right course of action, what Sayer calls 'mundane reflexivity' (Sayer 2005a). Moreover, the intersubjective context of the gappers' stories, written as a blog for a real or imagined audience, can be seen in shared understandings and explicit evaluations of worth. I argue we need to consider how gap year narratives of identity work emerge in a 'context-specific, shared, but negotiated, social lifeworld' (Bottero 2010: 5).

The Enterprising Gapper

There is a general consensus that gap years are a 'good thing' for those who take them. A review for the Department of Education and Skills suggests the following benefits:

- improved educational performance;
- formation & development of educational and career choices;
- reduced likelihood of future 'drop out' from education, training or employment;
- improved 'employability' & career opportunities;
- non-academic skills & qualifications;
- social capital;
- life skills;
- developing social values. (Jones 2004: 58)

Jones suggests employers have a positive view of young people who take a gap year, and that they actively recruit graduates with such experiences on their CV. This is because the gap year is considered as a way to develop desirable 'soft skills', like interpersonal abilities, and 'life skills' such as leadership and self-discipline (Jones 2004: 13). These benefits are reminiscent of the 'enterprising worker' as described by du Gay, who displays 'certain enterprising qualities –

such as self-reliance, personal responsibility, boldness and a willingness to take risks in the pursuit of such goals' (du Gay 1996: 56). Discourses of enterprise (along with ethics and enjoyment) are prevalent in the discourses that determine what sort of gap years are worthwhile (Cremin 2007).

In an analysis of the 'professionalisation of youth travel', Simpson notes how the gap year has become institutionalised in recent years, so that young people are encouraged to develop 'marketable commodities' through volunteering (and may find themselves at a disadvantage if they do not) (Simpson 2005b: 450). The good taste of cultural cosmopolitanism also demonstrates a young person is 'cultivated'. Taking a gap year before university potentially gives a young person some positional advantage when looking for a job after graduation in a context of increased participation in higher education. By developing a 'personality package' (Brown et al. 2003) consisting of soft skills/life skills like independence and leadership, young people can distinguish themselves in a competitive job market (Heath 2007). Studies suggest that young people who take gap years think they gain confidence, maturity and independence through these experiences, which they consider to be beneficial for their future employability (King 2011: 353).

As a result, the gap year has become a 'training ground for future professionals' (Simpson 2005b: 455). For Simpson, this is at the expense of pedagogically-informed gap years that engage with critical views of development and issues of social justice. Her focus is volunteering placements in the 'Third World'. It is these structured, formal placements that are often viewed as the most worthwhile. The gap year market is hierarchically structured, with some types offering more opportunities for accumulating cultural capital than others (Heath 2007: 95). The value associated with simply going overseas, however, should not be underestimated. Travel itself is seen to have inherent value, as long as it is the 'right kind' of travel, which leads to cosmopolitan encounters.

Worthwhile Experiences

Making the Most of It

Gap years provide an opportunity to do things that would not be possible at other stages in life with the pressures of study, work, and other responsibilities. Before she leaves for her gap year in South America and the USA, Alicia [14] contemplates being separated from her family for six months. Although she will miss them, Alicia considers her gap year to be worth it:

> But then I realise that I'm running away for half a year and doing all the things that I was too busy, or skint, or lazy to do, and that I'll have no responsibilities apart from self-preservation, and I don't mind all those goodbyes so much. (Alicia [14])

The gappers are sometimes apprehensive, but they look forward to the chance to temporarily live a different kind of life. Ingrid [4] wonders whether she should leave her 'comfortable life' to travel. She reasons that staying home would make her 'go crazy', especially if she turns down the chance to have 'amazing experiences'. Gap years thus give young people the space and time to do new and exciting things. For example, a number of the gappers want to try adventure sports while travelling. Harri [36] looks forward to being able to do things that are 'new' and 'crazy' in New Zealand like bungee jumping and sky-diving.

This concern with new experiences helps to explain the value of framing gap years as cosmopolitan. By consuming the difference between home and away, the gappers can claim to have access to unique experiences. As this is only temporary, they must use the time wisely. Jason [9] is very keen not to 'waste' time during his gap year in Australia:

> I'm on a bloody gap year! There'll be plenty of time to eat shit, waste days sleeping in, etc. when I get back to my real life in Not-So-Great Britain. But whilst I'm here, I'm going to make every day count! (Jason [9])

Gap years are time out from the everyday as they are a distinct period, which has a start and end point, so they need to be utilised fully. The bloggers note that gap years are significant life events, using phrases like: 'once in a lifetime'; 'trip of a lifetime', 'first day of the rest of our lives' and 'defining point'. These are clearly life-defining experiences for the gappers. Lisa [3] talks about how her gap year is enabling her to tick items off a list a book called *101 Things to Do Before You Die*. The importance of travel as central to getting the most out of life is stressed by Bryony [35]: 'it may sound daft but OH MY GOD you haven't LIVED until you've seen the night sky and stars from the middle of a desert'. For Jenny [13], it is 'only when you go away & see what's out there that you realise how much more there is to life than you previously thought', and her gap year has a profound effect on her. Similarly, Louise [11] finds Niagara Falls 'like nothing [she has] ever seen before'. The participants project the resulting benefits beyond the end of their time out; these are not just stories to tell now, but can be told in the future. Andy [26] thinks that watching a performance by a quirky international band in Japan is something to 'write about in Christmas cards'. 'Seeing the world' and doing something different from their normal lives is an investment in life experience.

The cultural capital of these gap years is based on the idea that the right kinds of travel will bestow the right kinds of life experience. By exercising the good taste of 'proper travel', gappers are able to broaden their horizons and develop the right kinds of cultural resources. Desforges notes that independent travel, when conducted in the right way, engenders a sense of status and authority:

> Through intellectualising travel into the collection of knowledge and experiences rather than, for example, sitting on a beach or going to Disneyland, young travellers define themselves as middle class, gaining entry to the privileges that go with that class status. (Desforges 1998: 177)

The status of the right sort of experience is acknowledged by Kevin [34] when he discusses the prospect of working in a fish factory in New Zealand. It is not only a way to make money, but also is a resource that can be drawn upon in years to come: 'also when i'm middle aged and middle class i can talk about it at dinner parties'. He projects himself into a middle-class future with the recognition of cosmopolitan value. Working in a manual job is not about *necessity*. In this context, it is an exotic life experience (as long as it takes place overseas, and is only temporary). Having such worldly knowledge is a valuable commodity, a form of cultural capital that can be converted into prestige and reputation (O'Reilly 2006: 1012–1013). This sort of investment is not unique to gap year travel, but it is these ideas about 'worldliness' that form part of the desirable skills base that gap years provide (Jones 2004). These are worthwhile experiences because they provide young people with opportunities that can be drawn on for future benefits.

In the interviews, the gappers talk about wanting to take advantage of the 'natural break' between school and university to 'do something different' (Peter [16i]. They give two main reasons for taking their gap years at this point: wanting to be sure about university choices, and wanting a break from studying. Gappers like Libby [8i] and Owen [37i] disclose they had misgivings about their initial choice of university course, and use their years out to be more certain about their studies. Others, like Francesca [6i], cite the pressures of A Levels as a reason for not heading straight to university. The exception is Daniel [31i], who did not receive any university offers, and so took his gap year to gain some relevant experience and reapply. He thinks that he probably would have gone straight to university if he had been given the opportunity at the time, but in retrospect his gap year was a positive and useful experience. This is not strictly leisure time but a chance to do something valuable. Christina [10i] sums up these motivating factors:

> After A levels, you work really hard for A Levels, you do your GCSEs, your AS, your A Levels, and I just couldn't face doing another! I really wanted to travel,

do something different rather than another year of exams! And like exploring and stuff … and I wanted to help people, do a gap year that was constructive, rather than just travel. (Christina [10i])

Making a Difference

Christina highlights another concern for many young gappers. In addition to having valuable life experiences during a gap year, helping people is also an appropriate indicator of gap year worth. The gappers who go on volunteering and teaching placements discuss doing something worthwhile in an altruistic sense, of 'making a difference'. Volunteering is a rewarding activity, which gives the gappers pleasure if they feel they have made an impact on the people and communities they encounter. Indeed, it has a profound effect on some of the gappers. Ingrid looks back on working as a camp counsellor in the USA, and feels that her actions have been significant:

> On the back of our staff shirts it said: "Be the change you want to see in the world" and this summer i've realised how true that is I mean, i haven't done much yet but i know that i've affected some kids lives for the better and that's an amazing feeling. (Ingrid [4])

Similarly, Francesca [6] talks about teaching in Russia as being very rewarding, an 'emotional high'.

As noted in Chapter 5, the gappers are able to claim a cosmopolitan status as they are 'there', located in places of difference. This also shows they are global citizens, demonstrating that they care and are willing to travel to where there is need. Anna [29] suggests that the volunteers are appreciated by the teachers at her placement school in South Africa simply because they are there, 'which is what counts'. Although Louise [11] is working at a summer camp in the USA (rather than a 'needy' country), she also comments she is not working for payment but is 'here for the kids'. The gappers' presence alone is enough to help. Simpson (2004) critically reflects on such discourses and the idea that young people volunteering is enough to make an impact on host communities. Significantly, she highlights how the term 'development' is rarely mentioned in gap year promotional literature (apart from self-development), but that placements promote 'good intentions' and 'doing something worthwhile' (Simpson 2004: 683).

The bloggers do acknowledge at times that such placements may not make a big difference, but they still think the projects are important, as at least they are doing *something*. Libby [8] is told that her missionary outreach work in China 'refreshed' the local prayer house, and she feels that her work was indeed worthwhile: 'I feel we really fulfilled our calling in Shanghai! Even if that was all that we had achieved, I'd be happy'. Not all of the participants feel that they are making an impact, however. Daniel [31] reflects on the fact that the volunteer work he can do in Botswana is rather limited, but he looks to a future time when he may be able to offer more help: 'I'd like to imagine that I'll be able to come back once I've got some medical training under my belt, so I can be a bit more useful' (Daniel [31]).

Making (Moral) Distinctions

The gappers on placements genuinely want to do something that is beneficial for the communities they visit. At the same time, they frame their accounts with the discourses of anti-tourism and authentic experiences. In order to define what is worthwhile, they make reference to the experiences of others as *not worthwhile*. For example, Paul [32] discusses his desire to work on a project when planning his trip, 'Rather than just pass through loads of countries'. There is a *moral* distinction between just passing through – like a tourist – and having cosmopolitan encounters. Having good taste in travel is bound up with these preferences, which are seen as intrinsically better. During his time in Thailand, Ewan decides to stay in South-East Asia after his first period of teaching, and continue to volunteer:

> The realisation that there are so many amazing things you can do has really hit me today. There is absolutely no need at all to be a sightseer. Whether it is teaching, working at a rescue centre or building furniture for Tsunami victims (as [Friend], one of the other GAPpers is), working in a place gives you so much more than just passing through and seeing the sights. Getting to know a place, networking with the Thais – learning the lingo and having fun, is infinitely more rewarding. (Ewan [1])

Ewan's thoughts about what gap years should involve encapsulate the cosmopolitan impetus at the heart of such experiences. If gap years overseas are not cosmopolitan, they are not worthwhile, but simply inauthentic tourism and a waste of time.

Consequently, the gappers distance themselves from their peers before, during and after their gap year. The bloggers who volunteer overseas can claim moral distinctions through altruism, and all the gappers make value judgements based on ideas about proper travel. Paul [32] blogs about being irritated with his friends while he is planning his gap year, who are just preoccupied with 'getting drunk'. The gappers also express some distaste for people they encounter 'on the road' who are not doing proper travel. Helen [27] discusses, with a sense of incredulity, conversations amongst other people on a backpacking tour she takes in China. The other 'tourists' discuss how the use of chopsticks is unhygienic and forks are more 'evolved', and they are thankful they come from a 'proper country'. Helen, understandably, does not want to spend time with people expressing such overtly stereotypical views. What is interesting, however, is that her explanation for their attitudes is that they are on an organised tour, and so are not invested in cosmopolitan experiences – even though she is taking part in the tour herself.

Another instance of creating distance from other travellers can be found in Jessica & Celia's [19] blog:

> Some say that the point of travel is to open the mind to other cultures and we have found this to be mostly true. However, we've also developed a certain amount of scorn for the english based on the average backpacker we meet. Three girls arrived and, somewhere in between their complaints about ants and bemoaning the loss of their hair straighteners, we came to love Nacula.[1] (Jessica & Celia [19])

Home comforts identify the 'average backpacker' as different from those undertaking proper travel like Jessica & Celia. They define themselves as 'not average', because they are able to have a more sophisticated approach to the travel experience. Jessica and Celia's comments also suggest some distain for female travellers who cannot 'rough it' and are too interested in their appearance. Again, there is an implicit suggestion that 'girls' who are too concerned with possessions and conditions might not be good travellers.

This idea of doing things differently means that there are distinctions to be made upon their return as well. When Katy blogs about starting university after her gap year is over, she doesn't feel like she has much in common with other students:

> flats mates keep getting a bit funny with me about the fact im always out … apparently i never just sit and watch tv with them and hang out … .well maybe watching tv isnt all there is to life. (Katy [5])

Katy has learned to do something worthwhile with her time. Her gap year experiences have changed her, and have accumulated so that she can continue to draw on the skills, knowledge and sense of value during university and beyond.

Making It Count

The importance of doing something 'productive' and 'different' was also a topic of discussion in the interviews with the bloggers. In particular, taking a gap year overseas rather than at home is important. Lisa [3i] explains that

---

1 An island in Fiji.

she wanted to travel as she wanted to explore, as did Christina [10i], and Francesca [6i] specifically states that she didn't want to 'do something in the UK'. As Heath notes, gap years in the UK can lack the prestige of overseas trips (Heath 2007: 96). Status is also determined by the importance of 'helping people'. The interviews show, however, that the gappers have quite realistic understandings of the contribution that their gap year programmes may have on host communities. For example, Daniel [31i] notes the difference between the expectations he had for his volunteering and what he found when he arrived at his placement:

> I realised that I could have done anything with my gap year, but I was volunteering, so it wouldn't be a holiday, it would be productive, and you could maybe feel like you'd left something behind. But when I was actually there I realised that what I was doing over there wasn't actually what I expected, because I thought I would go over there and 'save Africa' but in reality I was just another pair of hands, I don't have specialist training. (Daniel [31i])

Such limitations are also discussed by Christina [10i], who reflects that if she had not undertaken her placement, someone else would have done. For Christina, the experience was 'more about what you're learning'. However, she also draws upon the notion of being active and organised in evaluating some additional voluntary work she took part in, suggesting that this made more of a difference. The gappers' narratives suggest that being active and enterprising is worthwhile.

Such ideas are more apparent when the interviewees discuss what is *not* worthwhile. These are, on the whole, prompted by the question whether a gap year would be suitable for everybody. Lisa [3i] suggests that gap years should be taken for the right reasons and not because the person is 'lazy'. Similarly, Francesca [6i] suggests that it is important to be interested in the activity in the first place, and criticises other gappers she encountered who did not make an effort to learn the local language. She questions the 'point' of spending an extended period of time somewhere without being interested in developing language skills. Although some interviewees place more emphasis on the importance of volunteering as a worthwhile activity, not all make the distinction between backpacking and more structured placements, suggesting that hierarchies of experience depend on a number of factors; it is 'what you get out of it' that is important.

This last point is reinforced in the discussion with Owen [37i], who is the only interviewee to have taken an unstructured gap year (although he had undertaken a brief volunteer placement in Kenya through Army cadets while still at school). Owen [37i] is particularly explicit about making the most of his time out. For him, becoming an accomplished traveller and accruing the accompanying personal benefits was a key goal at the start of his gap year. He makes distinctions between his own activities, and the gap years of friends and acquaintances that are less worthwhile:

> The idea had always been there but I was concerned about wasting my time. I'd seen a lot of friends, er, take a year off, even just a couple of guys from halls, took a year off and just worked in Edinburgh the whole holiday and went out drinking and buying clothes and stuff. I was quite concerned I would get stuck in that rut. (Owen [37i])

Throughout the gap year narratives, therefore, run implicit counter-narratives that gap years might not be worthwhile if incorrect decisions are made. In both the blogs and the interviews, the gappers present an account of experience that is framed within a particular narrative: of making worthwhile choices that enable benefits to be accrued.

These notions of value and worth in gap years are moral judgements, which normalise middle-class experiences (Skeggs 2004a). Employing cultural resources in this way is a classed process. It is the good taste of middle-class travel, of being adventurous and independent, and crucially being cosmopolitan, that is held up as the ideal. Altruism is important, and is another way of making distinctions. Yet status claims to do something different can still be made even if the gappers are 'just travelling'. This is particularly true if the gappers recognise the limitations of their volunteering placements, as they can still make claims to worth through the development of personal benefits. At work here is the drawing of boundaries, between what is and what is not worthwhile. Sayer highlights how morality comes into play in such cases:

> the way in which social groups often distinguish themselves from others in terms of moral differences, claiming for themselves certain virtues which others are held to lack: we are down-to-earth, they are pretentious; *we are cosmopolitan, they are parochial,* we are hard-working, they are lazy, and so on. (Sayer 2005b: 953; my italics)

Claiming the status of a young person on a worthwhile gap year, and the subsequent benefits, requires others to be engaged in non-worthwhile activities. For someone to be cosmopolitan, others need to be 'normal tourists'.

Making Time for Fun

What is fascinating is how the gappers are also able to reconcile their own less salubrious behaviour into an experience that is worthwhile overall. They are young people away from home, enjoying their freedom and independence, and having a break from education. Unsurprisingly, they want to have a good time. The bloggers tell humorous stories about nightclubs, pubs, and going to parties. For gappers who visit Thailand, the infamous 'Full Moon Party' on Koh Phangnan is a common attraction:

> On the night of the full moon we went to a party down on the beach, saw another fire show, and damn those buckets,[2] we got hammered! :D[3] Was a brilliant night! (Dave [7])

The space afforded by being away gives the gappers a sense they are outside ordinary life. Owen [37] talks about how 'time seems to be inverted' on Kho Phangnan – he sleeps during the day and goes out in the evening. The blogs tell stories of excess, often involving alcohol. Rich [22] amusingly relates a night in which one friend vomits in the sink, and another passes out on the sofa, and Jason [9] and his friends develop a reputation as 'those scousers who are always drinking'. Although there are some gender differences in the levels of gratuitous detail provided in such stories, they are not limited to male participants. Molly [24], for example, notes on a photo of her and two friends: 'drinking for three days with about 2 hours sleep … probably not the best time to take a photo'. Nearly all of the blogs recount some instance of visiting pubs and clubs.

The gappers who spend all or the majority of their time backpacking have more opportunities for hedonism, but those on structured placements still enjoy similar excesses. Sian [39] celebrates the end of a trek in Belize as follows:

> we arrived back late into Davis Falls (HOME!) and were greeted by rum, fried jacks, onion bargees [bhajis] and peach crumble. Didn't get to bed until gone 3am (after I hurled on my clean clothes I had been saving to wear after trek) Before we got drunk we all went down to the river and washed in the light of the full moon, skinny dipped and streaked through the camp. (Sian [39])

These hedonistic tales do not seem to contradict an overarching concern with a worthwhile gap year. Ewan [1], who stresses the importance of doing something 'rewarding', also hints at the 'atrocious stories' that could be told about his 'partying'. Some bloggers hold back the full details of their exploits: 'Saturday afternoon involved a great deal of hitherto unknown heights of craziness, which I feel I don't want to disclose right now' (Zoe [38]).

The interviewees also mention this editing, particularly as the readers of their blogs are likely to include people who had sponsored their trip. Daniel [31i], for example, states he missed out certain details, such as when he 'passed out' after drinking. Christina [10i] had to be careful as the 'vicar would be reading' her blog, along with sponsors from her church. She contrasts her blog with that

---

2 Plastic buckets filled with Thai whiskey, cola, ice, and energy drink.
3 This is the 'emoticon' for a laughing face.

of a friend who had gone backpacking in South America, who wrote a funny and more personal journal. However, story management is also discussed by Owen [37i], who exclusively travelled during his gap year. He specifically set up a separate private Facebook account to interact with his friends to keep his blog as an account of his experience that he would be happy to share with anyone.

Having fun does not stop anyone having a worthwhile gap year, although some bloggers seem to be aware that they should manage the public presentation of anything too excessive. The interviewees also mention that gap years are opportunities to get this behaviour out of their system before starting university. Some make distinctions between their more mature attitude and young students who go out every night. When asked about the differences between people who had and had not taken gap years, Libby [8i] replies:

> I think, something as simple as Freshers' Week. Like, I don't like getting pissed … Now I've come to university, and I'm like, I don't wanna get drunk, and have to be carried home! So in a way, I feel like I've grown up a lot, and I've learned there's so much more than that. (Libby [8i])

Other interviewees make similar comments: that having a good time on their gap year enables them to take their studies more seriously. Research that analyses gap year industry discourses suggests that having fun is a key part of 'official' accounts. In an analysis of promotional material, Cremin notes the similarities between enjoyment and the imperative to be enterprising:

> It is *really* living: it is fun, expressive, happy and spontaneous. It is the choice of reflexive agents making the most of their opportunities and having fun, so that once the chrysalis has ruptured the butterfly can leave its gap year cocoon and work for people friendly, interpersonal, flexible, team-based organizations. (Cremin 2007: 532)

Having fun on a gap year is bound up with being 'well-rounded' in all aspects of one's life, attributes that make for ideal workers. A key part of the successful gap year is a recognition that it is a 'contingent moment' (Cremin 2007) in which enjoyment is an intrinsic part of the experience, as long as orientations to doing something worthwhile – in Cremin's terms, being enterprising subjects and making the right choices – are also evident.

Making the Right Choice

This idea of enterprise helps to explain the imperative to do something *constructive* during a gap year. The period between school and university is a transitional moment in young people's lives. The uncertainty of late modernity means that such periods are more difficult and protracted than in previous generations (Furlong and Cartmel 1997). While class, gender and 'racial' divisions remain central to determining life chances, young people still feel individual responsibility for their life course:

> Blind to the existence of powerful chains of interdependency, young people frequently attempt to resolve collective problems through individual action and hold themselves responsible for their inevitable future. (Furlong and Cartmel 1997: 114)

Young people consequently see their progression as requiring individual negotiation and decision-making. This notion of individual responsibility for life chances is evident in the gappers' concerns to ensure that their gap year is worthwhile. When they think about how to spend their time out, they must negotiate a range of choices and make decisions regarding what constitutes a constructive use of time. This means that their gap year experiences should not be ordinary, but life-enhancing. Yet for all this talk of choice, not everything counts as a valid gap year experience.

Cremin writes a parody gap year 'case study'[4] about a young woman from a troubled background who steals money and runs away to France at 16, but has to abort her trip when she loses her passport and ends up supporting herself by doing casual work in London (Cremin 2007: 531). This fictitious young woman 'Jackie' would likely need to demonstrate the independence and self-sufficiency that gap years are supposed to provide. Without the sort of cosmopolitan encounters expected by middle-class travellers, however, roughing it loses its appeal. Cremin's fictional case study illustrates an invalid experience. Of course, a casual worker in London is likely to interact with a wide range of people from migrant backgrounds, but this form of cosmopolitanism is unlikely to count. Moreover, Cremin suggests that not being able to demonstrate enterprise is framed as an individual problem: 'Jackie has not "bounced back", she has not turned her trauma into a marketable or commodified asset' (Cremin 2007: 531). The bloggers' narratives are shaped by ideas of choice, yet they all share very similar ideas about worth, aligned with wider dominant values. These notions of choice and individual responsibility for self-development obscure the privileged nature of gap year experiences.

---

4 These are often used by gap year companies in marketing material to illustrate what young people might do during their gap years.

Gap Years as a Learning Experience

Learning through Adversity

By overcoming difficult situations, like the uncomfortable travel presented in the previous chapter, the bloggers assign worth to their activities to distinguish them from tourism. This is certainly the picture of gap years presented by the industry, who tend to stress they offer personal development rather than tourist products (Jones 2005: 6). Gap years are presented as an opportunity to learn, not as leisure. Young people are often given daunting tasks on their structured placements. Charlotte [12] worries about how she and her fellow volunteers will be able to plan lessons on their placement in Thailand as 'none of us have any teaching experience – oh and we can't speak a word of Thai'. The gappers sometimes undertake very difficult work, like Duncan [21] who has to photograph patients' eyes at a health clinic in Ghana, which he says is 'just about as hard as it sounds'. Simpson notes that the gap year industry provides work placements to gappers in fields that would normally require formal qualifications, such as teaching, medicine and construction (Simpson 2005a: 112). There is evidence throughout the blogs of gappers undertaking this sort of work. Whether such efforts are beneficial for the host communities is disputable. What is important for the *gappers* is that they learn something. Kevin [34] describes how his placement at a Christian mission in India enables him to learn through being challenged:

> went to 2 church services yesterday … we introduced ourselves by interviewing each other and then i spoke on transformation (i think i learn far more (and get way more challenged) from teaching others than being taught. (Kevin [34])

Kevin also positively discusses events that are not directly related to the programme, and which involve overcoming additional challenges, such as more adventurous activities like cave-walking. There is worth associated with difficulty and effort. According to Cremin, individuals are required to be 'active' in all aspects of life (not just at work), so that all uses of time should involve worthwhile activity and be orientated towards future goals (Cremin 2007: 530). Notions of enterprise and activity are central to the gap year experience because they help young people to demonstrate being active in these ways. This is especially clear in gap years that involve volunteering and work, but can also be seen during periods of travel.

Looking Ahead to Education and Employment

Framing gap years with the requirement that they need to be worthwhile means that the gappers look ahead to the benefits they can enjoy when they return. As well as being a break from formal study, there are also indications that this period of time out is, in fact, another form of education. Worthwhile gap years enable the acquisition of specific skills and knowledge that will be useful when the gappers go home. Such skills may be connected to their future university courses for example, particularly when they have chosen structured placements. Lisa [3] has plans to study drama and French on her return to the UK, and in an early blog post, she looks forward to working at a boarding school in the USA because she hopes to be involved in its drama and modern language provision. During her time at the school Lisa performs with one of the students, helps others with their French homework, and finds time to do some studying of her own:

> After lunch, I did some work from the French text book I bought over Spring Break (I thought I'd best refresh my French seeing as I haven't done any for nearly a year, and yet I'm studying it at uni in September!!). (Lisa [3])

Other gappers spend their year out visiting specific countries to develop their language skills. Both Andy [26] and Bryn [2] teach English in Japan and plan to take a Japanese degree. Similarly, Francesca [6] teaches in Moscow in her gap year before studying Russian at university.

Gap years can also provide other sorts of experience, like Daniel's [31] placement at a hospice in Botswana. This gives him some knowledge of what it is like to work in a clinical environment before he begins his medical degree. Direct links to potential plans such as these are not always possible, however. Ingrid [4] jokes that this is what gap years should be aiming for, although it may not work in practice. She intends to study geography on her return and makes a light-hearted reference to this while describing her travel in Australia:

> I have been outside solidly for the last week, but I think I would fry today (westerly winds travelling acororss [across] the contintent [continent] -makes them hot) see I am doing something vaguely geographical. (Ingrid [4])

While their gap year experiences may not directly relate to their university subject, the blogs do suggest that generic skills might be obtained that will be beneficial in future employment. The advantage that gap years have over other forms of work experience is the associated cosmopolitan cultural capital. When Jenny [13] returns to the UK, her father tells her she has more 'knowledge about the world'. This is something she explicitly regards as 'one for the CV'. The interviewees also note the potential benefits of gap years for the future. Lisa [3i] describes her placement at the US boarding school as 'work experience'. In a globalised marketplace, overseas gap years may provide some highly useful benefits: both Peter [16i] and Christina [10i] state they now have the confidence to work overseas in the future. They have accumulated what Murphy-Lejeune (2002) calls 'mobility capital' and have acquired a 'taste for living abroad'.

The responsibilities of structured placements in particular mean that the gappers develop a sense of what might be expected by employers. For example, Ewan [1] has to attend a formal reception during his teaching placement in Thailand, attended by local dignitaries. Ewan blogs about needing to remain professional at the event; about being asked at short notice to give speeches; and about 'making polite chatter with important people'. These experiences are seen by Ewan as helpful for prospective *professional* employment. Louise [11] recognises that some aspects of her placement are less fun, but they will help to prepare her for the future:

> So Monday morning came along and I had such a boring day had to sit through meetings and people talking from 8:30 am until 4:45pm. But I guess I should get used to it as that is what I will have to do one day. (Louise [11])

Gap years give young people a flavour of the responsibilities of a professional career.

Becoming Independent

Gap years therefore provide some potentially useful experiences that the gappers directly link to education and employment. More generally, however, they also provide other opportunities for self-development that are less specific, centred on growing up and becoming a well-rounded person. One of the key elements of self-development is the widely-accepted view that gap year travel helps young people to become more independent. The idea of becoming self-sufficient is mentioned throughout the gap year blogs. Being away from home, in a place defined by Otherness, enables the gappers to establish that they are able to take care of themselves. The blogs document the young people cooking, cleaning and earning money. If any activities are challenging, they are even more valuable. Independence is something to be earned, rather than bestowed. Young people with comfortable lives back home see this as an achievement:

> All the simple tasks like cooking, cleaning, washing and shopping have become huge tasks because [because] I'm not used to doing them on my own ... or at all for that matter. (Anna [29])

The 'Travel Buddies' [20] also proudly report they are 'fending for themselves' in Australia by doing their own laundry and cooking. Being responsible in such ways is framed by the bloggers with a sense of achievement, and that they are adults who can deal with life's realities.

There are overlaps once again with the values associated with proper travel. Gap years should not involve pampering, and independence is important. This also means that when the gappers are not travelling independently, or are faced with the prospect of organised travel, they feel like part of the experience is missing. When Zoe [38] has to rely on her gap year provider to organise the next stage of her travel, she resents her loss of freedom:

> Having been travelling independently for so long, having my travel plans spoon fed me – in such a way that I never get to see the full picture, is intensely annoying at best. (Zoe [38])

Similarly, Owen [37] discusses how he and his friends want to negotiate their own deal for a snorkelling trip in Thailand rather than take an organised package. There are also symbolic struggles over what counts as a 'proper' gap year in relation to being independent:

> At the moment there's a group of people my age who are doing their gap year (3 months in south america, thats it) … (they get a 'team leader' and absolutely everything already organised for them – I think it kind of defeats the object of a gap year, but you know …). (Adam [28])

The hierarchy of gap year experiences is up for debate, as asserting autonomy through independent travel means that the gappers can be seen as capable young people.

This sense of control is something that Lisa [3] misses when she returns home from the USA, as experiences like finding her own way around New York City had given her positive feelings of autonomy. However, fending for themselves can overwhelm the bloggers at times. Even though Alicia [14] classes herself as 'pretty damn independent', she finds some of the demands of travel a little too much:

> It's funny, I'm pretty damn independent and I was doing really well in the airport and with the first leg of trying to get a visa but there is a moment, pretty much when you have burst into tears in an embassy, that you just want someone's advice, and someone to help you out. (Alicia [14])

The gappers develop an ability to cope and be self-reliant by negotiating testing experiences. These feelings of self-sufficiency sometimes have limits, perhaps due to gap years taking place during a transitional period for the gappers. They are learning to assert their independence but also recognise when they need the help and advice of others.

This form of work on the self, of developing as a person, is a form of embodied cultural capital: the 'long lasting dispositions of the mind and body' that need labour, investment and time to acquire (Bourdieu 1997 [1986]: 47–48). Good taste in gap year travel, characterised by independence, engenders the development of traits that are advantageous, particularly in relation to graduate employment. Heath notes:

> the widespread view that the gap year is hugely beneficial to young people, the presumed benefits including the acquisition of soft skills, greater maturity, enhanced self-awareness and increased independence. (Heath 2007: 100)

In the graduate market place, charismatic 'personal qualities' are valuable, thanks to the development of more flexible forms of work and organisations. In this context, the 'whole person' is assessed in performance (Brown 1995: 41). As Heath (2007) argues, gap years are a way for young people to show that they have such skills, and this view is adopted by the bloggers.

Gap Years and Personal Development

Growing as a Person

Before he leaves for his work during the ski season in France, Tim [23] looks ahead to the opportunities for personal development he expects:

> This trip is going to offer me so much, such as a good step up the career ladder, becoming more independent, and realizing how lucky I am to have things in life I do take for granted. (Tim [23])

Tim's thoughts encapsulate the benefits that are ascribed to gap years: benefits for future employment, life skills and a broader perspective. This is a prospective idea of what gap years can offer, which plays out in the reflections on the day-to-day occurrences during the bloggers' time overseas. They discuss the benefits of meeting the challenges presented by gap years, such as gains in confidence, independence and practical life skills. Again, the responsibilities that come with structured placements in particular enable gappers to develop and push themselves to further challenges. Francesca [6] blogs about feeling more and more confident when she is teaching in Moscow, taking classes on her own and feeling able to lead discussions. Being somewhere 'away' is also a key factor in driving the development of these qualities for Ewan:

> Also: my confidence has gone through the roof, maybe because of the completely different social environment, maybe because I'm in Thailand and maybe because I'm just really looking forward to teaching next week. (Ewan [1])

The benefits of gap year travel presented in the blogs match those identified in the existing literature: increased confidence from being outside existing networks of support; ideas about worldliness; the ability to negotiate problems; and personal qualities such as communication skills (Jones 2005: 10–11). They are accumulating embodied cultural capital in the form of desirable personal qualities.

Gap years are framed as beneficial although it is not always explicit exactly what has been achieved. Anna [29], for example, simply states that when one stage of her gap year is over: 'I've learnt a lot about myself and made a lot of friends'. Precisely what Anna has learned is not clear, as she is excited about the next part of her trip. This is balanced with a recognition that she has been homesick at times, underlining how challenges need to be overcome in order to move on and develop. More specifically, Louise [11] is pleased that she has developed her interpersonal skills, and now sees herself as someone who can support others. While working as a camp counsellor in the USA she comforts and calms down one of the young campers. She is 'proud' of herself as she has 'never dealt with anything like that before'. In addition, gap years are an opportunity to modify one's personal behaviour, like Jason's reflections that he has been too hedonistic:

> After a few hard weeks living in 'the now', I think its time to start kickin' back and looking ahead. After giving up alcohol (I lasted a week, now I'm going for moderation instead of firm abstinence), I felt it was time to start reigning in my other bad habits. (Jason [9])

Jason wants to make sure that he doesn't waste time on his gap year, but instead thinks about doing things that are worthwhile, and looks towards the future. Jenny [13] also reflects on changes in her behaviour that are driven by her experiences. For example, she notes that she is more relaxed and 'chilled out', and on a trip to a shopping centre, is more careful with her purchases then she would have been previously, asking herself: 'Do I really need this?' Economising and generally being more thoughtful regarding her actions during her gap year lead Jenny to reflect on aspects of her behaviour that have improved.

Changing as a Person

One crucial piece of gap year identity work is the development of a cosmopolitan attitude. Katy [5] suggests that she doesn't think her gap year has changed her as such, but she has been instilled with a passion for seeing the world. The idea of global knowledge is seen as very valuable, with some gappers viewing this as something quite profound. Their reflections include the ephemeral – looking at the world differently – and more substantial, such as changes in travel practices:

> It still makes me smile how at home I would never travel so long for four days, and yet here I think nothing of it. It's just a fun thing to do. I also think this weekend may have got me addicted to the whole travelling thing – I want to stay here for ever and ever! (Sian [39])

Cosmopolitan encounters provide the space for young people to contemplate their changing perspectives. Being somewhere that is 'away' allows for reflections on 'home'. Bryn [2], for example, notes that the way he views home itself changes while he is overseas. One of Tim's [23] school friends tell him he has 'totally changed' upon meeting him when he goes home. This leads Tim to frame his experiences in comparison to home, which he sees as unchanging and static.

Not all of the gappers continue to blog on their return to the UK, but feelings of change and transition are notable in the narratives of those who do. As well as making distinctions between herself and her peers, Ingrid [4] feels a certain dissonance with the person she 'used to be':

> You know those kids toys where they have to put the round block in the round hole and the square block in the square hole. Well right now i am a square block trying to fit into a round hole. I feel like i've changed so much this summer, or pretty much this year really and now i can't quite fit back into my old life. (Ingrid [4])

Ingrid's reflection, once again, is from being 'out of place'. However, not all of the bloggers reflect on their self-development in this way, and when they do mention such topics, it is not necessarily something that is explored in much detail. Of course, this does not mean that they do not have such thoughts, or do not reflect in these ways. The point is that blogs offer us an insight into how gap year narratives are framed, and in the case of many of the stories, this is a taken-for-granted presentation of change and self-development. Helen [27], for example, simply states that she has 'visited all those places' and that the experience was 'fun, exciting, enlightening and life-changing'. There is an assumption in these accounts that doing something worthwhile will provide the expected benefits. The belief that gap years should be life-changing is also evident in Zoe's [38] thoughts about returning home: 'I want to think that I've changed as a person in some way. For me not to have done, after all that I've seen/done this year, would be rather saddening, I feel'. The standard narrative of gap year travel incorporates 'changing as a person', and it is these expectations that can structure how the experience is understood.

Gap Year Narratives and Reflexive Identity Work

Travel as identity work is well-established in both academic literature and the popular imagination. As explored in Chapter 3, researchers exploring contemporary forms of travel practice draw on Giddens's (1991) concept of reflexive projects of the self. Desforges's (2000) work on travel biographies, for example, suggests the narration of self-identity has particular relevance for longer periods of independent travel as this often takes place at 'fateful moments'. New travel experiences are resources at transitional points like finishing education or changing career, which help individuals to move their identity towards a rewarding future self (Desforges 2000: 935). We can see some elements of these themes in the gap year narratives, such as self-development with an eye on future benefits, and the profound effect on some of the gappers' sense of self. Yet the blogs do not provide compelling evidence for the model of the reflexive gapper explored in Chapter 3. Reflexivity is not just concerned with using events to narrate identity; it is the ability of the self to stand outside and know itself, a form of possessive individualism (Skeggs 2004a: 81). Reflection is not the same as reflexivity, and expectations of what gap years 'should' be about frame many of the gappers' narratives. In reproducing these standard narratives regarding gap year travel, such as requirements to be enterprising or to make the most of it, the majority of the blogs show how such stories are concerned with representing the 'right type' of experience. Moreover, the resources drawn upon include discourses of the exotic Other, and authentic travelling is bound up with class distinctions. Structural disadvantages are thus implicated in these stories.

As discussed, the gappers frame their narratives with reference to requirements to be enterprising, in keeping with views of self-regulatory identity work (Cremin 2007; du Gay 1996; Rose 1999). Although self-development is important, there are very few instances of *explicit* critical reflection from the gappers in the form of working on their 'bodies and souls' on order to transform them (Foucault 1988: 8). There were some notable exceptions to this, however, when situations involving dialogue prompt the gappers' reflexive considerations. Libby [8] spends her year out at a discipleship training school in New Zealand. This experience is grounded in learning to be a 'better Christian', and her blog is the only case of consistent, in-depth self-reflection in the sample.

Like the other gappers, Libby spends time describing the day-to-day aspects of her placement – where she goes, the daily activities and routines, and the food she eats. She also writes and reflects on exactly what she needs to change about herself in order to achieve her goals. Libby is self-critical, and thinks about how she 'should' behave. This seems to be enabled through the learning and self-analysis guided by her discipleship studies. Although Libby is not the only blogger enrolled on a placement with a Christian organisation, the extent to which she reflects on her personal shortcomings and what she needs to do to overcome them is striking compared to the other gappers:

> I was so humbled this week. I realised what a baby Christian I am, living my life focussed on my sin, not living free but just sinning, feeling guilty about it and then repenting rather trying to live like a saved person. Time for change! (Libby [8])

This self-reflexive discussion examines areas for development. It is not directly achieved through cosmopolitan encounters, nor the gap year experience per se. Instead, it is generated by an intense programme of study, dialogue and reflection. In other posts, Libby writes about the need to 'take responsibility for where [she] has ended up', and how 'wrong' she has been. She discusses the identity work required, and her religious belief is central for her to achieve these changes.

Libby was also one of the bloggers interviewed, and in the interview she discloses a key motivation for her gap year was to 'sort things out'. Her faith and mission work are important to her, but she also talks about some issues with her mental health, and that the gap year experience had helped her to 'fix' things. When asked what she had hoped to get out of her gap year, and whether she was successful in this, she answers:

> a lot of it was trying to sort myself out, as a person, because I was a bit of a mess. To be honest, I'm so much happier now than I was. And yeah, I guess, I put a lot of pressure on myself to get better, ah, a bit of background and stuff [discloses problems]. That had been happening for a year before I went away. And then, I was really hoping that would be a time for me to just work out what the problems were. Work out what was wrong, and how do I fix that. It's so much better now, and in the end, I think that was my biggest aim was to be happy, and secure in who I was, and I am. (Libby [8i])

For Libby, her gap year is worthwhile because her placement is based upon dialogue and introspection. It takes place at a particularly troubling time for her, and allows her to deal with specific issues and problems.

The identity work that Libby engages in is rather different from that promoted by official gap year discourses. It arises out of a very specific context that has little to do with employability or global knowledge. What Libby's case does show is how we can theorise how and why reflexivity may emerge, in 'the mutual obligation and influence that agents bring to bear upon each other' (Bottero 2010: 16). In the context of an intensive period of Bible study and 'discipleship training', Libby is *challenged* to work on herself.

For the most part, the readers of the blogs leave comments that reinforce the taken-for-granted benefits of gap year travel. There is tacit agreement that their gap years are worthwhile, as the bloggers' stories are not challenged. There is one striking incident of disagreement, however, in Katy's [5] blog. A tsunami in India prompts a friend to leave a comment on a blog post written towards the end of Katy's time in Nepal, as the friend is worried that Katy would be affected. An anonymous commenter then sarcastically dismisses this idea, suggesting that Katy's friend has limited geographical knowledge. He then attacks Katy herself:

[Comment] Katy you do sound naïve. its no wonder that you have learnt so much because you knew so little to begin with. I quote 'I don't think that there is a class barrier in Britain' … Maybe you should see your own country before jetting off around the world and working in private [Charity] schools where you aren't really needed because the kids are already fluent … Personally I think GAP years are all about the participating individual and are geared to 'developing character' and giving the 'Gapper' a 'life-changing experience' instead of really helping people, but at least if that's the case we went to a deserving cause. (Katy [5])

The anonymous author seems to be another gapper that Katy has met during her travels. He echoes many of the same criticisms that have been levelled at gap years: that they do not help the host communities but are focused on the gappers' identity work. At the same time, the commenter makes assertions that his own volunteering placement is more worthwhile.[5] Katy does not delete the comment, but instead defends herself and the Nepalese school where she volunteers. This is framed with developing global knowledge, while recognising the limitations of her contribution:

the school isnt just a private school. its a charity school, and can only continue to work as it has been doing with the support of volunteers, donation, and [Charity] … i wish i could have done more here, i dont feel like ive 'made a difference' (a naïve thing to say i know). (Katy [5])

---

5 It is assumed that the anonymous commenter is male due to an insult that he uses.

It is external criticism and dialogue that prompts Katy's reflexive consideration on whether her gap year is worthwhile.

Talking About Self-Development

The gap year stories generated in the interviews also tend to stick to standard frames of identity work. Providing the interviewer with an interesting and exciting account of the experience of being in another country appears to be important, rather than critical reflection upon change (with the notable exception of Libby [8] discussed above). This is not to say that the interviewees do not view their experience as profound. Daniel [31i] states that his gap year was 'the most interesting thing about him' and that his family said he 'left a boy, and came back a man' (Daniel [31i]). Nor did it mean that when asked, the interviewees do not thoughtfully discuss the benefits and changes they feel have occurred. For example, Lisa [3i] reflects on how she used to get in trouble when she was younger for being a little impulsive when talking to people, and thinks that her gap year has enabled her to deal with social situations more successfully. Most of the interviewees express such sentiments in terms of gains in maturity and life experience – exactly what gap years are supposed to do.

Some of the interviewees are aware of the standard narratives that frame such experiences:

> I was thinking about stuff that everyone says when they're going to take a gap year, like 'I felt much so much more confident', those kind of things you definitely write down, but definitely some of the things I wasn't expecting will be more useful. (Christina [10i])

Christina goes on to add that the unexpected elements of her experience have helped her to be more self-reliant on her return to the UK. Francesca [6i] notes that self-development in terms of future prospects was not a priority when planning her gap year:

> I had a really good experience – OK, speaking in practical terms I suppose it is good for a CV, but I'm not really bothered about that to be honest … . For me, it was about having an interesting experience, and I definitely had that. (Francesca [6i])

We can see that both Christina and Francesca are aware of the ways in which gap years are typically framed. They make some status claims using their narratives of identity work in order to distinguish themselves from others, but at the same time this reproduces the common discourse that they are doing something different – just like everybody else!

Conclusion: Identity Work in Gap Year Narratives

In this chapter, I have suggested that gap year stories contain judgements about morality. Some activities are worthwhile and have value, and some are not. The gappers' narratives suggest that being a cosmopolitan traveller who has authentic experiences is constructive, as is being an altruistic global citizen. The bloggers also discuss the benefits that they can accrue during gap years that will help them in the future. Yet the extent to which this is *self-reflexive* is questionable. I have not referred to all of the blogs in this chapter, simply because they did not make much mention of the worthwhile aspects of their gap year, nor the resulting potential for self-improvement. One explanation for this is that some of the gappers are able to tell the right story more successfully than others. There are indications, however, that the benefits of gap years are taken-for-granted. The examples given of reflexivity in the gappers' narratives are prompted by interactions and dialogue, either online or offline. This highlights how the stories of self-development that young people tell need to be situated (King 2011). King suggests that young people can be aware they are making moral judgements, and this might not always be appropriate: 'accounts of Gap Year experiences can act as different resources, in different contexts, for different purposes' (King 2011: 354). Comparisons can be made to the use of cosmopolitan frames as contextual and '*periodically* articulated, embodied and materialized, rather than being an inherent property of particular individuals, groups or situations' (Skey 2012: 473).

Narrating a story of self-development, therefore, is not necessarily a reflexive process; it merely supposes a model of identity that depends on the ability to accrue value (Skeggs 2004b: 75). The self-improvement discussed by the gappers follows *standard narratives* that are well-established in ideas regarding the benefits of travel, and gap year travel in particular. The blogs demonstrate explicit reflections on self-development to varying degrees, ranging from those that are predominantly concerned with factual representations of experience to more reflexive discussions which tended to be prompted by others. This is more evident in the interviews, in which the gappers provide a variety of justifications and motivations for gap year travel in the context of self-development, but which are all within a recognisable framework.

Doing something worthwhile and enterprising, to be active in self-development, implies that individuals have to make the right choices. This obscures the effects of structure on young people's life chances (Furlong and Cartmel 1997). The idea that everyone is able to work to develop their cosmopolitan identities and become more employable seems to be uncritically adopted by the gappers. The interviewees, for example, speak about non-worthwhile behaviour as a matter of choice or personality, rather than circumstance. Middle-class cosmopolitanism is therefore normalised. While there is little evidence of extensive critical reflection upon the 'self' in the accounts, the narratives of gap year travel suggest that young people should 'choose' the correct experience for self-development in line with future goals. The dispositions and tastes of the young people who undertake gap year travel are those which, when they are prompted, are concerned with telling the right story about identity work.

The bloggers' approaches to this self-development do not share many similarities with the reflexive gapper. Their narratives suggest their experiences are more like Bourdieu's (1990) strategies of capital accumulation as driven by the dispositions of the habitus: worthwhile gap years are considered appropriate. At the same time, the picture of the habitual gapper does not accurately capture the tensions that run through gap year narratives, and the gappers' moments of critical reflection cannot only be attributed to being 'out of place' or 'times of crisis' as Bourdieu suggests. Moreover, claims to cosmopolitan encounters have a moral dimension, which Sayer argues needs to be brought into the concept of habitus (along with emotional dispositions) (Sayer 2005a: 142).

The final chapter revisits the overarching argument made throughout this book: rather than a progressive experience, the gap year tends to confirm existing frameworks of understanding. This influences the ways that difference is encountered, the sorts of travel experiences that are valued, and how this is understood as worthwhile self-improvement. Gap year stories are framed by the references of home, and describe experiences that will be advantageous when they return. Cosmopolitanism is a valuable resource, a form of capital that gappers can draw on in globalising education and employment markets. The reproduction of established frames means we can question the moral distinctions that are employed in proclaiming the benefits of gap years, and the discourses of choice and individual responsibility that are at work in dominant notions of worth. Although the reproduction of established discourses in the gappers' accounts suggests an overall lack of critical reflection, there is also evidence of some reflexivity, and a degree of variety and agency in their experiences. Consequently, I revisit theories that suggest more mundane or habitual forms of reflexivity; the moral aspects of social practice; and the relevance of intersubjectivity in identity work (Bottero 2010; Crossley 2001; Sayer 2005a).

Chapter 8
Conclusion

In a humorous collection of emails sent home by young gappers, the authors state:

> The whole and entire point of a gap year is to have bizarre experiences of the type you could never have at home ... (Hoggart and Monk 2006: 1)

Gap years take place away from home in order to be out of the ordinary and exciting. Yet the ways that young people understand and present their experiences are learned at home, and their narratives are predominantly directed to audiences back home. Shared, habitual frames structure the experience and are imported into these liminal spaces. This period of liminality or 'apartness' (Turner 1974) marks the gap year as a rite of passage. Liminality reverses or inverts the norm (elsewhere in opposition to home, for example, or affluence contrasted with simplicity) (Graburn 1983: 21). The gap year narratives explored in this study frame the experience as different yet draw on home for a point of comparison.[1] The types of gap years that are worthwhile have value which can be carried back through embodied cultural capital. Young people are not necessarily 'freed' from their identity, and their identity work may reflect home values (Johan 2009).

What are the implications for gap years as a cosmopolitan practice? The gappers certainly are oriented towards experiencing diversity, and can make status claims regarding cosmopolitan competence. However, the level of 'global reflexivity' in their accounts is limited, and therefore we can question whether the cultural practice of gap years *in and of itself* fosters political or ethical cosmopolitanism. The empirical research presented here is built upon three key questions:

- How do young people frame their encounters with difference in their gap year stories?
- What frames do they draw upon to distinguish good taste in gap year travel?
- Do the participants frame their own narratives with reference to self-development and to what extent is this a reflexive process?

---

1 It should be noted that Turner reserves the term liminality for religious rites, and uses the term 'liminoid' for secular/leisure activities. I would also suggest that the rules of home are not completely suspended during gap years.

In this final chapter, I summarise the findings of this study, and reflect on how discourses of cosmopolitanism inform contemporary forms of cultural capital and notions of selfhood. While gap years may provide an example of 'actually existing cosmopolitanism' (Robbins 1998), I argue for caution in applying the term when the view of the Other reproduced in such narratives is not always progressive and when the frames surrounding such experiences are rooted in structural inequalities.

Gap Year Debates: Cosmopolitanism, Cultural Capital, and Self-Development

Chapter 2 identified cosmopolitanism as a multi-dimensional concept with social, political, cultural and ethical aspects. We should not collapse the differences between these conceptualisations, and the contribution of cultural practices based on consumption to progressive attitudes towards difference is not straightforward. Gap years are not just about consumption, but they are a commodified experience that can be bought, as indicated by the growth of a specialised industry, and particularly the development of commercial organisations. Both cultural cosmopolitanism more generally, and gap years in particular, can be criticised as elitist, doing little to foster cosmopolitan ideals while serving as a way for the privileged to make status distinctions. As suggested in Chapter 3, gap years are institutionalised and legitimate, demonstrate good taste, and provide potential advantage in terms of increased employability. This cultural capital is accumulated and exercised through the gap year experience, and can operate in overlapping fields. The associated values are aligned with good cosmopolitan taste. Moreover, the embodied qualities of being well-travelled can be transferred to the fields of education and employment, centred on this idea of employability.

Current research suggests there are multiple cosmopolitanisms, including banal forms, when exposure to diversity becomes part an implicit part of everyday life, and reflexive forms that critically engage with difference. The latter is associated with more progressive politics and ethics, although this association needs to be viewed with caution. Some work on cosmopolitanism links these more engaged forms with self-reflexivity, and indeed travel is also viewed as a means of uncovering or working on the self. However, I have suggested some theoretical problems with seeing travel as simultaneously an exercise in reflexive self-development and as a means of accumulating cultural capital. One potential theoretical perspective is to view the gapper as a reflexive social agent (Giddens 1991; Beck 1992). Cultural capital, on the other hand, is part of Bourdieu's wider theory of practice, which emphasises the structural constraints to agency and reflexivity and the reproduction of advantage (Bourdieu 1984; 1990; Bourdieu and Wacquant 1992). In Chapter 3, I introduced criticisms that there is too little agency in Bourdieu's account, and suggested theories of 'habitual' or 'mundane' reflexivity (Sweetman 2003; Crossley 2001; Sayer 2005a) as a way of addressing this. Such work encapsulates the everyday reflection that is involved in social practice, which is a part of everyday cosmopolitanism, but still retains a central concern with how social practices are constrained by and reproduce inequality.

Researching Gap Year Narratives

To explore representations of the gap year experience, I have drawn on Goffman's (1974) concept of framing to look at how people understand events and experiences, and communicate them to others. In this study, the online narratives of young people on gap years were collected and analysed, supplemented by semi-structured interviews with a sub-set of the bloggers. The spontaneous narratives found in blogs help to identify the frames used by young people to describe experiences. Blog analysis considers what the bloggers themselves deem to be important to communicate, without the concerns of a researcher guiding the story. In Chapter 4, I suggested that analysing gap year blogs provides insight into some common frames and shared understandings of worth and value. However, this innovative use of methods presents a number of methodological and ethical challenges. Concerns over reliability, authenticity and representativeness may pose a problem when using online data. Despite these concerns, the methods employed were appropriate, as the research was concerned with representations of gap year experiences, rather than 'truthful' or 'accurate' accounts. Combining the blog data with interviews also meant that themes identified through the blog analysis could be discussed with some of the gappers.

Although it is not possible to make any generalisations regarding the structural position of individuals who take gap years, the accounts in this study are those of relatively advantaged young people. They may not be a cosmopolitan elite, but they are privileged compared to their peers in the UK, and even more so in a global context, given they have the resources to engage in this legitimate form of mobility. In their narratives, we can see evidence of the tacit, dominant values that are part of the gap year experience. So, while it may not be possible to make claims regarding the direct reproduction of structural inequality using this data, the gappers' narratives reproduce ideas about what kind of experiences have value. Blog analysis is a valuable way of accessing how people think and talk about their experiences. Such work does present some tricky ethical dilemmas, in term of whether the blog data can be considered publically available and whether the gappers can be considered human subjects or authors. Adopting an ethical stance of sensitivity to context means that employing 'moderate disguise' (Bruckman 2002) has been deemed the best approach to presenting the data. The following sections summarise the insights from this analysis to show how gappers engage with difference, make distinctions and undertake identity work.

Difference, Distinction and Identity Work

Encountering the Other

The gap year industry is criticised for the way that young volunteers engage with host communities. An alternative activity – travel – is also criticised for the persistence of historical narratives of contact with the Other (Said 1978; Galani-Moutafi 2000), which shape contemporary tourist practices. Both of these critiques suggest that established images of people and places are reproduced rather than challenged when difference is encountered. In exploring how the bloggers frame their contact with the Other in Chapter 5, I argued that their accounts employ a limited number of ways to describe people and places. These shared representations stress the differences between 'home' and 'away'. Some frames evoke images of the exotic from the popular imagination, like references to the tropical beaches of desert island fantasies. These secluded locations are out of the ordinary as they are seen as the opposite to 'Western' modernity. Such places are clearly 'away'. In the blogs, the gappers recount the consumption of local food and meeting local people, and talk about being out of place. Feelings of embodied difference are reflected upon, such as standing out physically and being unfamiliar with etiquette. Even stereotypical notions of local people are referred to at times.

The gappers often exhibit a genuine desire to understand their host communities. Those on structured placements see these types of gap years as aiding this understanding, as they spend longer in one location. This leads to more extended interaction, and consequently the gappers use this as an opportunity to develop local knowledge and a deeper appreciation of people, places and cultures. There is cosmopolitan value placed on interacting with difference in ways that demonstrate sensitivity and sophistication. For some, this leads to more reflective considerations of inequalities and difference. Yet it is important to reiterate that such cosmopolitan openness is not evident in all of the blogs. Moreover, there is a pervasive tendency to represent the Other using established ideas about exoticism, naturalness or authenticity, even for those with a more reflexive standpoint. The blogs also show that gap year interactions are not always positive, especially if the ideal of the Other is challenged by negative experiences such as 'hassle'.

Another element of these less progressive interpretations is when the gappers draw attention to perceived deficiencies of the places visited, particularly in the global South. For example, the need for volunteers is highlighted by the bloggers making comparisons between the disorder of the gap year location and the rationality and modernity of 'the West' (Simpson 2004). Other frames used to contrast away with home include tradition, poverty, danger and risk. Most of these comparisons are made while in the global South, but these are also evident in the stories of bloggers in the USA and Japan, who highlight differences along racialised and classed lines.

Overall, then, we can see a tension in the gappers' accounts between global reflexivity and global reproduction. There is a cosmopolitan desire to learn about and understand the Others encountered, and instances of reflection upon global issues. The gappers want to experience what places are 'really like' and broaden their horizons. Yet their representations are structured by established discourses about the Other, a figure who is exoticised, romanticised, or even rejected. The gappers' blogs should not be classified as either globally reflexive or globally reproductive, because this is a continuum to be negotiated. Gap year companies claim that volunteering placements benefit host communities and that independent travel leads to a greater understanding of cultural difference. Both types of gap year product are infused with discourses of global citizenship. These experiences are framed by *novelty*, however; the desire to go away, rather than be at home. The endurance of existing ways of understanding the Other signifies continuing asymmetric relationships, and how they are represented. As I have discussed, there is some debate regarding the benefits of gap year placements for host communities. Critics such as Simpson (2004) argue that many volunteering organisations, particularly commercial enterprises, do not engage with issues of development. Moreover, they are criticised for reproducing established ideas about the Other. This was indeed borne out in many of the gappers' accounts. The continuum in their accounts from reflexive to reproductive representations of difference suggests a more nuanced framing is required, however. There is the *potential* for global perspectives to be generated through gap year experiences (Jones 2005). As Skey (2012) argues, exploring cosmopolitanism in practice requires us to recognise that people move *between* cosmopolitan and uncosmopolitan attitudes; that local identities continue to matter; and that cosmopolitanism may be expressed to suit a particular purpose or need (Skey 2012: 476). *When* gap years engender cosmopolitan sentiments is therefore a critical question, rather than simply assuming that they do.

We might expect differences in levels of global reflexivity between those on gap year placements and those who just travel. Reflexive inclinations do seem to be more apparent in the blogs of those who spend an extended period of time in one place. Yet cosmopolitan desires are not exclusive to the gappers on placements, and simplistic, negative or uninterested accounts of the Other are not limited to backpackers. What emerges in both types of narratives is close to what Savage, Bagnall and Longhurst (2005) term 'self-referential cosmopolitanism'. Savage, Bagnall and Longhurst use this term to refer to cosmopolitan identity claims that are concerned with aligning oneself with other cosmopolitans, rather than engaging with cultural difference. The orientation to the Other in the gappers' accounts indicates that experiences are framed within established contexts of understanding. By its very definition, gap years are bounded periods of time that are separate from the normal course of things, framed by this difference between home and away. Home is an implicit element of these frames rather than, say, cosmopolitan commitments to global citizenship. Overseas gap years take place somewhere that is definitely not home, but status can be gained among a home audience, as encountering the Other is evidence of good cosmopolitan taste.

Good Taste in Gap Year Travel

The bloggers' accounts of their travel practices draw on established notions of contemporary good taste. In Chapter 6, I noted that the historical distinction between mass tourists and independent travellers continues to have relevance (Wang 2000). This shapes the presentation of gap year experiences, centred on the idea of 'proper travel' as the most appropriate way to engage with difference. Even when the gappers are settled in one place, such as while they are on a placement, they frame their narratives using this discourse of proper travel to define experiences as cosmopolitan. Indeed, the aim of proper travel is to get to know what a place is 'really like', something that the placements offer. As well as defining their own practices, the gappers make distinctions between themselves and others. I noted that there is another 'other' in gap year narratives: the figure of the inauthentic tourist who does not engage in proper travel. The blogs contain negative descriptions of those defined as tourists, whose approach to travel is seen as inauthentic. By transplanting the comforts and practices of home to away, tourists are viewed as engaging in fake experiences. The gappers therefore adopt the cosmopolitan's critique of 'home plus' (Hannerz 1990). Authenticity is very important, and some also distance themselves from the mass of backpackers. As independent travel grows in popularity, new hierarchies of taste emerge.

There were some occasions when it is acceptable to act like a tourist, to save time or to have a break from travelling 'properly'. This is because, as noted, consuming a place via independent travel involves going without the comforts of home (Loker-Murphy and Pearce 1995; Munt 1994; Elsrud 2001). There is a sense of achievement in coping with basic facilities and taking low cost, uncomfortable transport. Events are framed by narratives of exploration and risk, evoking the cosmopolitan adventurer, who is spontaneous and mobile. If something is difficult or even dangerous, it can still be brought into a successful narrative of cosmopolitan competence, as such experiences demonstrate the difference between 'proper travel' and the ease of being a tourist. The gappers' willingness to experience 'real life' aligns with their cosmopolitan concerns. This, again, is in contrast to home, with access to the inside of an authentic place demonstrated by talking, acting or thinking like a local. Language skills are a mark of distinction, so those who can communicate in the host language see this as something to be prized as they are able to access the inside in an authentic way, whereas others find the lack of these skills frustrating. The consumption of food is also a way to access the authentic, and eating in local places is valued. Thus the cultural capital that is accumulated through proper travel is based on accumulating knowledge about a place through a connection to the 'inside' that is distinct from mass tourism (Munt 1994). The gappers can impart this knowledge in their blogs, which are lent an air of authority as they are 'there'. Some bloggers also talk about local history and culture, showing some understanding of the issues that affect the community. This embodied knowledge is demonstrated through the collection of places, the ability to impart advice to others, and being able to make authoritative statements about what such places are like.

Taking a gap year has many similarities with the perceived benefits of independent travel more generally. The recognised status of being a well-travelled person legitimates taking an overseas gap year rather than staying in the UK, and is indicative of wider trends in good middle-class taste in cultural consumption: cosmopolitanism, albeit 'self-referential' (Savage, Bagnall and Longhurst 2005), omnivorousness (Peterson 1992) and authenticity (Urry 2002: 86). The implications for these findings in defining contemporary cultural capital are explored below. There is also an implicit classed dimension to these taste expressions. The reference point for making distinctions is the uncultured masses, those who are not open to the Other and consume only touristic experiences. In making these judgements of worth, the gappers are reproducing them (Bourdieu 1990). When they tell their gap year stories, they draw on the 'correct' way to experience something in order to describe it, which in turn legitimises these tastes. However, while there are hierarchies of experience in gap years (Heath 2007), this might not be as straightforward as structured placements being more legitimate than backpacking. Young people who travel independently from more privileged backgrounds may be able to tell the right story about such events. There is still a certain kudos that can be obtained and celebrated through travelling in the right way. Being a cosmopolitan, well-travelled person is crucial, and this structures how the gappers frame what is worthwhile.

The Worthwhile Gap Year

There are clear overlaps between good taste in overseas gap years and the quality of being employable. Across popular, government and academic discourses, there is an agreement that these experiences offer young people future advantages. Although the bloggers do not always explicitly discuss self-development, they do judge what they consider to be worthwhile. A central motivating factor for taking some time out is to have a break from education, but this is a period that has to be used wisely. Gap years are a 'once-in-a-lifetime' experience, when you have to 'make the most of it'. This suggests that cultural capital needs to be accumulated. Young people undertaking voluntary work frame their activities with the additional dimension of altruism. They have a genuine concern to demonstrate their global citizenship and to do something beneficial for their host communities, but there are moralising claims at work here, as the volunteers can, once again, distance themselves from people who are tourists. Moreover, doing something different, by definition, is a way of being distinctive. The gappers discuss how other travellers have poor taste, or how their peers don't 'get it'. These discussions draw moral boundaries (Sayer 2005a; 2005b) between what is, and what is not worthwhile, which are framed by references to restricted cultural resources.

For many, if not all, of the gappers, gap years are an opportunity to enjoy oneself. These activities still fit within an overall framework of a successful gap year, as they give young people a space to get these inclinations 'out of their system' before they start university. Having some fun in a *legitimate* context is fine, and can be included as part of an overall narrative of growing up. If young people enjoy their gap years, it does not mean they are not doing something constructive and worthwhile. Enjoyment is part and parcel of 'really living' (Cremin 2007), part of a frame of legitimation and justification. Some of the gappers, including those interviewed, draw on the ideology of choice in discussing worthwhile activity: that it is down to the individual to make the right decisions about their gap year, for the right reasons. There are also references to the specific skills and knowledge that can be gained, including language skills and relevant work experience, along with personal qualities like independence, confidence and self-sufficiency. Crucially, one of the more ephemeral benefits is a cosmopolitan knowledge about the world. Gap years function as evidence of this intangible but increasingly validated disposition. Moreover, it is the difficulties of proper travel and encounters with the Other that contribute to the development of the other associated benefits and skills.

The benefits of taking a gap year can be conceptualised as embodied cultural capital (Bourdieu 1997[1986]). Such benefits take the form of skills, knowledge and 'personality factors', as suggested by Heath (2007). So, the gap year is a project of self-improvement, but this is something that seems to be taken-for-granted, even when the bloggers reflect on this (and not all of them do). Some exceptions to this were discussed in Chapter 7, where a direct challenge, or 'calls to order from the group' (Bourdieu 1977: 15) prompt more critical reflection, but throughout the narratives, there is little evidence of a reflexive consideration of social position. Consequently, there are few indications of the examination of 'unthought categories of thought' (Bourdieu 1982, cited in Bourdieu and Wacquant 1992: 40). Chapter 5 suggested that encounters with difference *can* provide the point of disjuncture to prompt self-definition in a global context, but not *always*.

As well as questioning the extent of reflexive cosmopolitanism as part of the gap year experience, the gappers' blogs also provide a challenge to the idea of these experiences as reflexive identity work as understood by Giddens (1991). When the gappers do reflect on their self-development, they engage in a more mundane form of reflexivity (Sayer 2005a). Gap years tend to be viewed as having inherent qualities which, when experienced, accrue value in the self without the need for critical reflection. The judgements made about what counts as worthwhile are then embodied in the form of desirable 'personal qualities' and knowledge. Such framing parallels the (global) inequalities in who 'gets' to be cosmopolitan.

Prospects for Gap Years and Global Citizenship

What, then, are the prospects for gap years as cosmopolitan journeys? The evidence from the gappers' narratives explored in this study could be seen as evidence of banal cosmopolitanism (Beck 2002). This would suggest these encounters with difference are a consequence of increased mobility and cultural pluralism becoming a part of everyday life (for the privileged, at least). I do not think this does justice to the gappers' sincere attempts to engage with the Other, however. Alternatively, gap years may be a form of 'ordinary cosmopolitanism', for example that described by Skrbis and Woodward (2007). Ordinary cosmopolitanism identifies how tolerance for cultural diversity becomes part of everyday life, a repertoire to draw on. Rather than examining the cosmopolitan elite, Skrbis and Woodward explore tolerance to increased cultural diversity amongst the broadly defined middle classes, and suggest that cosmopolitan dispositions are restrained by 'personal, local and national anchors' (Skrbis and Woodward 2007: 735). In their study, there is a greater tendency towards cosmopolitanism when it is linked to positive experiences. There are some parallels with the gappers' encounters with difference, in that they are more likely to resort to stereotypes during unpleasant experiences.

Germann Molz sees the practices of independent travellers as evidence of 'actually existing cosmopolitanism' due to their 'mobility, tolerance and openness to difference' (Germann Molz 2006: 5). However, the cosmopolitanism of the travellers in Germann Molz's study speaks from a particular position of privilege, and is primarily concerned with adopting a mobile, flexible cosmopolitan identity, rather than progressive views towards difference. As Skey notes, cosmopolitanism has been used to describe such a wide range of cultural practices that this 'does not tell us much about the significance of such processes for those involved or their relative importance in generating or sustaining a more open attitude towards others' (Skey 2012: 472). There is a tendency for any encounters with diversity to be *already* defined as cosmopolitan. We have seen some uncritical representations of difference in the gap year narratives, and the data from the gappers' accounts points to the continuing relevance of implicit, collective understandings of experience alongside more deliberative framings.

This raises the question of what might prompt global reflexivity, a question crucial for any discussion of cosmopolitanism as 'The key underlying characteristic of cosmopolitanism is a reflexive condition in which the perspective of others is incorporated into one's own identity, interests, or orientation in the world' (Delanty 2011: 634). For Bourdieu, reflexivity emerges at times of crisis, when there is a disjuncture between habitus and field (Bourdieu and Wacquant 1992). We might expect overseas gap years to provide this opportunity, helping young people encounter difference away from home. The embodied feelings of not fitting in and being somewhere away could be one factor that prompts reflection upon one's place in the world. However, the gappers' narratives in this study draw on frames that span the continuum between globally reproductive and globally reflexive. Although the tension between reproduction and reflexivity is negotiated by the gappers, the former is more prevalent. Consequently, the concept of self-referential cosmopolitanism is perhaps the most useful here. Gappers may adopt a cosmopolitan identity, but ultimately they are identifying with those who hold similar views. This is because their stories are framed by the references of their home contexts – the exotic Other, or proper travel – and are describing an experience that will be advantageous when they return. Cosmopolitanism, in the form of 'cosmopolitan cultural capital', may not solely be a property of a global elite, but it is an increasingly required resource in which it might be beneficial to invest. Like other forms of capital, this is unevenly distributed.

Cosmopolitan Cultural Capital and Good Taste

The gappers' narratives also indicate wider conceptions of what is considered to be good taste. Here, I consider three forms of cultural capital. Firstly, the gappers are not really concerned with 'high culture', which potentially suggests they are cultural omnivores. Secondly, while there is certainly some evidence of omnivorousness in these young people's tastes, as they are able to move between 'proper travel' and more conventional tourism, they still draw boundaries that have an implicit class dimension. Thirdly, I argue that the concept of cosmopolitan cultural capital better captures the status distinctions and desire to consume Otherness that define good gap year taste.

Snob Culture

The gappers do not seem to be primarily concerned with highbrow cultural tourism in terms of museums, art galleries and the like, as suggested by Craik (1997). This is not to say that these young people do not visit such places, and indeed there are frequent discussions of historical and cultural sightseeing. The sites/sights visited are important in terms of a to-do list of must-see places. Yet the emphasis is on authentic experiences and knowledge, as it is this that is valued, rather than a command of consecrated high culture. The content of cultural capital as described by Bourdieu in *Distinction* (1984) is not supported by the bloggers' accounts (although this does not, of course, challenge his overall model of status distinctions). Indeed, findings from a large-scale study of contemporary cultural taste in the UK notes that command of high culture is now less important, and instead it is orientations to cultural consumption rather than its content that marks class divisions (Bennett et al. 2009: 254). An example would be that lots of people may consume reality television, but it is the ways in which it is consumed (such as 'ironically') that mark boundaries. Does this lack of concern with snob culture mean that theories of the cultural omnivore (Peterson 1992; Peterson and Kern 1996; Peterson and Simkus 1992) are better placed to define the cultural capital of gap years?

Cultural Omnivorousness

The gappers do show signs of being cultural omnivores, and are able to switch between different styles of travel. They visit high cultural sites, but also value proper travel and a back-to-basics approach. Throughout their narratives of being on the move, they adopt the independent traveller's concern with being on a budget, alongside more expensive accommodation and food as a treat. Being a tourist *temporarily* is fine, as long as there is an overall concern with more authentic experiences. This is because not all travel practices are valued equally. Peterson and Kern (1996) define omnivorousness as antithetical to snobbish exclusion, but in the gappers' narratives, the tourist is a figure who is used as an unsophisticated counterpoint to real travel. Boundaries between travellers and tourists have an implicit class dimension, separating the former from the uncultured masses. The growth of international travel and tourist infrastructures means that 'exotic' destinations have been opened up to wider audiences. Visiting and consuming these locations is less of a marker of status in the past, and consequently they need to be experienced in the right way. So although the gappers are not snobs in the sense that they are only concerned with high culture, they draw boundaries between themselves and others who do not have the right sort of taste. Being omnivorous can, of course, be a form of distinction (Bennett et al. 2009). However, the way that gappers frame their varied activities with reference to authenticity suggest that cosmopolitan cultural capital is the most appropriate way of defining the type of cultural capital accumulated.

Cosmopolitan Cultural Capital

In a critique of 'white multiculturalism', Hage asks: 'who has the competence to enjoy ethnic diversity?' (Hage 1998: 204). According to Hage, the 'sophisticated internationalism' of cosmopolitanism is an elitist practice, one in which 'the other remains exotic' (Hage 1998: 205). This appetite for diversity as a means of making status distinctions can be observed in the gappers' narratives. They provide some evidence for the gap year as a way of accumulating cosmopolitan cultural capital that reproduces social advantage, while at the same time cosmopolitan dispositions are restrained by pre-existing discourses about the Other. This critical view of cultural cosmopolitanism generates some interesting problems, however. According to Brook (2008), Hage does not consider cosmopolitan (cultural) capital neutrally, but criticises the commodification of 'ethnic culture'. Consequently, Hage could be accused of having the same desire for authenticity as the cosmopolitans who are the target of his critique (Brook 2008: 215). When I use the term 'cosmopolitan cultural capital', I do not suggest that the gappers are engaged with inauthentic experiences, nor that wider critiques of cultural appropriation should be concerned with preserving the authenticity of the Other. Instead, I use it to recognise the status distinctions at work in gap year travel (and beyond) that draw on this idea of authenticity and which tend to utilise pre-existing ideas about difference.

Of course, there are overlaps between cosmopolitanism and omnivorousness, as both are concerned with openness – to variety, and to difference. They are both a product of cultural pluralism via globalisation. However, I suggest that cosmopolitan cultural capital is better placed to capture the possibilities for boundary drawing in the gap year experience. This includes how the taste for 'ethnic' difference can lie behind a discourse of cosmopolitanism (Hage 1998). Moreover, cosmopolitan dispositions may be valuable in an increasingly globalised context, but they have 'limits' when encounters with difference might be threatening or challenging (Skrbis and Woodward 2007). Viewing cultural cosmopolitanism as a means to accumulate cultural capital is also complementary to the concept of mundane or habitual forms of reflexivity (Sayer 2005a; Sweetman 2003). The practices of cosmopolitan consumption suggest that openness towards the Other is habitual rather than critically reflected upon, and is based on inequalities in the possession of valuable cultural resources and the exercise of good taste. Moreover, given the emergence of a global labour market, this may a resource in which it is increasingly beneficial to invest.

Cosmopolitan Cultural Capital, Global Education and Global Employment

Additional longitudinal research would be required to track the outcome of accumulating cosmopolitan cultural capital for the gappers in this study. However, we can see links between their experiences, and the associated skills and benefits, with broader trends in education and the employment market. In their work on student mobilities, Brooks and Waters note that studying overseas might be considered as identity work for the young people involved, but this should not lose sight of the associated educational inequalities, and indeed the limits to the inter-cultural learning that can be enabled. Instead, as noted in Chapter 1, attempting to gain a global outlook through educational experiences may be viewed as 'strategic cosmopolitanism' (Mitchell 2003), orientated towards future benefits. For example, Weenink (2007; 2008) discusses parents choosing to send their children to 'internationalised' schools[2] in the Netherlands in order to accumulate 'cosmopolitan capital'. Parents are concerned with the potential for upward social mobility this would confer in globalising social arenas, rather than concerns with openness to the Other (Weenink 2008).

These cosmopolitan experiences mean that young people have the opportunity to gain advantages in increasingly competitive graduate labour markets. Gap years may offer one solution for young people to set themselves apart from their peers in order to be more employable (Heath 2007). Certainly, the gappers' stories provided examples of such distinctions. The graduate labour market is arguably a global one, offering opportunities to work for multinational corporations, non-governmental organisations, and the like (Weenink 2007). In order to compete in the context of credential inflation, young people and their families may pursue a variety of strategies in order to succeed, including postgraduate study, internships, extra-curricular activities, work experience and attending high status universities (Brooks and Waters 2011: 31).

---

2 These are state schools where half of the curriculum is taught in English and pupils take part in exchange programmes and extra-curricular activities 'with an international outlook' (Weenink 2008: 1090).

Those experiences that can be framed as cosmopolitan are likely to offer considerable advantages. We can see similar rhetoric in the discourses surrounding international education as those promoting gap years:

> For students, a period of study or work abroad brings positive benefits, both personally and professionally. It enhances their understanding of other languages and cultures, and increases their confidence and self-reliance. In a global economy, these skills and competences are increasingly sought by employers, and students with this experience will find that their employability is higher than without it. (Fielden 2007, cited in Brooks and Waters 2011: 151)

Moreover, if gap years before university inculcate what Murphy-Lejeune (2002) calls 'mobility capital', or a taste for living overseas, then this may lead to further opportunities. Brooks and Waters suggest that gap years increase young people's interest in international study (Brooks and Waters 2011: 139).

Underlying these trends is the rhetoric of choice. The contemporary provision of education is shaped by market theory and models of rational decision-making (Reay, David and Ball 2005). Young people and their families are expected to make the right choices and make the most of the opportunities that are available. As Reay, David and Ball (2005) demonstrate, however, higher education choice is structured by class, with elite students colonising the higher status institutions. Brooks and Waters (2009) suggests that similar trends can be observed in global education markets, with a small minority of privileged UK students choosing to study overseas when they do not gain access to prestigious home institutions. What is problematic here is that, while taking a gap year might be strategic, it is not seen as such. Instead, it is seen as an individual decision to embark on a gap year and to *choose* to make this time out worthwhile. This neglects how less affluent students face restrictions, for example having to work during their gap year in order to save for university (Bradley and Ingram 2013: 60).

Gap Year Identity Work

The decision to take a gap year is often portrayed as a matter of individual choice, a young person choosing the most appropriate path. As demonstrated throughout this book, this obscures both inequalities in access to such experiences, and the workings of class in defining legitimate identity work. In Chapter 3 I outlined two hypothetical figures: the reflexive gapper, inspired by Giddens (1991); and the habitual gapper, inspired by Bourdieu (1990). Although the concept of choice appears in the gappers' accounts, the ways in which their narratives are structured by acceptable practice and agreements concerning value questions the voluntarism of the reflexive model. There are a limited number of narratives that are available to tell a successful, cosmopolitan gap year story, centred on making the most of time to have fun; become an experienced traveller through proper travel; gain skills and knowledge that will have future benefits; and help others. Some of the gappers' stories cover all of these elements, and some focus on just one. These closely match established understandings of what gap years should be about: the imperatives of enjoyment, employability and ethical behaviour (Cremin 2007). This obligation to undertake something worthwhile is pervasive. We can also see requirements for young people to be 'enterprising' (du Gay 1996; Rose 1999). A discourse of choice does not mean that these gappers are free to choose.

Moreover, the trends of individualisation and detraditionalisation associated with the reflexive self do not fit well with the gappers' use of structural frameworks of understanding. Their narratives of self-development make use of the other: both the exotic Other and the uncultured masses. These frames are used with little evidence of critical reflection. It is taken-for-granted that gap years are a 'good thing' and such well-established ideas are, for the most part, unreflexively adopted. Consequently, there is a strong case for considering the habitual gapper as the model that best captures the gap year experience. The gappers have a 'feel for the game' (Bourdieu 1990: 66), and are aware of the correct way to do things. They rarely reflect on their social and political position, and the taken-for-granted quality of their accounts suggests that their narratives of self-development can be understood as the working of the habitus. Gap years are something that young people from certain (relatively privileged) backgrounds do, they are 'normal' behaviour. Although the concept of habitus is often criticised as being overly deterministic (Jenkins 2002), improvisation and adaptation *can* be accounted for within Bourdieu's theory:

> the habitus, like every 'art of inventing', is what makes it possible to produce an infinite number of practices that are relatively unpredictable (like the corresponding situations) but also limited in their diversity … the habitus tends to generate all the 'reasonable' 'common-sense', behaviours (and only these) which are possible within the limits of these [objective] regularities, and which are likely to be positively sanctioned. (Bourdieu, 1990: 55)

As such, gappers' narratives are not all the same, and draw on different frames, but are still limited by structural constraints, and fit within defined parameters of 'worthwhile' behaviour.

At the same time, there is some variety and flexibility in the gappers' narratives. In Chapter 5, I noted that some situations prompt a version of 'global reflexivity' (Savage, Bagnall and Longhurst 2005), when the gappers consider their place in the world in relation to the Other. Their stories suggest some negotiation between globally reflexive and globally reproductive positions. Similarly, there were different degrees of reflection on the process of self-development, and we need to account for those instances of self-awareness. How can we understand this without resorting to the ideology of choice? As suggested in Chapter 3, a model which incorporates intersubjectivity and morality, and which moves beyond Bourdieu's rather narrow definition of reflexivity, is best placed to do this.

As Archer (2007) suggests, the inner conversations of reflexivity arise from the interplay between our thoughts and social context, and individuals can engage in varied forms of reflexive thought. While the evidence presented by the gap year narratives suggests that tacit routines and collective knowledge do continue to shape young people's identity work, in contrast to Archer's conclusions, their presentations of experience require a consideration of context: not only objective factors, but intersubjective frameworks. Indeed, this is something that is suggested by Bourdieu's early work, what King calls the 'intersubjective sense of the game' (King 2000: 420). Actions are guided by thinking about what others might find appropriate:

> a sense of honour, a disposition inculcated in the earliest years of life and constantly reinforced by calls to order from the group, that is to say, from the aggregate of the individuals endowed with the same dispositions, to whom each is linked by his dispositions and interests. (Bourdieu 1977: 14–15)

Being cosmopolitan is something that is generally agreed to be a 'good thing', an appropriate way to engage with the world.

The gappers' stories are told in an intersubjective context, either to the readers of their blog or to me as an interviewer. For the most part, the gappers' narratives fit within shared understandings of acceptable practice, and their dispositions are reinforced. What counts as 'worthwhile', for example, involves subjective and intersubjective moral evaluation, as suggested by Sayer (2005a). Moments of reflexivity are prompted by conflict ('calls to order from the group'), ongoing dialogue, or when the available frames do not fit their experience. Frames are a way of understanding context, according to Scheff (2005). The concept of framing captures the mutual awareness of meaning, which has an emotional element: we feel pride when our interpretations are attuned to others, and shame when they are not (Scheff 2005: 377). For Scheff, frame analysis is a way of modelling this subjective and intersubjective context (Scheff 2005: 384). To be able to describe experiences, we have to draw on the shared resources available. In this book, I have highlighted how the gappers' narratives are aligned with the understandings of others and agreements regarding moral hierarchies of worth.

While young people may have good intentions and genuine commitments to cosmopolitanism, critical reflection on the gap year experience is limited by the intersubjective context, as well as structural constraints. Gap years need to be worthwhile (or at least presented as such), and hence there is a shared understanding of what the outcomes should be. They are also guided by classed distinctions of taste, so that middle-class taste is normalised and misrecognised as differences in moral worth, obscuring the privileged nature of the activity. Their stories tend to reproduce dominant meanings and values: the exotic Other, or the embodied skills that should be acquired to be successful. Frames from back home are used to define their experiences. Yet there are also more reflexive accounts at times, prompted by points of disjuncture or as part of a dialogue. The narratives suggest something other than 'mundane consciousness' guiding action as suggested by Atkinson (2010). By considering the intersubjective context, we can also see how gappers' accounts can reproduce dominant meanings but also reflect critically upon them. This provides young people with greater agency, as well as capturing issues of morality as put forward by Sayer (2005a). Bottero (2010) suggests that greater emphasis on the intersubjective nature of practice, such as the generation of accounts and accountability through interaction, can overcome the 'problem of reflexivity' in Bourdieu's work.

What Next for Gap Years and Gap Year Research?

What, then, might encourage 'reflexive cosmopolitanism' as part of the gap year experience? There are some proposals in work on volunteer tourism for developing cross-cultural understanding. For example, Raymond and Hall offer the following suggestions for the gap year industry:

> First, they should develop programmes which will be of genuine value for the local communities. Second, the importance of approaching VTPs [volunteer tourism programmes] as a learning process rather than simply an 'experience' should be recognised through the use of experiential learning techniques. Third, opportunities for interaction with other cultures should be deliberately facilitated. (Raymond and Hall 2008: 530)

Simpson also calls for more pedagogically-informed gap years and recommends looking to 'adventure and experiential education, service learning and other travel-based programmes such as the Peace Brigade and VSO' (Simpson 2005a: 231). There is a case for encouraging critical reflection among backpackers as well, of course, although the nature of the activity can make intervention difficult. One entry point would be youth travel providers, yet this raises the thorny issue of the 'cosmopolitical terrain' of consumption (Germann Molz 2012a). Swain (2009) asks if tourism can be non-capitalistic, and points to insights from feminist economics that suggest new economies and ethical practices. This could include: 'ecotourism, social justice tourism, local co-operatives, alternative, hidden, informal economic activities and ethical transformation of poverty by the poor themselves [micro credit for example] with the collusion of tourism researchers' (Swain 2009: 523). Insights from critical cosmopolitan studies could provide examples of what this might look like, according to Swain, so that tourism acts as a force for good.

Education has an important role here. It is vital that young people should be encouraged to reflect critically on their experiences, and confront common-sense ideas that gap years are automatically a good thing. In a discussion of UK-based volunteering, Holdsworth and Quinn suggest that universities should help young people to link their own experiences to new, challenging academic knowledge (Holdsworth and Quinn 2012: 402). It is also crucially important not to lose sight of the fact that gap year travel is a privileged activity that is not open to everyone. A focus on developing reflexive cosmopolitanism among young people who take gap years has the potential to be implicated in reproducing a certain kind of cosmopolitan subject: one who is geographically mobile (including the able-bodied), affluent, 'sophisticated' and from the global North.

In this study of gap year narratives, I have focused on the ways in which these young people's stories featured classed distinctions of taste and moral boundaries. However, as Lovell argues, there is a danger in work influenced by Bourdieu to place 'sex/gender, sexuality, and even "race" as secondary to that of social class' (Lovell 2000: 12). There are some suggestions in the gappers' narratives that these journeys are also shaped by gender. For example, in Chapter 5, I noted that young women experience an additional limit to being able to 'fit in' when confronted with sexual harassment. Germann Molz argues that 'not all cosmopolitan bodies are cosmopolitan in the same way' (Germann Molz 2006: 17). Moreover, there are indications that a certain type of femininity is viewed at odds with 'proper travel', for example the 'girls' who have too much luggage, complain about the conditions or miss their hair and beauty products. This moral distancing shares some similarities with Skeggs's (2004a) work on working-class femininity as a boundary marker in urban cosmopolitan spaces, representing what is 'tasteless'.

There are multiple cosmopolitanisms, and we need to consider not only how people are cosmopolitan, but also how to challenge dominant cosmopolitanisms. Moreover, Rizvi (2009) argues that learning itself needs to become cosmopolitan, to enable an ethical understanding of global transformations. It would be historically aware; critical; conscious of the relationality of culture; and reflexive, helping young people to better understand both their own position and connectivities (Rizvi 2009). This is very different to the experiences currently promoted through many gap years:

cosmopolitan learning is not so much concerned with imparting knowledge and developing attitudes and skills for understanding other cultures per se, but with helping students examine the ways in which global processes are creating conditions of economic and cultural exchange that are transforming our identities and communities; and that, unreflexively, we may be contributing to the production and reproduction of those conditions, through our uncritical acceptance of the dominant ways of thinking about global connectivity. (Rizvi 2009: 265–266)

Such efforts are not concerned with ensuring that young people develop cosmopolitan cultural capital but with wider issues of global social justice.

To develop the field of gap year research, Lyons et al. (2012) suggest large scale, generalisable survey analyses to examine the relationships between backgrounds of gap year participants, the sorts of gap year experiences undertaken, and the broader impact of this. They also suggest this is combined with qualitative research that employs purposive sampling to explore such relationships. Overall, their argument is for gap year research to employ a more systematic framework (Lyons et al. 2012: 373–374). Future work could also evaluate how the cosmopolitan cultural capital accumulated is transferred into the fields of education and employment, for example by comparing the relative success of gappers to their peers. This would highlight the privileging processes at work and contribute to wider debates on the relationship between cosmopolitanism and structural advantage. I have focused on the experiences of young people from the UK, and it would be beneficial for future gap year research to explore similar phenomena beyond the British context. Given the points noted above, gender also requires much more attention in gap year research

In conducting this research, and in writing this book, it was not my intention to criticise young people who take gap years. Their stories are funny, thoughtful, entertaining, at times infuriating, even boring in places. They are also diverse and usually well-intentioned. My aim has been to critically explore cultural cosmopolitanism, and challenge the common-sense assumptions about gap years that can hide their role in reproducing inequalities. Not everyone is in a position to take a gap year, and gap years do not necessarily foster a critical engagement with difference. Structural effects are misrecognised, as young people who occupy a relatively advantaged position are able to claim what they do has intrinsic worth. Although gap year experiences are closed to those less fortunate, they are seen as a matter of individual choice. Moreover, gap years are implicated in problematic relationships with an exoticised Other. Such concerns present clear challenges to the idea of gap years as progressive 'cosmopolitan journeys'.

Appendix
Gapper Profiles

All of the bloggers were aged between 17 and 19 at the start of their gap year travels. The profiles below provide the bloggers' home locations and future degree programmes if this information is available. Additional background details are provided for those gappers who were interviewed.

Ewan [1] (blogspot.com)
Ewan is from the South West of England and plans to study English at university. He undertakes a teaching placement in Thailand, and sets up his blog specifically to record his year out. His original plans were to travel to Australia, New Zealand and Fiji, but he decides to continue to backpack and volunteer in South East Asia when his placement finishes rather than continue on his round-the-world journey.

Bryn [2] (Self-hosted using wordpress.org)
Bryn is from Wales and has a place to study Japanese at university after his year out. His blog, which demonstrates considerable technical competence, is set up especially to record his gap year, and includes photos and videos as well as descriptions of his experiences. Bryn's year is divided into six months teaching English in Japan, and six months travelling in Australia, New Zealand, and South America, although his blog ends before his promised 'final post'.

Lisa [3] – INTERVIEWEE (livejournal.com)
Lisa's gap year consists of a 12-month placement at a boarding school in the USA, although her blog starts before her application is accepted and continues after her placement ends. She sets up her blog on the community and blogging site LiveJournal, which links to her fundraising page. Lisa takes her gap year before going on to study for a French and drama degree, and she returns to visit the school the following summer. Lisa was eager to share her gap year during our interview, and brought along her scrapbook to show me. She is from the West Midlands and her parents are a nurse (her mother) and a business manager (her father). Lisa went to a comprehensive school, and took her A Levels at the affiliated sixth-form college.

Ingrid [4] (livejournal.com)
Ingrid's gap year consisted of a mixture of travel in Australia, New Zealand, Fiji and the USA along with volunteering on a conservation project and working as a youth camp counsellor. She is from London and plans to study geography at university. Her blog is hosted on LiveJournal, and she also uses the social networking functions of this website.

Katy [5] (livejournal.com)
Katy's blog records her gap year spent teaching in Nepal. She also spends a few weeks backpacking in India before she returns home. She is from the East Midlands, and goes on to study archaeology and anthropology at university. Her blog continues after the end of her gap year, and records further travel experiences, such as working as a camp counsellor in the USA and volunteering/ backpacking in Asia.

Francesca [6] – INTERVIEWEE (livejournal.com)
Francesca is a regular blogger on LiveJournal but sets up a separate account for her gap year. She is from London, and takes her time out before going on to study history and Russian at university. Most of her gap year is spent on a teaching placement in Russia. She also decides while she is overseas to take the Trans-Siberian Express to Mongolia to undertake an additional, shorter placement. During our interview, Francesca spoke about her parents who have both worked and volunteered abroad. Her father is Canadian and her mother is from a Polish background, and Francesca states that travel is a feature of her family's life. Francesca went to a comprehensive school and her parents are both educated to degree level, with her father working as a teacher and her mother working in the public sector.

Dave [7] (globenotes.com)
It was difficult to establish Dave's background details, although his blog indicates that he has sat his A Levels and is taking a gap year before university. Dave utilises a dedicated travel blog website to record his time backpacking in Africa, Australia and South East Asia. His travels in Eastern Africa are cut short due to the lack of a backpacker 'scene', and he prefers places where there is more of a travel infrastructure and nightlife.

Libby [8] – INTERVIEWEE (myspace.com)
Libby undertook a 'discipleship training' placement in New Zealand run by a Christian organisation, which involves study workshops, volunteering and outreach work. She also visits China with the scheme for an additional outreach programme. Upon her return to the UK she volunteers as a sailing instructor for a local charity before studying occupational therapy at university. Libby

is from the South East of England, and her parents work as a researcher in engineering, and as a carer. She was brought up in a Christian household and it was clear during the interview that her faith is extremely important to her.

Jason [9] (myspace.com)

Jason is from the North West of England. He was initially going to study psychology at university but then dropped his place, although it is not clear if he has gone on to study for an alternative degree. His blog is set up on his Myspace social networking profile, and records his period of backpacking in Hong Kong and Australia, which he partially funds with casual work once in Sydney.

Christina [10] – INTERVIEWEE (myspace.com)

Christina's blog describes her teaching placement at a school in Uganda, along with some additional volunteering she does at a hospital. She also undertakes some independent travel around Eastern Africa during the school holidays. She is from the North West of England, and goes on to study English literature at university, with an extra 'Erasmus' exchange year in France. Her mother is a lecturer who is studying for a doctorate, and her father is a graduate who works for an education assessment board. Christina went to a comprehensive school until 16, and then went to a private sixth-form college.

Louise [11] (blogspot.com)

Louise's gap year overseas was split into two parts. She works as a camp counsellor in the USA, travels, and then returns home for two weeks. She then travels to Australia, where she works in a boarding school. Louise's blog is set up specifically to record her gap year on a common blog-hosting website.

Charlotte [12] (fuzzytravel.com)

Charlotte is from London, and teaches English in Thailand during her gap year. She also travels in Thailand, Singapore and Australia. She uses a specialist travel blog website, and uploads a number of photos to her blog.

Jenny [13] (blogspot.com)

Jenny is from the North East of Scotland. She teaches maths and science at a school in Guyana on a 12-month placement, and goes on to study maths at university. In addition to recording her travel experiences, her blog also provides information on the organisation that provided her placement and details of her fundraising activities.

Alicia [14] (blogger.com)

Alicia is a regular blogger, and uses the medium as a diary and to share her poetry, asking for comments on work-in-progress from her readers. She is from

London. During her time spent overseas, she travels in South America and teaches in the USA. The blog seems to end before she starts university, and does not provide details about her studies beyond her discussion of her successful application to a prestigious institution.

Chris [15] (travellerspoint.com)
Chris is from the North West of England. He volunteers in Tanzania and also travels in South East Asia. He uses a specialist travel website to host his blog, which is incomplete.

Peter [16] – INTERVIEWEE (livejournal.com)
Peter undertakes his gap year before going on to study chemistry at university. He travels around New Zealand before undertaking a seven-month placement at a school in Australia. His blog on LiveJournal documents his time spent backpacking, but he does not blog about the placement as it was easier to keep in touch using other means. Peter was born in Greater London and attended an all-boys independent school. His mother is a teacher and his father is an accountant.

Neil [17] (livejournal.com)
Neil spends his gap year travelling in Thailand, Australia, New Zealand, Fiji and the USA. He works on a farm during his time in Australia. Neil's blog is incomplete, and does not extend beyond his time in Australia.

Jo [18] (fuzzytravel.com)
Jo backpacks around Singapore, Malaysia, Australia and New Zealand, and stops off in the USA on her way home. She uses a specialist travel blog website to record her travels and the casual work she undertakes during her trip. Jo goes on to study nursing at university after her gap year.

Jessica & Celia [19] (blogspot.com)
Jessica and Celia are two friends who write a joint blog about their gap year travels in India, New Zealand, Fiji, the USA and Mexico. They are both from East Anglia. Jessica and Celia take it in turns to write their blog posts, which include photos of their trip and tongue-in-cheek accounts of their experiences.

'Travel Buddies' [20] (blogspot.com)
This is a group blog set up to record the travels of a group of four female friends from Wales who undertake their gap year together. They take it in turns to write the posts and upload their photos onto the blog, which documents their gap year spent backpacking around South-East Asia, Australia, New Zealand and Fiji. The 'Travel Buddies' spend the entirety of their gap year together, apart

from when one of the friends breaks her leg and returns home for recovery before re-joining the group. They do not discuss what they will be studying on their return, although it is clear they are all going on to higher education.

Duncan [21] (blogspot.com)
Duncan is from London. He spends the first few months of his gap year volunteering on a community health project in Ghana, and then spends the rest of his time out travelling with a friend in Western Africa, India, China and Nepal, although his blog does not extend beyond his travels in Africa.

Rich [22] (myspace.com)
Rich is from the South East of England, and goes on to study Japanese at university. Rich's travels include some time spent backpacking in South Africa, Australia and New Zealand, after which he returns home before going to the USA and taking part in a car rally in South America.

Tim [23] (myspace.com)
Tim is a prolific blogger and user of Myspace, and uses his profile to share his screenwriting and film reviews, as well as to record his gap year experience. He also posts a number of video blog posts. Tim works at a ski resort in France during his gap year before studying psychology at university.

Molly [24] (myspace.com)
Molly's gap year is predominantly spent travelling in the USA, along with a period of backpacking in Australia. She blogs on her Myspace profile, and mainly posts photos of sight-seeing and nights out. Molly is from the North West of England, and she goes on to study politics at university.

Nicola [25]
Nicola's blog was initially included in the sample, but after contacting her for an interview, it emerged that she was undertaking her gap year during her second degree, having taking a sabbatical for health reasons. Consequently Nicola's blog was excluded from the final sample.

Andy [26] (Self-hosted using wordpress.org)
Andy sets up his blog on his own website to record his gap year spent teaching in Japan. He is from Yorkshire, and goes on to study Japanese at university. In addition to capturing his gap year experiences, he also presents a 'guide to Japan', and continues to write about the country on his return to the UK.

Helen [27] (livejournal.com)
Helen keeps two LiveJournal blogs, including one set up specifically to record her travels. She also maintains a fundraising and information website. Helen's

gap year involves travel in China and South East Asia. She states that she will be undertaking a placement in Nepal, although her blog does not record this, and her personal blog is set to 'private'. Helen states her intentions to study English literature and theatre on her return.

Adam [28] (blogspot.com)
Adam's gap year is mainly spent backpacking in South America, Australia and South East Asia, although he also spends a couple of weeks volunteering in an animal sanctuary. He sets up a blog especially to record his gap year, but also seems to have a personal blog. He discusses his forthcoming degree, but it is not clear what he will be studying.

Anna [29] (blogspot.com)
Anna undertakes a volunteering placement in South Africa, and then travels with her mother in Australia. Her blog is set up to specifically record her gap year experiences, using a common blog-hosting website, and is a complete record of her travels.

Lucy [30] – INTERVIEWEE (blogspot.com)
Lucy volunteers with a Christian organisation for four months in Ecuador during her gap year, and afterwards spends a few weeks travelling in South America, although she does not blog about this. During the interview she was very self-assured and confident, and discusses how she viewed her gap year as undertaking 'God's Work'. Her aspirations are to travel and volunteer every summer. Lucy is from the South East of England, and went to an independent girls' school. Both of her parents are vicars.

Daniel [31] – INTERVIEWEE (blogspot.com)
Daniel is from the North East of England, and volunteered in a clinic in Botswana during his gap year. The placement was not organised through a gap year provider but arranged through links between his church and one in Botswana. He spent a couple of weeks travelling, including trips to Zambia and South Africa, and spent four months overseas in total. In the interview, Daniel was quietly spoken but keen to share his experiences. He is studying medicine at university. His father is a police officer and his mother is a teaching assistant. Daniel attended a comprehensive school with a sixth-form attached.

Paul [32] (blogspot.com)
Paul writes a blog before the start of his gap year, and he discusses his decision to travel and the preparation for his trip. On his return, he sets up a website to sell photographs taken while he was away, and begins to blog about his travels,

although this is incomplete. Paul volunteered on a conservation project in Uganda, along with some periods of travel.

Hugo [33] (blogspot.com)
Hugo is from Scotland, and backpacks through South East Asia, Australia, New Zealand and the USA during his gap year. He sets up his blog especially to record his gap year. Although he talks about university, it is not clear what he will be studying, but he does mention that he went to 'prep school'.

Kevin [34] – INTERVIEWEE (blogspot.com)
Kevin is from the South West of England and took two years out between school and university, taking two overseas trips. The first involved volunteering at a Christian mission in India for three months. The second, extended trip encompassed independent travel in South East Asia (including volunteering at a youth camp), Australia, New Zealand (including a Bible studies course), Australia, Fiji and the USA. Kevin's father is a part-time GP and also works for his local church; his mother owns a gift shop. He attended a comprehensive secondary school and is studying graphic design at university.

Bryony [35] (livejournal.com)
Bryony has a private blog on LiveJournal, and sets up a special journal to record her gap year. She is from London, and spends her gap year backpacking in Asia. Bryony is the only participant who discusses being from a non-White ethnic background.

Harri [36] (offexploring.com)
Harri is from South East England and undertakes a round-the-world trip during her gap year. She spends some time in Russia, Mongolia (where she briefly volunteers), China, Hong Kong, Australia, New Zealand and the USA. Her boyfriend joins her for some of the trip and he also contributes some blog posts. Harri's blog is hosted on a specialist travel website, and records her overseas trips before and after her gap year, including spending a year the USA on an exchange programme while at university.

Owen [37] – INTERVIEWEE (Self-hosted using ProjectDX.org)
Owen was born in South Africa and his family moved to London when he was eight or nine. He travels in Europe for a few months during his gap year, backpacked in South East Asia for 3½ months then spent some time with his grandfather in South Africa, although his blog only documents his time spent in Asia. It is hosted on his family's website, although he was unable to complete his record due to a lack of internet connection while he was away. Owen is studying law at university and was very confident and career-orientated during

the interview. His parents met as lecturers but his father is now a director at a computer corporation and his mother is now a photographer. Owen attended a grammar school.

Zoe [38] (livejournal.com)

Zoe is from the West Midlands, and sets up her blog on LiveJournal, which she uses to write 'fan fiction' (stories using characters from popular literature, television and films, such as Harry Potter) and for social networking, as well as to record her gap year experiences. Zoe travels in India, South East Asia, Australia, New Zealand, South America and the USA. She volunteers in South America, and works as a camp counsellor in the US.

Sian [39] (livejournal.com)

Sian hosts her blog on LiveJournal, and utilises its social networking functions. She is from the West Midlands, and undertakes her gap year in Central America. Sian travels, teaches English, and studies Spanish during her time out.

Will [40] (blogspot.com)

Will is from the South West of England, and undertakes a mixture of independent travel and volunteering in Central America. He sets up his blog before his gap year to record his fundraising progress and updates this regularly, but the frequency of his posts declines once his trip is underway, although he does upload a number of photos.

References

Adams, M. (2006) 'Hybridizing Habitus and Reflexivity: Towards an Understanding of Contemporary Identity?', *Sociology*, 40 (3): 511–528.

Adkins, L. (2003) 'Reflexivity: Freedom or Habit of Gender?', *Theory, Culture & Society*, 20(6): 21–42.

Adler, J. (1985) 'Youth on the Road: Reflections on the History of Tramping', *Annals of Tourism Research*, 12(3): 335–354.

Allon, F. (2004) 'Backpacker Heaven: The Consumption and Construction of Tourist Spaces and Landscapes in Sydney', *Space and Culture*, 7(1): 49–63.

Ansell, N. (2008) 'Third World Gap Year Projects: Youth Transitions and the Mediation of Risk', *Environment and Planning D: Society and Space*, 26(2): 218–240.

Appadurai, A. (1990) 'Disjuncture and Difference in the Global Cultural Economy', *Theory, Culture and Society*, 7(2): 295–310.

Archer, M.S. (2007) *Making Our Way through the World: Human Reflexivity and Social Mobility*. Cambridge: Cambridge University Press.

Arioso, L. (2010) 'Personal Documents on the Internet: What's New and What's Old', *Journal of Comparative Research in Anthropology and Sociology*, 1(2): 23–38.

Atkinson, W. (2010) *Class, Individualization and Late Modernity: In Search of the Reflexive Worker*. Basingstoke: Palgrave Macmillan.

Bagnoli, A. (2009) 'On an "Introspective Journey": Identities and Travel in Young People's Lives', *European Societies*, 11(3): 325–345.

Ball, S.J. (2003) *Class Strategies and the Education Market: The Middle Class and Social Advantage*. London: Routledge/Falmer.

Banyai, M. and Glover, T.D. (2012) 'Evaluating Research Methods on Travel Blogs', *Journal of Travel Research*, 51(3): 267–277.

Barrett, D. (2010) 'Universities Chief Declares Death of "Gap Year" and Proposes "Bridging Year" Instead', *The Telegraph*, 15 August 2010.

Bassett, E.H. and O'Riordan, K. (2002) 'Ethics of Internet Research: Contesting the Human Subjects Research Model', *Ethics and Information Technology*, 2: 233–247.

Bates, C. (2004) 'Pack up your troubles', *BBC News Magazine*, 12 August 2004. Available online at: http://news.bbc.co.uk/1/hi/magazine/3556332.stm (Accessed 24 September 2013).

Beaulieu, A. and Estalella, A. (2012) 'Rethinking Research Ethics for Mediated Settings', *Information, Communication and Society*, 15(1) 23–42.

Beck, U. (1992) *Risk Society*. London: Sage

Beck, U. (1994) 'The Reinvention of Politics: Towards a Theory of Reflexive Modernization' in *Reflexive Modernization: Politics, Tradition and Aesthetics in the Modern Social Order*, pp. 1–55. Cambridge: Polity.

Beck, U. (2002) 'Cosmopolitan Society and Its Enemies', *Theory, Culture and Society*, 19(1–2): 17–44.

Beck, U. (2006) *Cosmopolitan Vision*. Cambridge: Polity Press.

Beck, U. and Beck-Gernsheim, E. (2002) *Individualization: Institutionalized Individualism and its Social and Political Consequences*. London: Sage.

Beer, D. and Burrows, R. (2007) 'Sociology and, of and in Web 2.0: Some Initial Considerations', *Sociological Research Online*, 12(5). http://www.socresonline.org.uk/12/5/17.html

Benford, R.D., and Snow, D.A. (2000) 'Framing Processes and Social Movements: An Overview and Assessment', *Annual Review of Sociology*, 26: 611–639.

Bennett, R. (2008) 'The Gap Year – A Must for any Self-Respecting Student', *The Times*, 13 August 2008.

Bennett, T., Savage, M., Silva, E.B., Warde, A., Gayo-Cal, M., and Wright, D. (2009) *Culture, Class, Distinction*. Abingdon: Routledge.

Billig, M. (1995) *Banal Nationalism*. London: Sage.

Binnie, J. and Skeggs, B. (2004) 'Cosmopolitan Knowledge and the Production and Consumption of Sexualized Space: Manchester's Gay Village', *The Sociological Review*, 52(1): 39–61.

Birdwell, J. (2011) *This is the Big Society Without Borders': Service International*. London: Demos.

Blank, G. (2008) 'Online Research Methods and Social Theory' in N. Fielding, R.M. Lee and G. Blank (eds) *The SAGE Handbook of Online Research Methods*, pp. 537–549. London: Sage

Blood, R. (2004) 'How Blogging Software Reshaped the Online Community' *Communications of the ACM December 2004*. Available online at: http://www.rebeccablood.net/essays/blog_software.html (Accessed 24 September 2013).

Bohman, J. (1999) 'Practical Reason and Cultural Constraint: Agency in Bourdieu's Theory of Practice' in R. Shusterman (ed.) *Bourdieu: A Critical Reader*, pp. 129–152. Oxford: Blackwell

Boorstin, D.J. (1961) *The Image: A Guide to Pseudo-Events in America*. New York: Harper & Row.

Bosangit, C., Dulnuan, J. and Mena, M. (2012) 'Using Travel Blogs to Examine the Postconsumption Behavior of Tourists', *Journal of Vacation Marketing*, 18(3): 207–219.

Bottero, W. (2010) 'Intersubjectivity and Bourdieusian Approaches to "Identity"', *Cultural Sociology*, 4(1): 3–22.

Bourdieu, P. (1973) 'Cultural Reproduction and Social Reproduction' in R. Brown (ed.) *Knowledge, Education, and Cultural Change: Papers in the Sociology of Education*, pp. 71–112. London: Tavistock.

Bourdieu, P. (1977) *Outline of a Theory of Practice*. Cambridge: Cambridge University Press.

Bourdieu, P. (1984) *Distinction: A Social Critique of the Judgement of Taste*. Cambridge, Massachusetts: Harvard University Press.

Bourdieu, P. (1990) *The Logic of Practice*. Cambridge: Polity Press.

Bourdieu, P. (1997[1986]), 'The forms of capital' in A.H. Halsey, H. Lauder, P. Brown and A.S. Wells (eds) *Education: Culture: Economy and Society*, pp. 46–55. Oxford: Oxford University Press.

Bourdieu, P. and Passeron, J.C. (1977) *Reproduction in Education, Society and Culture*. London: Sage.

Bourdieu, P. and Wacquant, L. (1992) *An Invitation to Reflexive Sociology*. Cambridge: Polity Press.

Boyle, D. (2000) *The Beach* [Film]. USA: 20th Century Fox.

Bradley, H. and Ingram, N. (2013) 'Banking on the Future: Choices, Aspirations and Hardship in Working-Class Student Experience' in W. Atkinson, S. Roberts and M. Savage (eds) *Class Inequality in Austerity Britain: Power, Difference and Suffering*. Basingstoke: Palgrave Macmillan.

Bradt, H. (1995) Better to Travel Cheaply? *The Independent on Sunday Magazine*, 12 February 1995.

British Sociological Association (2002) *Statement of Ethical Practice for the British Sociological Association*. Available online at: http://www.britsoc.co.uk/about/equality/statement-of-ethical-practice.aspx (Accessed 24 September 2013).

Brook, S (2008) 'Cultural capital and cultural diversity: some problems in Ghassan Hage's account of cosmopolitan multiculturalism', *Journal of Australian Studies*, 32 (4): 509–520.

Brooks, R. and Waters, J (2009) 'A Second Chance at "Success": UK Students and Global Circuits of Higher Education', *Sociology*, 43(6): 1085–1102.

Brooks, R. and Waters, J. (2011) *Student Mobilities, Migration and the Internationalization of Higher Education*. Basingstoke: Palgrave Macmillan.

Brown, P. (1995) 'Cultural Capital and Social Exclusion: Some Observations on Recent Trends in Education, Employment and the Labour Market', *Work Employment and Society*, 9(1): 29–51.

Brown, P. and Hesketh, A. (2004) *The Mismanagement of Talent: Employability and Jobs in the Knowledge Economy*. Oxford: Oxford University Press.

Brown, P., Hesketh, A., and Williams, S. (2003) 'Employability in a Knowledge-Driven Economy', *Journal of Education and Work*, 16(2): 107–126.

Bruckman, A. (2002) 'Studying the Amateur Artist: A Perspective on Disguising Data Collected in Human Subjects Research on the Internet', *Ethics and Information Technology*, 4(3): 217–231.

Bruns, A. and Jacobs, J. (2006) 'Introduction' in A. Bruns and J. Jacobs (eds) *Uses of Blogs*. New York: Peter Lang.

Bryson, B. (1996) '"Anything But Heavy Metal": Symbolic Exclusion and Musical Dislikes', *American Sociological Review*, 61(5): 884–899.

Butcher, J. (2003) *The Moralisation of Tourism*. London: Routledge.

Butcher, J. and Smith, P. (2010) '"Making a Difference": Volunteer Tourism and Development', *Tourism Recreation Research*, 35(1): 27–36.

Calhoun, C. (1993) 'Habitus, Field and Capital: The Question of Historical Specificity' in C. Calhoun, E. LiPuma and M. Postone (eds) *Bourdieu: Critical Perspectives*, pp. 61–88. Cambridge: Polity Press.

Calhoun, C. (2002) 'The Class Consciousness of Frequent Travellers: Towards a Critique of Actually Existing Cosmopolitanism' in S. Vertovec and R. Cohen (eds) *Conceiving Cosmopolitanism: Theory, Context and Practice*, pp. 56–109. Oxford: Oxford University Press.

Chan, T.W. and Goldthorpe, J.H. (2007) 'Social Stratification and Cultural Consumption: Music in England', *European Sociological Review*, 23(1): 1–19.

Cheah, P. (2006) 'Cosmopolitanism', *Theory, Culture and Society*, 23(2–3): 486–496.

City and Guilds (2013) *Profile of Achievement*. Available online at: http://www. cityandguilds.com/Courses-and-Qualifications/skills-for-work-and-life/ employability-personal-and-social-development/3791-profile-of-achievement (Accessed 24 September 2013).

Cohen, E. (1973) 'Nomads from Affluence: Notes on the Phenomenon of Drifter-Tourism', *International Journal of Comparative Sociology*, 14(1–2): 89–103.

Cohen, E. (1989) '"Primitive and Remote": Hill Tribe Trekking in Thailand', *Annals of Tourism Research*, 16(1): 30–61.

Cohen, E. (2004) 'Backpacking: Diversity and Change', in G. Richards and J. Wilson (eds) *The Global Nomad: Backpacker Travel in Theory and Practice*, pp. 43–59. Clevedon: Channel View Publications.

Cohen, S.A. (2011) 'Lifestyle Travellers: Backpacking as a Way of Life', *Annals of Tourism Research*, 38(4): 1535–1555.

Coppola, S. (2003) *Lost in Translation* [Film] USA: Focus Features.

Craik, J. (1997) 'The Culture of Tourism', in C. Rojek and J. Urry (eds) *Touring Cultures: Transformations of Travel and Theory*, pp. 113–136. London: Routledge.

Crawford, C. and Cribb, J. (2012) *Gap Year Takers: Uptake, Trends and Long Term Outcomes*. Department for Education Research Report No. 252.

Cremin, C. (2007) 'Living and Really Living: The Gap Year and the Commodification of the Contingent', *ephemera*, 7(4): 526–542.

Crossley, N. (2001) 'The phenomenological habitus and its construction', *Theory and Society*, 30(1): 81–120.

Davies, C. (2008) 'Hate Mail Hell of a Gap-Year Blogger', *The Guardian*, 17 February 2008.

Delanty, G. (2011) 'Cultural Diversity, Democracy and the Prospects of Cosmopolitanism: A Theory of Cultural Encounters', *The British Journal of Sociology*, 62(4): 633–656.

Department for Business Innovation and Skills (2011) *Participation Rates in Higher Education: Academic Years 2006/2007 – 2009/2010* (Provisional), 31 March 2013. Available online at: https://www.gov.uk/government/uploads/system/uploads/attachment_data/file/16208/participation_rates_in_he_2009-10.pdf (Accessed 24 September 2013).

Department for Business Innovation and Skills (2013) *Participation Rates in Higher Education: Academic Years 2006/7 – 2011/2012* (Provisional), 24 April 2013. Available online at: https://www.gov.uk/government/uploads/system/uploads/attachment_data/file/192188/13-p140-HEIPR_PUBLICATION_2011-12.pdf (Accessed 24 September 2013).

Desforges, L. (1998) '"Checking out the Planet": Global Representations/Local Identities and Youth Travel', in T. Skelton and G. Valentine (eds) *Cool Places: Geographies of Youth Travel*, pp. 175–192. London: Routledge.

Desforges, L. (2000) 'Traveling the World: Identity and Travel Biography', *Annals of Tourism Research*, 27(4): 926–945.

Devine, F. (2004) *Class Practices: How Parents Help Their Children Get Good Jobs*. Cambridge: Cambridge University Press.

Directgov (2012) *Planning a Gap Year*. Available online at: http://www.direct.gov.uk/en/YoungPeople/Workandcareers/Workexperienceandvolunteering/DG_066213 (Accessed 30 July 2012)

Donati, P.R. (1992) 'Political Discourse Analysis' in Mario Diani and Ron Eyerman (eds) *Studying Collective Action*, pp. 136–167. London: Sage.

Du Gay, P. (1996) *Consumption and Identity at Work*. London: Sage.

Duffy, R. (2004) 'Ecotourists on the Beach' in M. Sheller and J. Urry (eds) *Tourism Mobilities: Places to Play, Places in Play*, pp. 32–43. London: Routledge

Duncan, T. (2004) 'Livin' the Dream: Working and Playing in a Ski Resort', *Tourism and Leisure IGU Pre-Meeting*, Loch Lomond, August 13–15, 2004.

Duruz, J. (2004) 'Adventure and Belonging: An Appetite for Markets', *Space and Culture*, 7(4): 427–445.

Dutton, W.H. and Blank, G. (2011) *Next Generation Users: The Internet in Britain 2011*. Oxford Internet Institute, University of Oxford.

Dutton, W.H., Helsper, E.J., and Gerber, M.M. (2009) *The Internet in Britain: 2009*. Oxford Internet Institute, University of Oxford.

Elliott, J. (2005) *Using Narrative in Social Research: Qualitative and Quantitative Approaches*. London: Sage

Elsrud, T. (2001) 'Risk Creation in Traveling: Backpacker Adventure Narration', *Annals of Tourism Research*, 28(3): 597–617.

Enoch, Y. and Grossman, R. (2010) 'Blogs of Israeli and Danish Backpackers to India', *Annals of Tourism Research*, 37(2): 520–36.

Eynon, R., Fry, J. and Schroeder, R. (2008) 'The Ethics of Internet Research', in N. Fielding, R.M. Lee and G. Blank (eds) *The SAGE Handbook of Online Research Methods*, pp. 23–41. London: Sage.

Feifer, N. (1985) *Going Places*. London: Macmillan.

Fielden, J. (2007) *Global Horizons for UK Students: A Guide for Universities*. London: The Council for Industry and Higher Education.

Fisher, K. (1997) 'Locating Frames in the Discursive Universe', *Sociological Research Online*, 2(3). http://www.socresonline.org.uk/2/3/4.html

Footprint Travel (2013) 'Vietnam Trekking'. Available online at: http://www.footprint-adventures.co.uk/countrypackage-list.php?cat=85&country=52&id=619 (Accessed 25 September 2013).

Ford, L. (2005) 'The Year of Living Adventurously', *The Guardian*, 18 August 2005.

Ford, S.M. (2011) 'Reconceptualising the public/private distinction in the age of information technology', *Information, Communication and Society*, 14(4): 550–567.

Foucault, M (1988) 'Technologies of the Self' in *Technologies of the Self: Seminar with Michel Foucault*, L. Martin, H. Gutman and P. Hutton (eds) pp. 9–15. London: Tavistock.

Frankel, M. and Siang, S. (1999) 'Ethical and Legal Aspects of Human Subjects Research on the Internet', *American Association for the Advancement of Science Workshop Report*. Available online at: http://shr.aaas.org/projects/human_subjects/cyberspace/report.pdf (Accessed 24 September 2013).

Furlong, A. and Cartmel, F. (1997) *Young People and Social Change*. Buckingham: Open University Press.

Galani-Moutafi, V. (2000) 'The Self and the Other: Traveler, Ethnographer, Tourist', *Annals of Tourism Research*, 27(1): 203–224.

Garland, A. (1997) *The Beach*. Harmondsworth: Penguin.

Gapyear.com (2013) 'What is a Gap Year?' Available online at: http://www.gapyear.com/articles/90431/what-is-a-gap-year (Accessed 24 September 2013).

Germann Molz, J. (2006) 'Cosmopolitan Bodies: Fit to Travel and Travelling to Fit', *Body and Society*, 12(3): 1–21.

Germann Molz, J. (2007) 'Eating Difference: The Cosmopolitan Mobilities of Culinary Tourism', *Space and Culture*, 10(1): 77–93.

Germann Molz, J. (2012a) 'Cosmopolitanism and Consumption' in M. Rovisco and M. Nowicka (eds) *The Ashgate Research Companion to Cosmopolitanism*, pp. 33–51. Farnham: Ashgate

Germann Molz, J. (2012b) *Travel Connections Tourism, Technology and Togetherness in a Mobile World*. Abingdon: Routledge.

Giddens, A. (1991) *Modernity and Self-Identity: Self and Society in the Late Modern Age*. Cambridge: Polity Press

Goffman, E. (1959) *The Presentation of Self in Everyday Life*. Garden City, NY: Doubleday.

Goffman, E. (1974) *Frame Analysis: An Essay on the Organization of Experience* Boston: Northeastern University Press

Goldthorpe, J.H. (2007) '"Cultural Capital": Some Critical Observations', *Sociologica [Online]*, 2/2007, doi: 10.2383/24755.

Gordon, S. (2009). 'A-level results: top ten gap year ideas', *The Daily Mail*, 20 August 2009.

Graburn, N.H.H. (1983) 'The Anthropology of Tourism', *Annals of Tourism Research*, 10(1): 9–33.

Griffin, T. (2004) *A Discourse Analysis of UK Sourced Gap Year Overseas Projects.* M.A. thesis, University of West England.

Griffiths, T. (2009) 'Constructive Gap Years Help Students Stand Out to Employers and Universities', *The Independent*, 17 August 2009.

The Guardian (2008) 'Max, 19, Hits the Road' *The Guardian*, 14 February 2008. Available online at: http://www.guardian.co.uk/travel/blog/2008/feb/14/skinsblog (Accessed 24 September 2013).

Guttentag, D.A. (2009) 'The Possible Negative Impacts of Volunteer Tourism', *International Journal of Tourism Research*, 11(6): 537–551.

Hage, G. (1997) 'At Home in the Entrails of the West: Multiculturalism, Ethnic Food and Migrant Home-Building'. In H. Grace, G. Hage, L. Johnson, J. Langsworth and M. Symonds (eds) *Home/world: Space, Community and Marginality in Sydney's West*, pp. 99–153. Annandale: Pluto.

Hage, G. (1998) *White Nation: Fantasies of White Supremacy in a Multicultural Society*, Annandale, N.S.W.: Pluto Press.

Halsey, A.H., Heath, A.F. and Ridge, J.M. (1980) *Origins and Destinations: Family, Class and Education in Modern Britain*. Oxford: Oxford University Press

Hannerz, U. (1990) 'Cosmopolitans and Locals in World Culture' in M. Featherstone (ed.) *Global Culture: Nationalism, Globalization and Modernity*, pp. 237–252. London: Sage.

Haverig, A. and Roberts, S. (2011) 'The New Zealand OE as Governance Through Freedom: Rethinking "The Apex of Freedom"', *Journal of Youth Studies*, 14(5): 587–603.

Heaphy, B. (2007) *Late Modernity and Social Change: Reconstructing Social and Personal Life*. London: Routledge

Heath, S. (2007) 'Widening the Gap: Pre-University Gap Years and the "Economy of Experience"', *British Journal of Sociology of Education*, 28(1): 89–103.

Herring, S.C., Scheidt, L.A., Bonus, S. and Wright, E. (2004) 'Bridging the Gap: A Genre Analysis of Weblogs', *Proceedings of the 37th Annual Hawaii International Conference on System Sciences*. 5–8 January 2004. Big Island, Hawaii, USA.

Hinchman, L.P. and Hinchman, S.K. (1997). 'Introduction' in L.P. Hinchman and S.K. Hinchman (eds) *Memory, Identity, Community: The Idea of Narrative in the Human Sciences*, pp.xiii–xxxii. New York: SUNY Press.

Hine, C. (2011) 'Internet Research and Unobtrusive Methods', *Social Research Update*, 61, University of Surrey.

Hoggart, S., and Monk, E. (2006) *Don't Tell Mum: Hair-raising Messages Home from Gap-Year Travellers*. London: Atlantic Books

Holdsworth, C. and Quinn, J. (2012) 'The Epistemological Challenge of Higher Education Student Volunteering: "Reproductive" or "Deconstructive" Volunteering?', *Antipode*, 44(2): 386–405.

Holt, D. (1997) 'Distinction in America? Recovering Bourdieu's Theory of Tastes from its Critics', *Poetics* 25: 93–120.

hooks, b. (1992) *Black Looks: Race and Representation*. Boston: South End Press.

Hookway, N. (2008) '"Entering the blogosphere": Some Strategies for Using Blogs in Social Research' *Qualitative Research*, 8(1): 91–113.

Hudson, J.M. and Bruckman, A. (2005) 'Using Empirical Data to Reason about Internet Research Ethics', in H. Gellersen et al. (eds) *ECSCW 2005: Proceedings of the Ninth European Confernece on Computer-Supported Cooperative Work*, 18–22 September 2005. Paris, France.

Huxley, L. (2004) 'Western Backpackers and the Global Experience', *Tourism, Culture and Communication* 5(1): 37–44.

ICS (2013) 'How it Works', *International Citizen Service*. Available online at: http://www.volunteerics.org/how-it-works (Accessed 24 September 2013).

Inkson, K., and Myers, B.A. (2003) '"The big OE": Self-Directed Travel and Career Development', *Career Development International*, 8(4): 170–181.

Jenkins, R. (2002) *Pierre Bourdieu*. London: Routledge.

Johan, N. (2009) 'Gap Year Travel: Youth Transition or Youth Transformation?' in R. Brooks (ed.) *Transitions From Education to Work: New Perspectives from Europe and Beyond*, Basingstoke: Palgrave Macmillan.

Jones, A. (2004) *Review of Gap Year Provision*, Research Report No 555, Department for Education and Skills.

Jones, A. (2005) 'Assessing International Youth Service Programmes in two Low Income Countries', *Voluntary Action: The Journal of the Institute for Volunteering Research*, 7(2): 87–100.

Jones, C. and Leshkowich, A.M. (2003) 'The globalization of Asian dress: re-orienting fashion or re-orientalizing Asia?', in *Re-Orienting Fashion: The Globalization of Asian Dress*, S.A. Niessen, A.M. Leshkowich and C. Jones (eds.) Oxford: Berg, pp. 1–48.

Karlsson, L. (2006) 'The Diary Weblog and the Travelling Tales of Diasporic Tourists', *Journal of Intercultural Studies*, 27(3): 299–312.

Kaya Volunteer (2013) 'Community Building Projects for Rural Minority Groups'. Available online at: http://www.kayavolunteer.com/gapyear/project/7/Community-Building-Projects-for-Rural-Minority-Groups.html (Accessed 25 September 2013).

Kelle, U. (1997) 'Theory Building in Qualitative Research and Computer Programs for the Management of Textual Data', *Sociological Research Online*, 2(2), http://socresonline.org.uk/2/2/1.html.

Kenco (2006). *Kenco Coffee Range: Kenco Decaff Gap Year Student/Kenco Instant Coffee Beans Argument/Kenco Pure Coffee Exam* (30 seconds). Television/cinema advertisements. Screened 2006–2007.

Kendall, G., Woodward, I. and Skrbis, Z. (2009) *The Sociology of Cosmopolitanism*. Basingstoke: Palgrave Macmillan.

King, A. (Andrew) (2011) 'Minding the gap? Young people's accounts of taking a Gap Year as a form of identity work in higher education', *Journal of Youth Studies*, 14(3): 341–357.

King, A. (Anthony) (2000) 'Thinking with Bourdieu against Bourdieu: A "Practical" Critique of the Habitus', *Sociological Theory*, 18(3): 417–433.

Lamont, M. (1992). *Money, Morals and Manners: The Culture of the French and the American Upper-Middle Class*. Chicago: University of Chicago Press.

Lamont, M. and Aksartova, S. (2002) 'Ordinary Cosmopolitanisms: Strategies for Bridging Racial Boundaries amongst Working-Class Men', *Theory, Culture and Society*, 19(4): 1–25.

Lamont, M. and Lareau, A. (1988) 'Cultural Capital: Allusions, Gaps and Glissandos in Recent Theoretical Developments', *Sociological Theory*, 6(2): 153–168.

Lash, S. (1993) 'Pierre Bourdieu: Cultural Economy and Social Change', in C. Calhoun, E. LiPuma and M. Postone (eds) *Bourdieu: Critical Perspectives*, pp. 193–212. Cambridge: Polity Press.

Law, K. (2011) 'Matt Lacey – Man of the Yah', *London Evening Standard*, 14 October 2011.

Lees, R.M. (2000) *Unobtrusive Methods in Social Research*. Buckingham: Oxford University Press.

Li, D., and Walejko, G. (2008) 'Splogs and Abandoned Blogs: The Perils of Sampling Bloggers and Their Blogs', *Information, Communication and Society*, 11(2): 279–296.

Loker-Murphy, L. and Pearce, P.L. (1995) 'Young Budget Travelers: Backpackers in Australia', *Annals of Tourism Research*, 22(4): 819–843.

Lomborg, S. (2013) 'Personal Internet Archives and Ethics', *Research Ethics*, 9(1): 20–31.

Lonely Planet (2013) 'The Lonely Planet Story', *Lonely Planet.com*. Available online at: http://www.lonelyplanet.com/about/ (Accessed 24 September 2013).

Lovell, T (2000) 'Thinking Feminism with and against Bourdieu', *Feminist Theory*, 1(1): 11.

Lynch, M. (2011) 'Blogging for beauty? A critical analysis of Operation Beautiful', *Women's Studies International Forum*, 34(6): 582–592.

Lyons, K., Hanley, J., Wearing, S. and Neil, J. 2012 'Gap Year Volunteer Tourism: Myths of Global Citizenship?', *Annals of Tourism Research*, 39(1): 361 – 378.

MacCannell, D. (1992) *Empty Meeting Grounds: The Tourist Papers*. London: Routledge.

MacCannell, D. (1999) *The Tourist: A New Theory of the Leisure Class*. Berkeley: University of California Press.

Markham, A.N. and Buchanan, E.A. and the AoIR ethics working committee (2012) *Ethical decision-making and Internet Research: Recommendations from the AoIR Ethics Working Committee*. Available online at: http://aoir.org/reports/ethics2.pdf (Accessed 24 September 2013).

Mason, J. (2002) *Qualitative Researching*. London: Sage.

McCabe, S. and Foster, C. (2006) 'The Role and Function of Narrative in Tourist Interaction', *Journal of Tourism and Cultural Change*, 4(3): 194–215.

McGehee, N. (2012) 'Oppression, Emancipation, and Volunteer Tourism: Research Propositions', *Annals of Tourism Research*, 39(1): 84–107.

McNay, L. (1999) 'Gender, Habitus and the Field: Pierre Bourdieu and the Limits of Reflexivity', *Theory Culture and Society*, 16(1): 95–117

McNay, L. (2001) 'Meditations on Pascalian Meditations', *Economy and Society*, 30: 139–154.

Miller, D. (2011) *Tales from Facebook*. Cambridge: Polity Press

Mintel (2005) 'Gap Year Travel: International' *Travel and Tourism Analyst no 12*. London: Mintel.

Mitchell, K. (2003) 'Educating the National Citizen in Neo-Liberal Times: From the Multicultural Self to the Strategic Cosmopolitan', *Transactions of the Institute of British Geographers*, 28:387–403.

Mitra, A., and Cohen, E. (1999) 'Analyzing the Web: Directions and Challenges', in S. Jones (ed.) *Doing Internet Research: Critical Issues and Methods for Examining the Net*, pp. 179–202. Thousand Oaks: Sage.

Moore, J. (2013) 'The great escape: our guide to gap year travel', *The Independent*, 16 August 2013.

Mowforth, M., and Munt, I. (1998) *Tourism and Sustainability: New Tourism in the Third World*. London: Routledge.

Munt, I (1994) 'The "Other" Postmodern Tourism: Culture, Travel and the New Middle Classes', *Theory Culture and Society* 11(3): 101–123.

Murphy-Lejeune, C. (2002) *Student Mobility and Narrative in Europe: The New Strangers*. London: Routledge.

Nave, K. (2013) 'Gap Year Kids are Not the New Face of the Imperial Raj', *The Times*, 29 June 2013.

Nowicka, M. and Rovisco, M. (2009) 'Introduction: Making Sense of Cosmopolitanism' in M. Nowicka and M. Rovisco (eds) *Cosmopolitanism in Practice*. Farnham: Ashgate.

Nussbaum, M. (1996) *For Love of Country?: Debating the Limits of Patriotism.* Boston: Beacon Press.

O'Reilly, C.C. (2006) 'From Drifter to Gap Year Tourist: Mainstreaming Backpacker Travel', *Annals of Tourism Research* 33(4): 998–1017.

Papi, D. (2013) 'Viewpoint: Is Gap Year Volunteering a Bad Thing?' *BBC News Magazine.* Available online at: http://www.bbc.co.uk/news/magazine-22294205. (Accessed 24 September 2013).

Pauwels, L. (2006) 'Ethics of Online (Visual) Research', *Visual Anthropology,* 19(3–4): 365–369.

Peterson, R.A. (1992) 'Understanding Audience Segmentation: From Elite and Mass to Omnivore and Univore', *Poetics* 21(4): 243 – 58.

Peterson, R.A. and Kern, R.M. (1996) 'Changing Highbrow Taste: From Snob to Omnivore', *American Sociological Review,* 61(5): 900 – 909.

Peterson, R.A. and Simkus, A. (1992) `How Musical Tastes Mark Occupational Status Groups ', in M. Lamont and M. Fournier (eds) *Cultivating Differences,* pp. 152–186. Chicago: University of Chicago Press.

Philpott, V. (2013) 'A Level Results: "1000s" now Debating Going on a Gap Year', *gapyear.com,* 15 August 2013. Available online at: http://www.gapyear. com/news/206115/a-level-results-1000s-now-debating-going-on-a-gap-year (Accessed 24 September 2013).

Polkinghorne, D.E. (1995) 'Narrative Configuration in Qualitative Analysis', in J.A. Hatch, and R. Wisniewski (eds), *Life History and Narrative,* pp. 5–23. London: Falmer Press

Price, J. (2008) 'What Kind of Journey Suits You?', *The Guardian,* 16 August 2008.

Rapport, N. (1995) 'Migrant Selves and Stereotypes' in S. Pile and N. Thrift (eds) *Mapping the Subject: Geographies of Cultural Transformation,* pp. 246–263. London: Routledge.

Raymond, E.M. and Hall, C.M. (2008) 'The Development of Cross-Cultural (Mis)Understanding Through Volunteer Tourism', *Journal of Sustainable Tourism,* 16(5): 530–543.

Reay, D. (2004) 'Education and Cultural Capital: The Implications of Changing Trends In Education Policies', *Cultural Trends,* 13(2): 73–86.

Reay, D., David, M. and Ball, S. (2005) *Degrees of Choice: Social Class, Race and Gender in Higher Education.* London: Trentham Books.

Reed, W. (2012) 'Gap Year: Why take a gap year?', *Prospects.* Available online at: http://www.prospects.ac.uk/gap_year_why_take_a_gap_year.htm (Accessed 24 September 2013).

Responsible Travel (2013) 'Karen homestay, Thailand'. Available online at: http://www.responsibletravel.com/holiday/1364/karen-homestay-thailand (Accessed 25 September 2013).

Rettberg, J.W. (2008) *Blogging.* Cambridge: Polity Press.

Richards, G. and Wilson, J. (2004) 'Widening Perspectives in Backpacker Research' in G. Richards and J. Wilson (eds) *The Global Nomad: Backpacker Travel in Theory and Practice*, pp. 253–279. Clevedon: Channel View Publications.

Riley, P.J. (1988) 'Road Culture of International Long-Term Budget Travelers', *Annals of Tourism Research*, 15(3): 313–328

Ritzer, G. and Liska, A. (1997) '"McDisneyization" and "Post-tourism": Complementary Perspectives on Contemporary Tourism', in C. Rojek and J. Urry (eds) *Touring Cultures: Transformations of Travel and Theory*, pp. 96–112. London: Routledge

Rizvi, F. (2009) 'Towards Cosmopolitan Learning', *Discourse: Studies in the Cultural Politics of Education*, 30(3): 253–268.

Robbins, B. (1998) 'Actually Existing Cosmopolitanism' in B. Robbins and P. Cheah (eds) *Cosmopolitics*, pp. 1–19. Minneapolis: University of Minnesota Press.

Robertson, R. (1992) *Globalization: Social Theory and Global Culture*. London: Sage.

Rojek, C. (1997) 'Indexing, Dragging and the Social Construction of Tourist Sights', in C. Rojek and J. Urry (eds) *Touring Cultures: Transformations of Travel and Theory*, pp. 52–74. London: Routledge.

Rose, N. (1999) *Governing the Soul: The Shaping of the Private Self* (2nd edn). London: Free Association Books.

Rovisco, M. and Nowicka, M. (2012) 'Introduction' in M. Rovisco and M. Nowicka (eds) *The Ashgate Research Companion to Cosmopolitanism*, pp. 1–14. Farnham: Ashgate

Rowley, T. (2013) 'Goodbye "gap yah", hello good works', *The Telegraph*, 27 July 2013.

Said, E. (1978) *Orientalism: Western Concepts of the Orient*. Harmondsworth: Penguin.

Savage, M. (2000) *Class Analysis and Social Transformation*. Buckingham: Open University Press.

Savage, M., Bagnall, G., and Longhurst, B.J. (2005) *Globalisation and Belonging*. London: Sage.

Sayer, A. (2005a) *The Moral Significance of Class*. Cambridge: Cambridge University Press.

Sayer, A. (2005b) 'Class, Moral Worth and Recognition', *Sociology*, 39(5): 947–963.

Scheff, T.J. (2005) 'The Structure of Context: Deciphering "Frame Analysis"', *Sociological Theory*, 23(4): 368–385.

Scott, J. (1990) *A Matter of Record: Documentary Sources in Social Research*. Cambridge: Polity Press.

Shepherd, J. (2008) 'Hands Up if You Want to be Useful', *The Guardian*, 16 August 2008.

Sherifi, M. (2013) 'The History of the Gap Year' Available online at: http://www.gapyear.com/articles/175601/the-history-of-the-gap-year (Accessed 24 September 2013).

Silverman, D. (2001) *Interpreting Qualitative Data: Methods for Analysing Talk, Text and Interaction (2nd ed.)*. London: Sage.

Simmel, G. (1971) *On Individuality and Social Forms*. Chicago: The University of Chicago Press.

Simpson, K. (2004) 'Doing Development: The Gap Year, Volunteer-Tourists and a Popular Practice of Development', *Journal of International Development*, 16: 681–692.

Simpson, K. (2005a) 'Broad Horizons: Geographies and Pedagogies of the Gap Year', PhD thesis, University of Newcastle-upon-Tyne.

Simpson, K. (2005b). 'Dropping Out or Signing Up? The Professionalisation of Youth Travel', *Antipode*, 37(3): 447–469.

Sin, H.L. (2009) 'Volunteer Tourism: "Involve me and I will learn"?', *Annals of Tourism Research*, 36(3): 480–501.

Skeggs, B. (2004a) *Class, Self, Culture*. London: Routledge.

Skeggs, B. (2004b) 'Exchange, Value and Affect: Bourdieu and "the self"', *The Sociological Review*, 52:2: 75–95.

Skey, M. (2012) 'We Need to Talk about Cosmopolitanism: The Challenge of Studying Openness towards Other People', *Cultural Sociology*, 6(4): 471–487.

Sklair, L. (2001) *The Transnational Capitalist Class*. Oxford: Blackwell.

Skrbis, Z. and Woodward, I. (2007) 'The Ambivalence of Ordinary Cosmopolitanism: Investigating the Limits of Cosmopolitan Openness', *The Sociological Review*, 55(4): 730–747.

Snee, H. (2013) 'Making Ethical Decisions in an Online context: Reflections on Using Blogs to Explore Narratives of Experience', *Methodological Issues Online*, 8(2): 52–67.

Snow, D.A., Rochford, E.B., Worden, S.K., and Benford, R.D. (1986) 'Frame Alignment Processes, Micromobilization and Movement Participation', *American Sociological Review*, 51(4): 464–481.

Sugden, J. (2009) 'Gap-Year Graduates to be Funded by Taxpayers', *The Times*, 1 August 2009.

Sutcliffe, W. (1997). *Are You Experienced?* London: Penguin.

Swain, M. (2009) 'The Cosmopolitan Hope of Tourism: Critical Action and Worldmaking Vistas', *Tourism Geographies*, 11(4): 505–525.

Sweetman, P. (2003) 'Twenty-First Century Dis-Ease? Habitual Reflexivity or the Reflexive Habitus', *The Sociological Review*, 51(4): 528–549.

Swidler, A. (1986) 'Culture in Action', *American Sociological Review*, 51(2): 273–286.

Swidler, A. (1995) 'Cultural Power and Social Movements' in H. Johnston and B. Klandermans (eds) *Social Movements and Culture*, pp. 25–40. London: UCL Press.

Szerszynski, B. and Urry, J. (2002) 'Cultures of cosmopolitanism', *The Sociological Review*, 50(4) 461–481.

Szerszynski, B. and Urry, J. (2006) 'Visuality, Mobility and the Cosmopolitan: Inhabiting the World from Afar', *The British Journal of Sociology*, 57(1): 113–131.

Thorne, R. (2013) 'Gap Year: An Extra Year to Develop Talents', *The Independent*, 19 August 2013.

Tickell, A. (2001) 'Footprints on *The Beach*: Traces of Colonial Adventure in Narratives of Independent Tourism', *Postcolonial Studies*, 4(1): 39–54.

Tobin, L. (2009) 'Student Gap Years – The Advisers Weigh In', *The Guardian*, 22 August 2009.

Triandafyllidou, A. (1995) *Second Project Report: A Frame Analysis of Institutional Discourse*. Sustainable Development Research Project, Centre for European Social Research, Cork, Ireland.

Turner, V. (1974) *The Ritual Process*. Harmondsworth: Penguin.

UCAS (2013) *Analysis Tables: Deferring for one year* Available online at: http://www.ucas.com/data-analysis/data-resources/data-tables/deferring-one-year (Accessed 24 September 2013).

Urry, J. (1995) *Consuming Places* London: Routledge.

Urry, J. (2002) *The Tourist Gaze: Leisure and Travel in Contemporary Societies (2nd ed.)*. London: Sage.

van Eijck, K. (2000) 'Richard A. Peterson and the Culture of Consumption', *Poetics* 28(2–3): 207–224.

Vertovec, S. and Cohen, R. (2002) 'Introduction: Conceiving Cosmopolitanism' in S. Vertovec and R. Cohen (eds) *Conceiving Cosmopolitanism: Theory, Context and Practice*, pp. 1–22. Oxford: Oxford University Press.

Wakeford, N. and Cohen, K. (2008) 'Fieldnotes in Public: Using Blogs for Research', in N. Fielding, R.M. Lee & G. Blank (eds) *The SAGE Handbook of Online Research Methods*, pp. 307–326. London: Sage.

Wang, N. (2000) *Tourism and Modernity: A Sociological Analysis*. Oxford: Elsevier Science.

Ward, L (2007) 'You're Better off Backpacking – VSO Warns about Perils of "Voluntourism"', *The Guardian*, 14 August 2007.

Warde, A., Martens, L. and Olsen, W. (1999) 'Consumption and the Problem of Variety: Cultural Omnivorousness, Social Distinction, and Dining Out', *Sociology*, 33(1): 105–127.

Warde, A., Wright, D. and Gayo-Cal, M. (2007) 'Understanding Cultural Omnivorousness: Or, the Myth of the Cultural Omnivore', *Cultural Sociology*, 1(2): 143–164.

Wearing, S. (2001) *Volunteer Tourism: Experiences That Make a Difference.* Wallingford: CABI Publishing.

Weenink, D. (2007) 'Cosmopolitan and Established Resources of Power in the Education Arena', *International Sociology*, 22(4): 492–516.

Weenink, D. (2008) 'Cosmopolitanism as a Form of Capital: Parents Preparing their Children for a Globalizing World', *Sociology*, 42(6): 1089–1106.

Welk, P. (2004) 'The Beaten Track: Anti-Tourism as an Element of Backpacker Identity Construction', in G. Richards and J. Wilson (eds) *The Global Nomad: Backpacker Travel in Theory and Practice*, pp. 77–91. Clevedon: Channel View Publications.

Werbner, P. (1999) 'Global Pathways: Working Class Cosmopolitans and the Creation of Transnational Ethnic Worlds', *Social Anthropology*, 7(1): 17–35.

Wilkinson, D. and Thelwall, M. (2011) 'Researching Personal Information on the Public Web: Methods and Ethics', *Social Science Computer Review*, 29(4) 387–401.

Year Out Group (2013) 'Benefits of Gapping'. Available online at: http://www.yearoutgroup.org/benefits-of-gapping/ (Accessed 24 September 2013).

.

Index